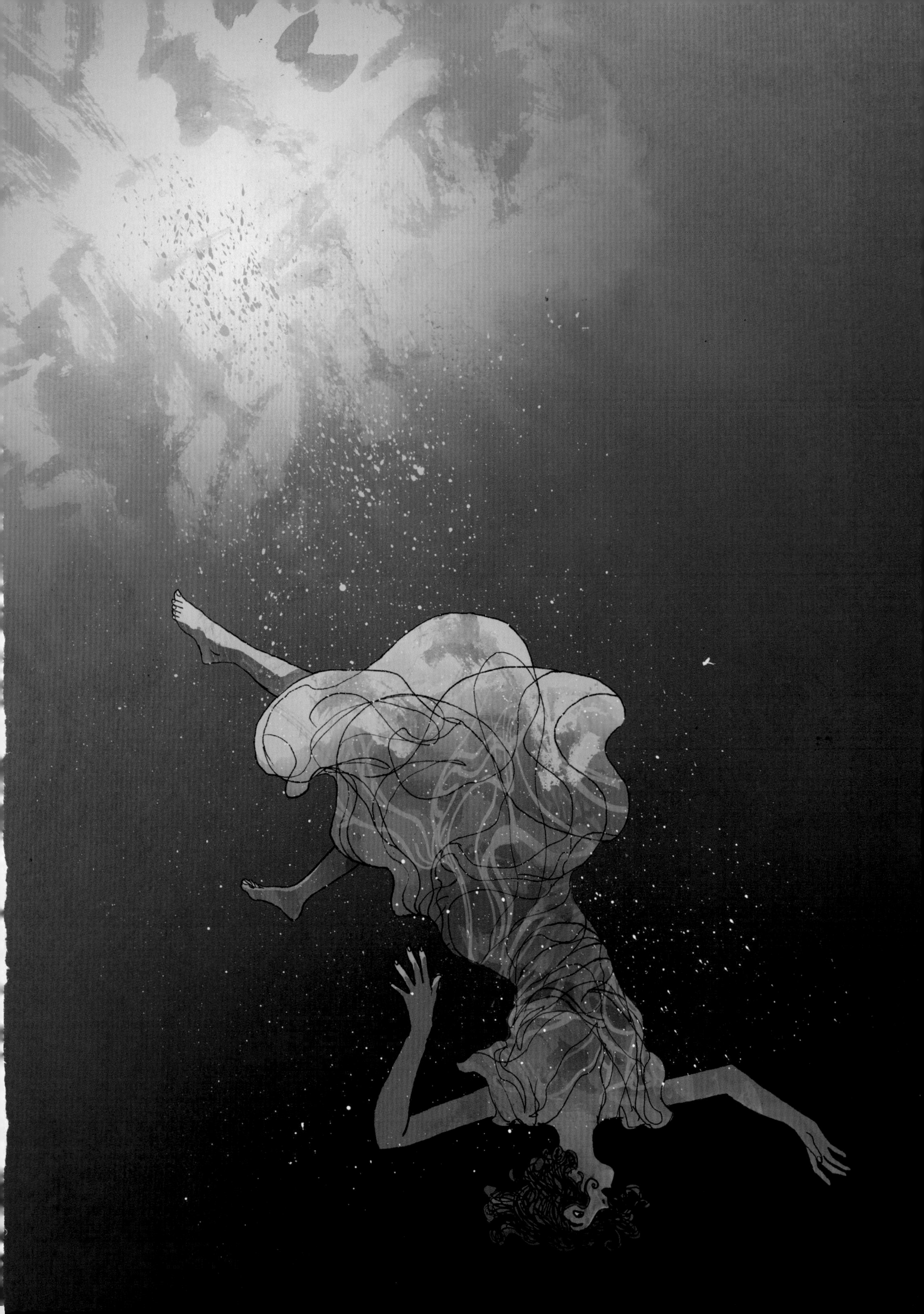

Emma G. Wildford

Written by Zidrou
Art by Edith

STATIX
PRESS

TITAN®
COMICS

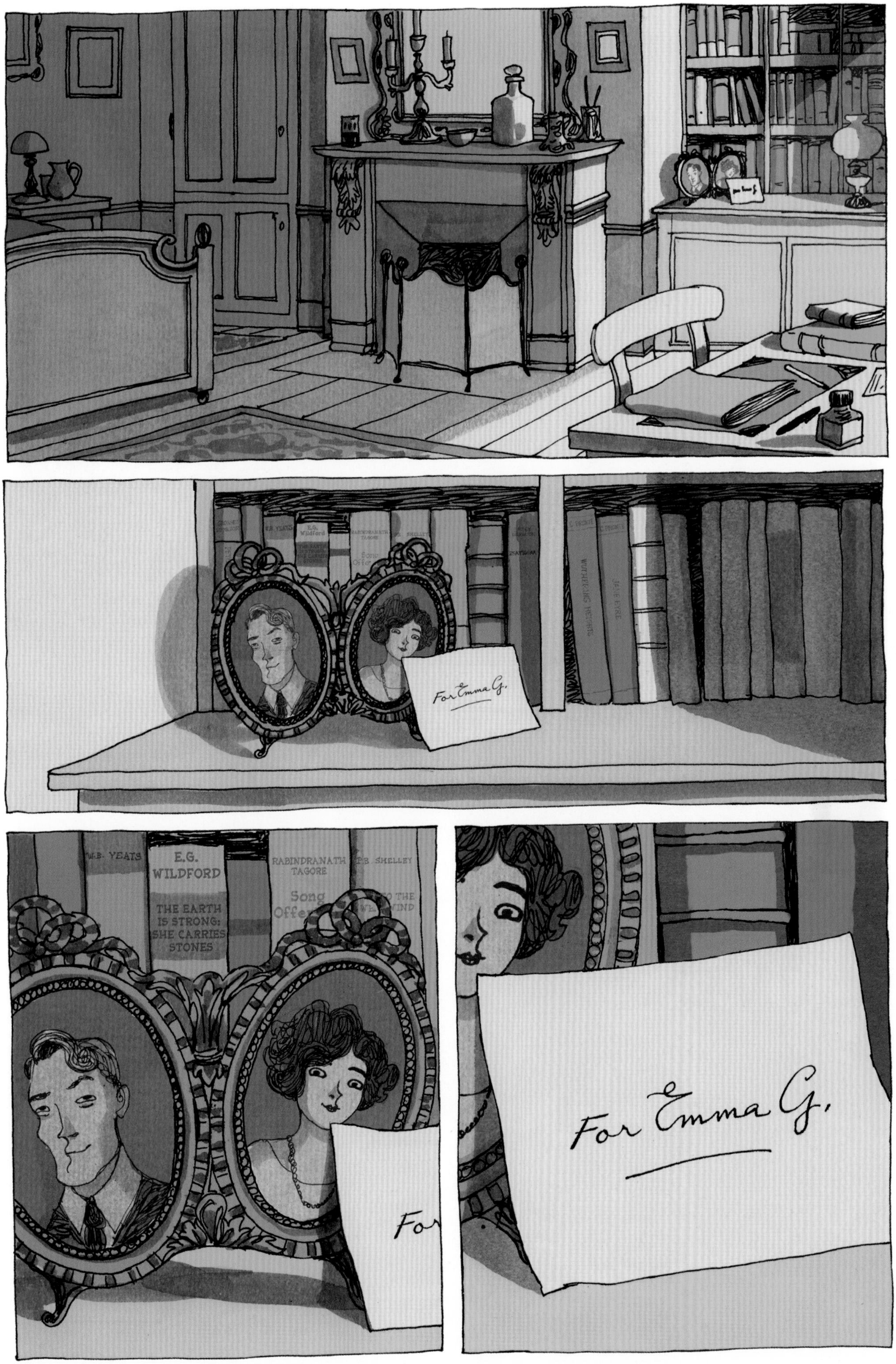
For Emma G.
W.B. YEATS
E.G. WILDFORD
THE EARTH IS STRONG: SHE CARRIES STONES
RABINDRANATH TAGORE
P.B. SHELLEY
For Emma G.

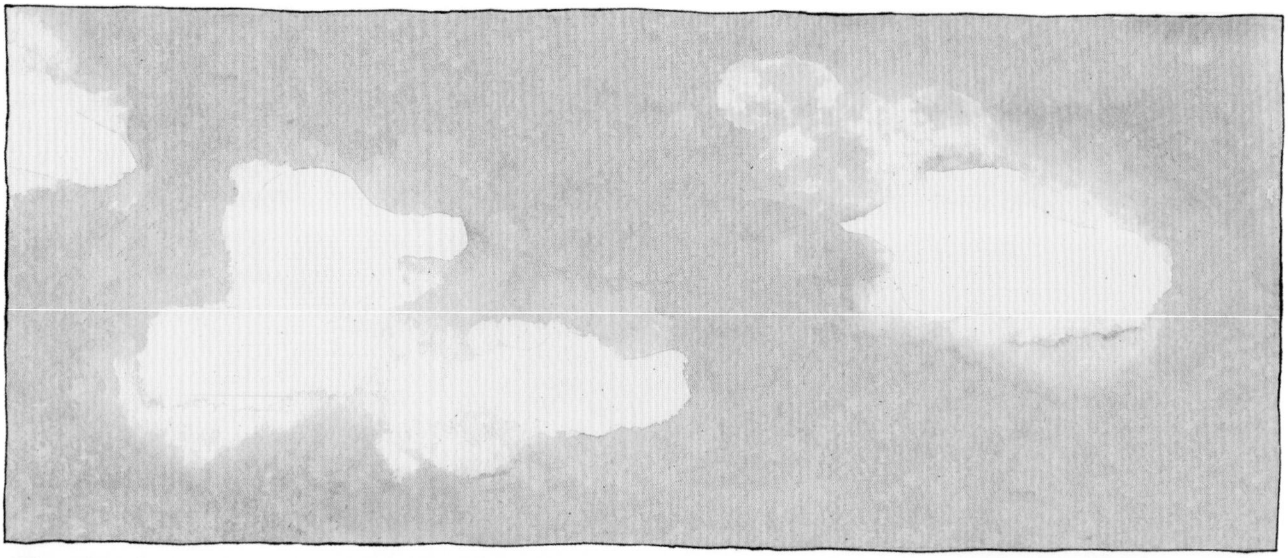

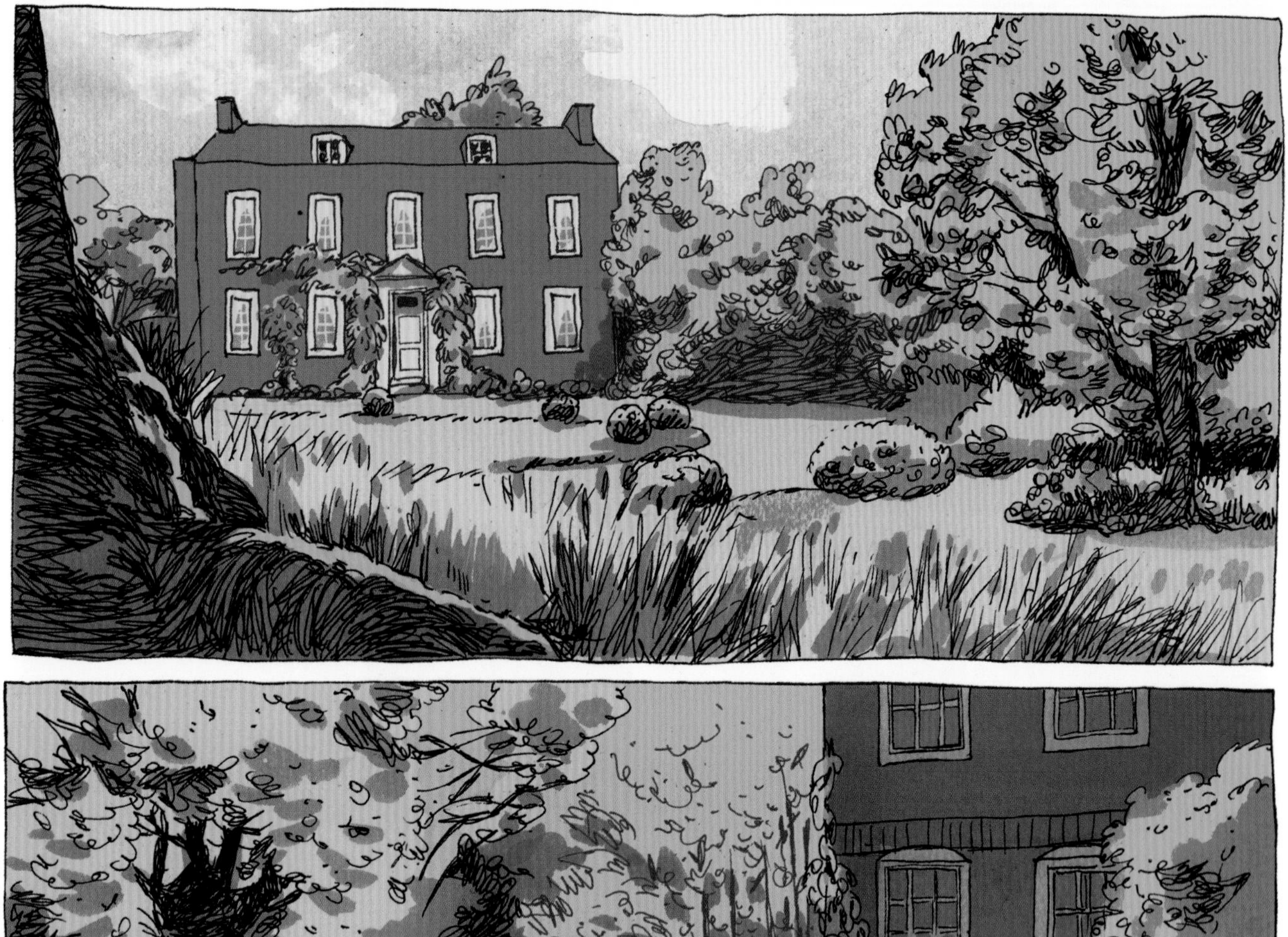

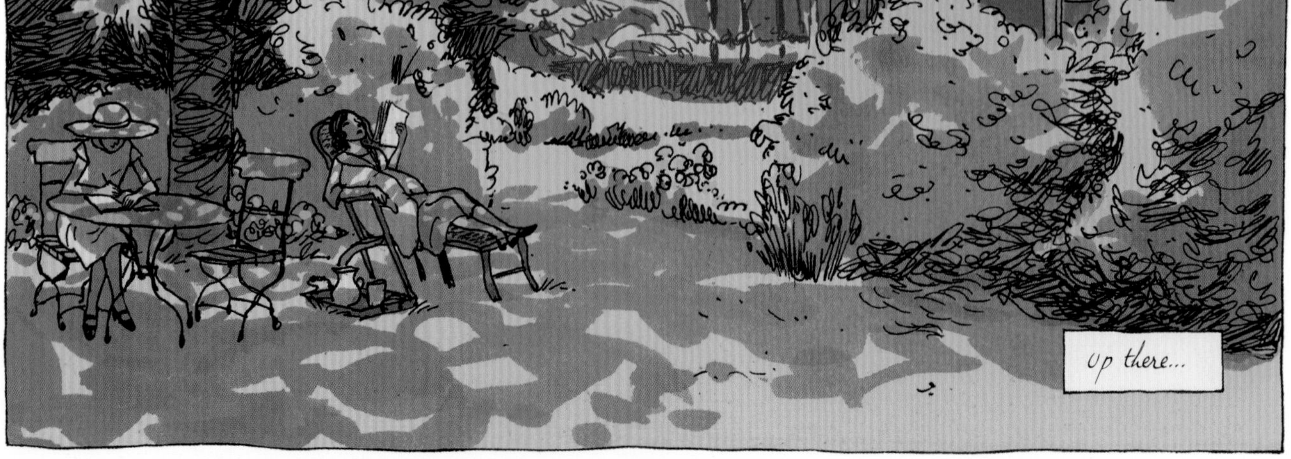
Up there...

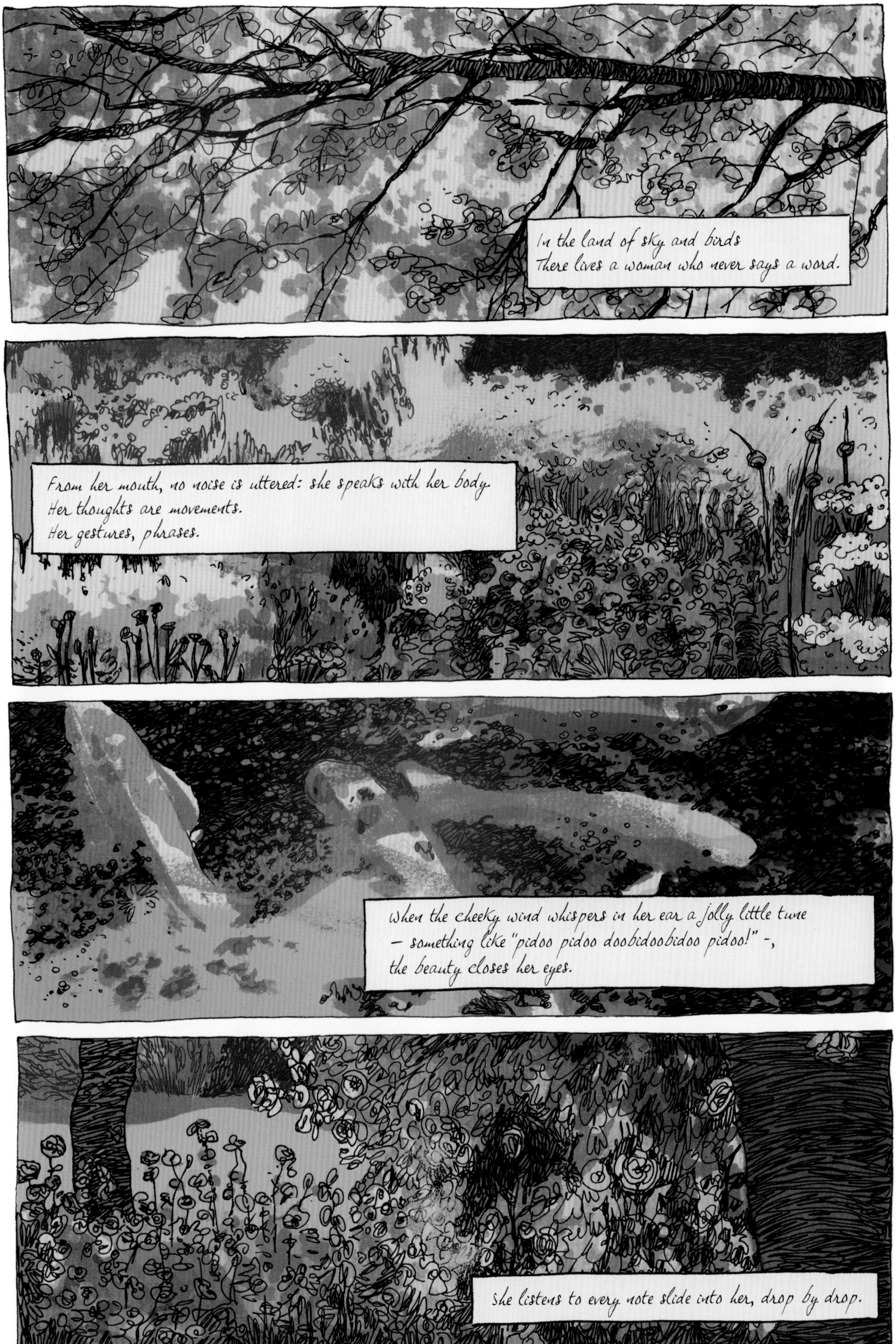
In the land of sky and birds
There lives a woman who never says a word.
From her mouth, no noise is uttered: she speaks with her body.
Her thoughts are movements.
Her gestures, phrases.
When the cheeky wind whispers in her ear a jolly little tune
– something like "pidoo pidoo doobidoobidoo pidoo!" –,
the beauty closes her eyes.
She listens to every note slide into her, drop by drop.

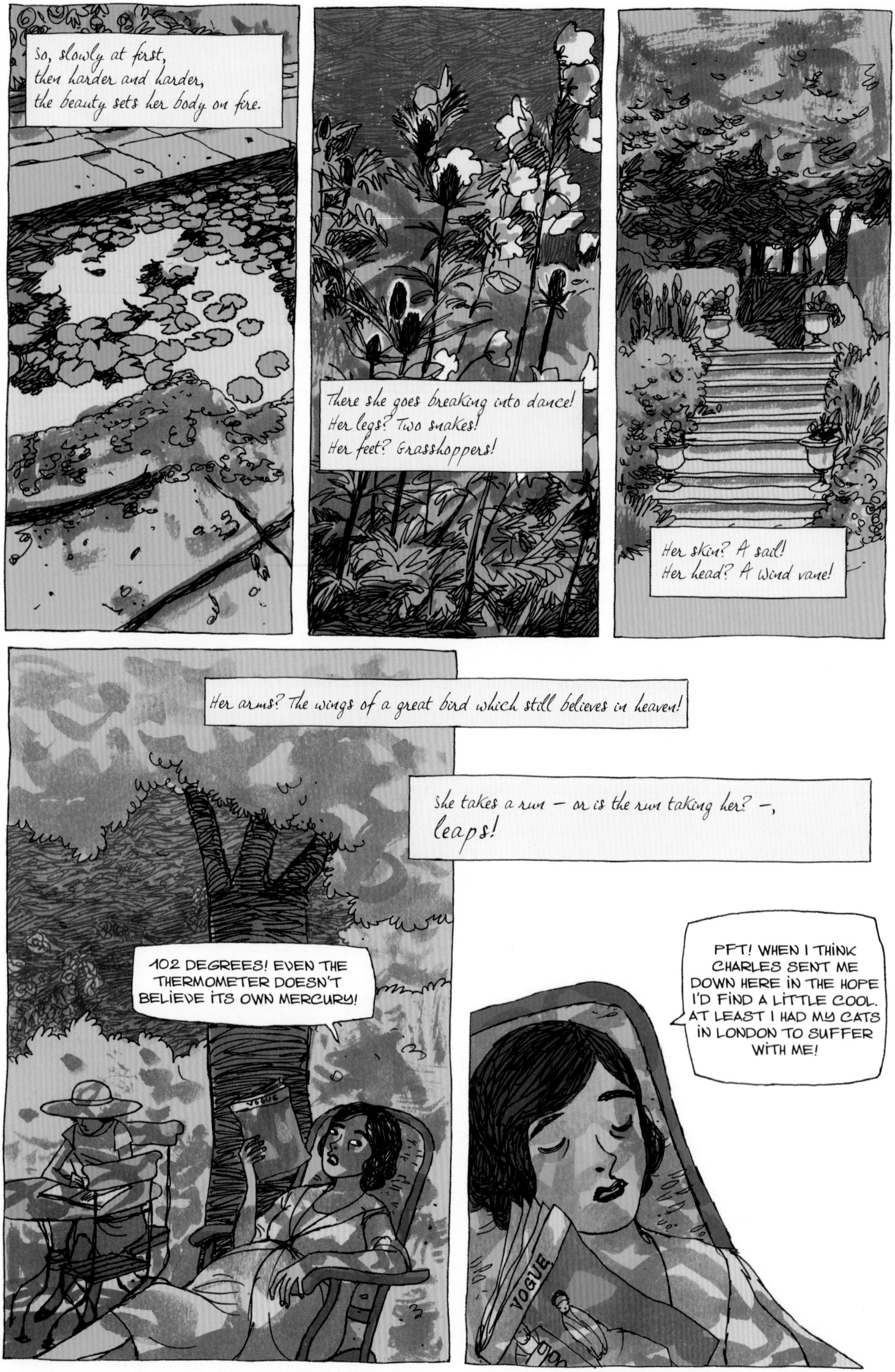
So, slowly at first, then harder and harder, the beauty sets her body on fire.
There she goes breaking into dance! Her legs? Two snakes! Her feet? Grasshoppers!
Her skin? A sail! Her head? A wind vane!
Her arms? The wings of a great bird which still believes in heaven!
She takes a run – or is the run taking her? –, leaps!
102 DEGREES! EVEN THE THERMOMETER DOESN'T BELIEVE ITS OWN MERCURY!
VOGUE
PFT! WHEN I THINK CHARLES SENT ME DOWN HERE IN THE HOPE I'D FIND A LITTLE COOL. AT LEAST I HAD MY CATS IN LONDON TO SUFFER WITH ME!
VOGUE

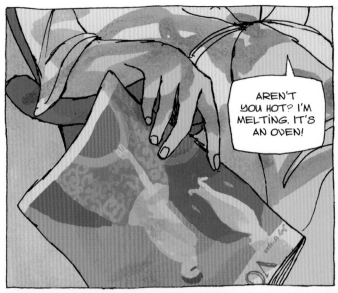

AREN'T YOU HOT? I'M MELTING. IT'S AN OVEN!

I DON'T MIND THE HEAT...

...NOR THE COLD, EITHER.

IT'S BEEN THREE WEEKS!

WHO KNOWS, MAYBE THE TROPICS HAVE DECIDED TO SETTLE HERE, IN ESSEX? AFRICA CONQUERS ENGLAND; IT'D BE A JUST REVERSAL, AFTER ALL.

JUST WAIT AND SEE, MY 'BETH. THERE'LL BE PALM TREES ALONG THE THAMES, LIONS IN NOTTING HILL, MONKEYS PICKING AT THEIR FUR IN BUCKINGHAM PALACE!!!

ENOUGH WITH SUCH HORRORS!

BY SAINT GEORGE! IF ONLY WE WEREN'T FORCED TO WEAR THESE HEAVY DRESSES!

WHO SAID WE WERE FORCED TO WEAR THEM?

?!

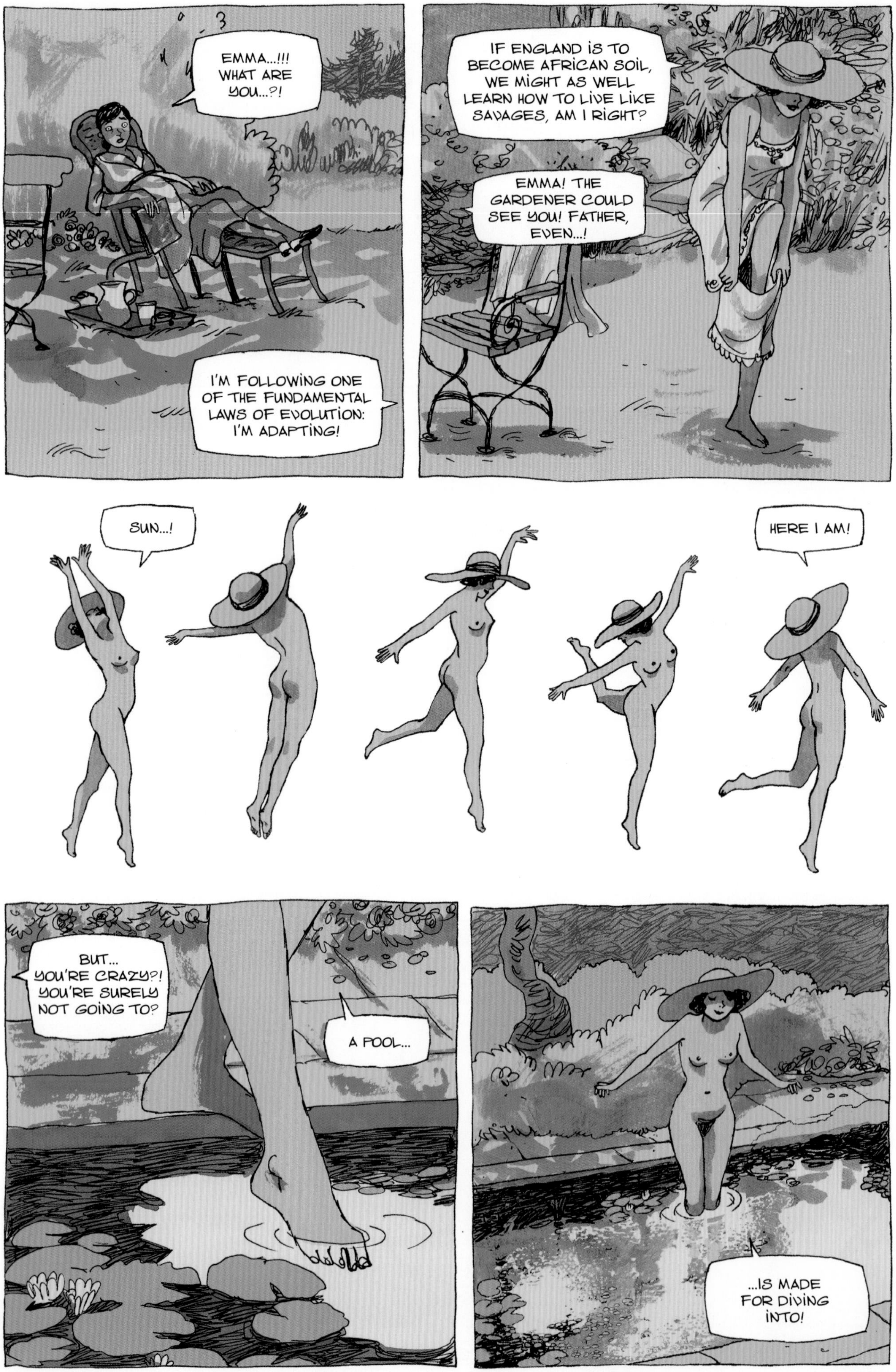
EMMA...!!! WHAT ARE YOU...?!
I'M FOLLOWING ONE OF THE FUNDAMENTAL LAWS OF EVOLUTION: I'M ADAPTING!
IF ENGLAND IS TO BECOME AFRICAN SOIL, WE MIGHT AS WELL LEARN HOW TO LIVE LIKE SAVAGES, AM I RIGHT?
EMMA! THE GARDENER COULD SEE YOU! FATHER, EVEN...!
SUN...!
HERE I AM!
BUT... YOU'RE CRAZY?! YOU'RE SURELY NOT GOING TO?
A POOL...
...IS MADE FOR DIVING INTO!

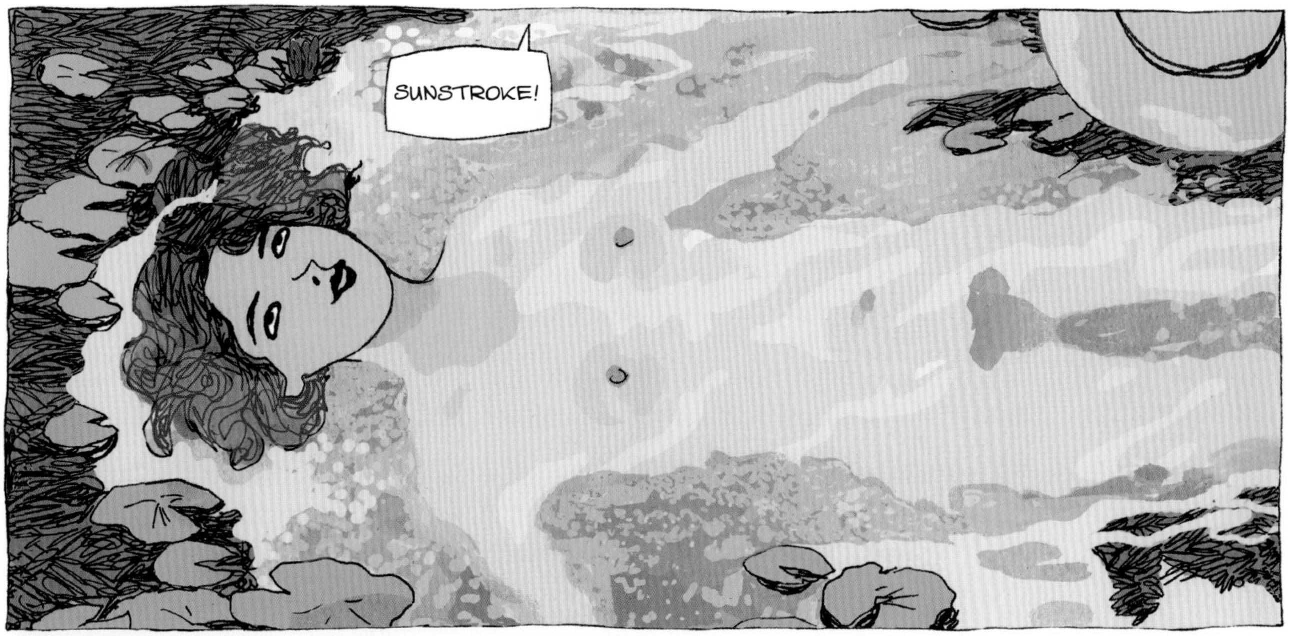
SUNSTROKE!

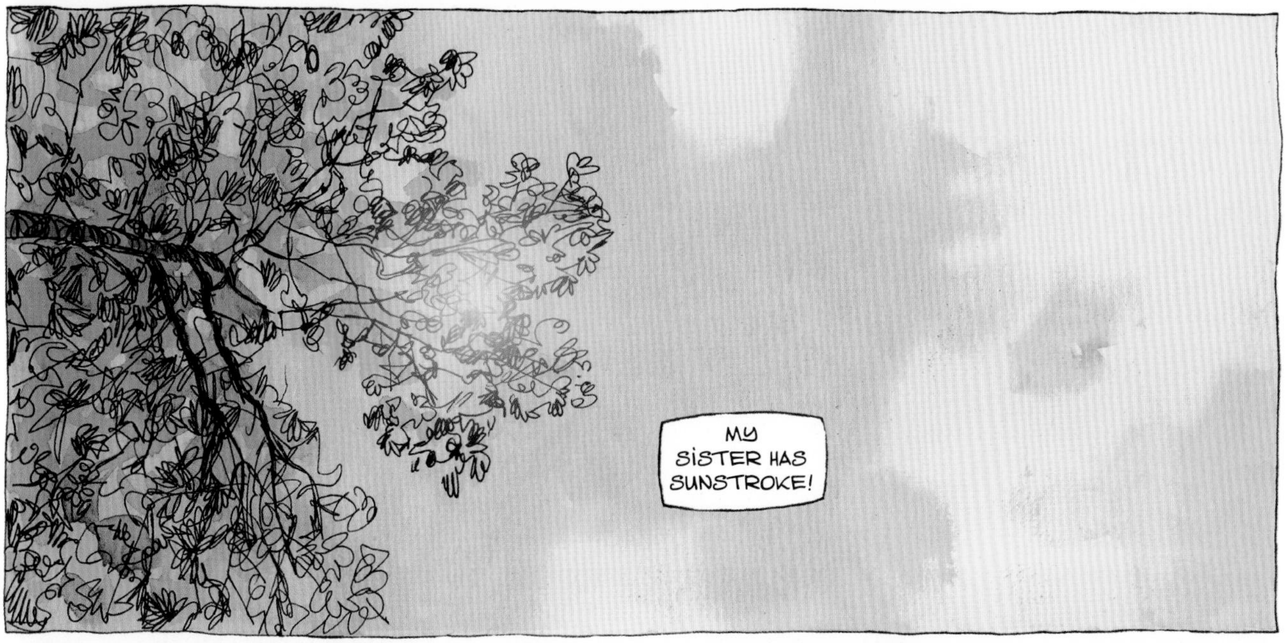
MY SISTER HAS SUNSTROKE!

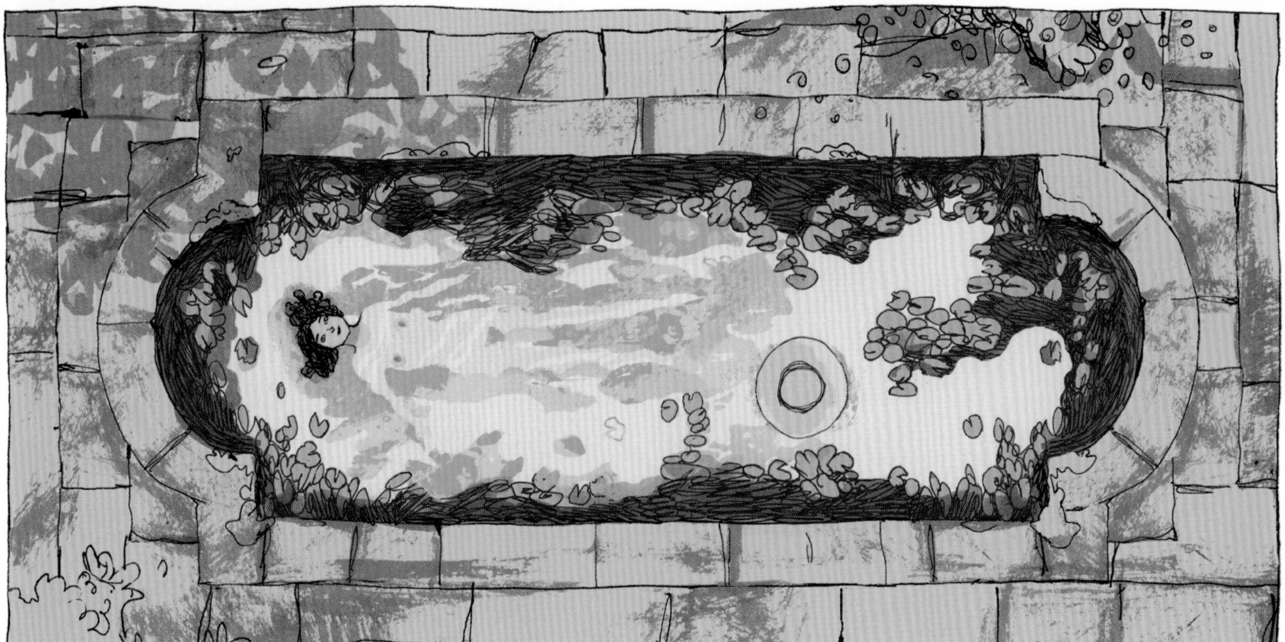

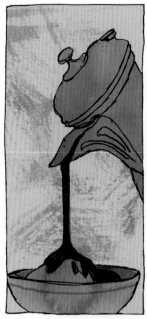

THANK YOU, DORIS!

I REALISE IT'S NOT THE BEST THING FOR MY FIGURE BUT, IN MY OPINION, A DAME BLANCHE IS THE ONLY THING THAT JUSTIFIES THE STRONG SUMMER HEAT.

HERE, HERE! TO THINK YOUR HUSBAND SMELT THE HOT CHOCOLATE ALL THE WAY FROM THE CITY!

YOU'LL HAVE TO EXPLAIN TO ME ONE DAY HOW YOU MANAGED TO MARRY THAT LOCK BOX ON LEGS.

OTHER THAN HELPING PUT ANY FINANCIAL CONCERNS TO REST, BANKERS ALSO POSSESS ANOTHER NOTEWORTHY ADVANTAGE...

...THEY DON'T, FOR ONE, GO OFF ALL THE TIME TO EXPLORE SAVAGE HOSTILE LANDS!

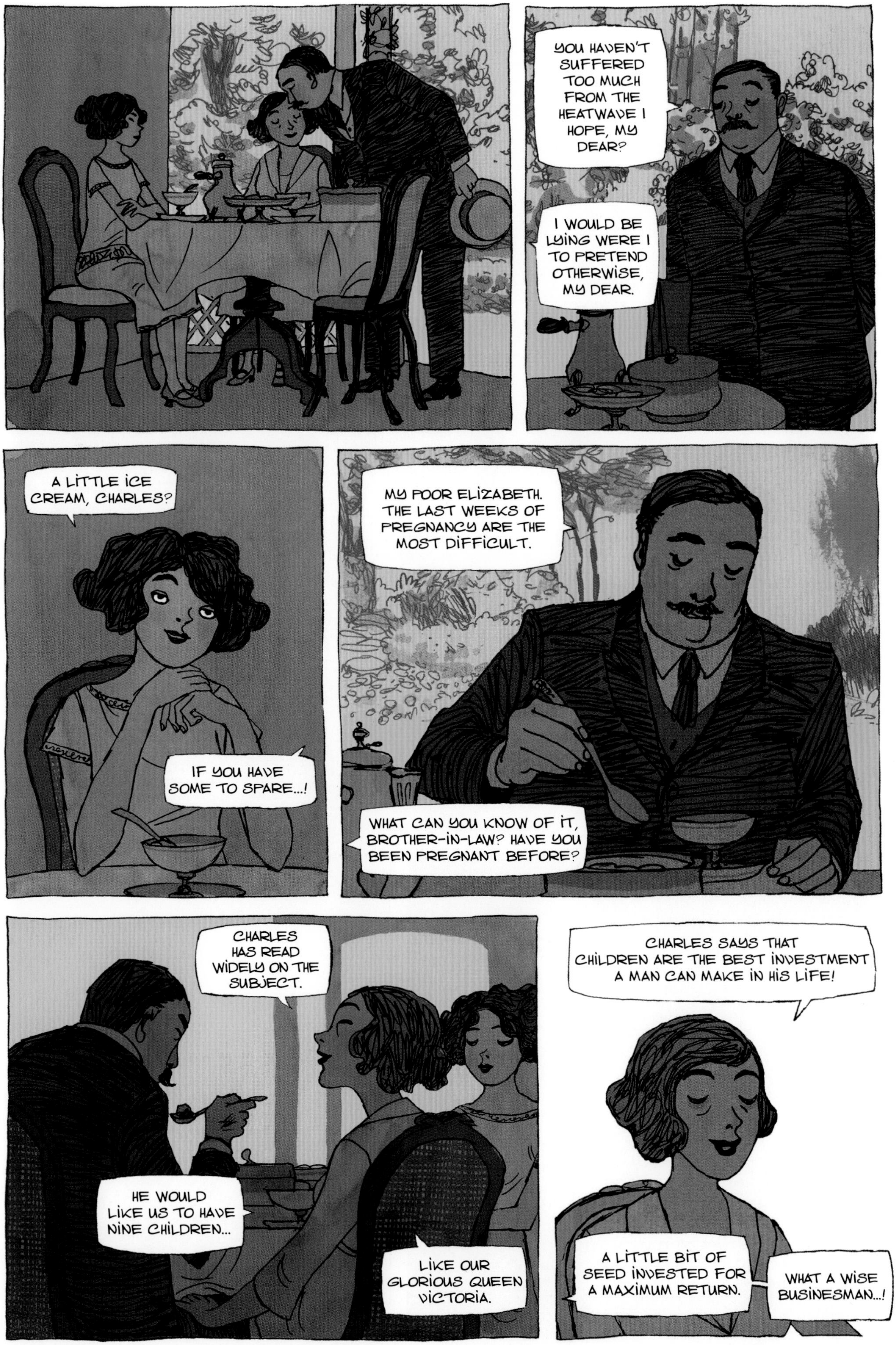

YOU HAVEN'T SUFFERED TOO MUCH FROM THE HEATWAVE I HOPE, MY DEAR?
I WOULD BE LYING WERE I TO PRETEND OTHERWISE, MY DEAR.
A LITTLE ICE CREAM, CHARLES?
IF YOU HAVE SOME TO SPARE...!
MY POOR ELIZABETH. THE LAST WEEKS OF PREGNANCY ARE THE MOST DIFFICULT.
WHAT CAN YOU KNOW OF IT, BROTHER-IN-LAW? HAVE YOU BEEN PREGNANT BEFORE?
CHARLES HAS READ WIDELY ON THE SUBJECT.
HE WOULD LIKE US TO HAVE NINE CHILDREN...
LIKE OUR GLORIOUS QUEEN VICTORIA.
CHARLES SAYS THAT CHILDREN ARE THE BEST INVESTMENT A MAN CAN MAKE IN HIS LIFE!
A LITTLE BIT OF SEED INVESTED FOR A MAXIMUM RETURN.
WHAT A WISE BUSINESSMAN...!

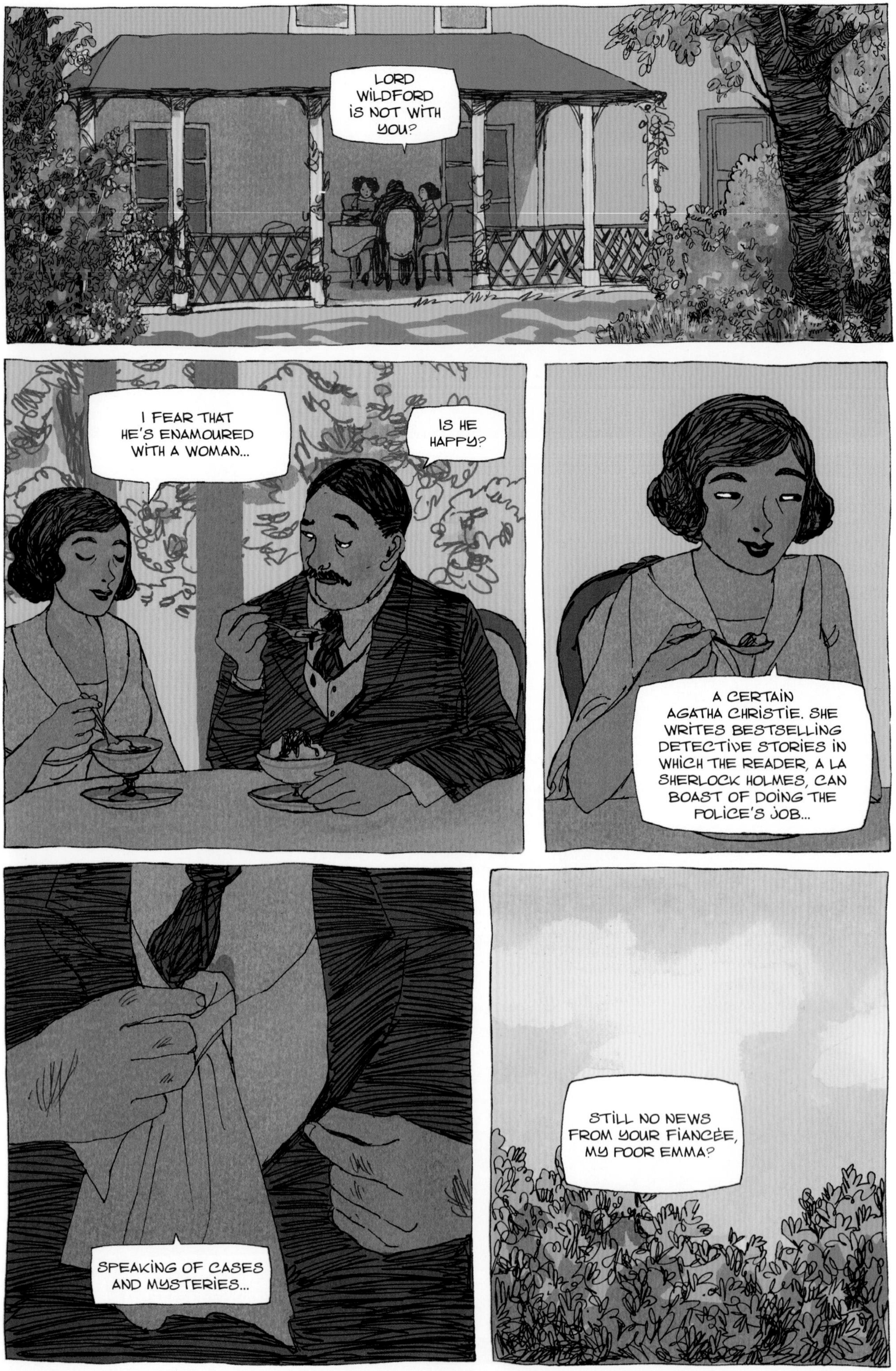
LORD WILDFORD IS NOT WITH YOU?
I FEAR THAT HE'S ENAMOURED WITH A WOMAN...
IS HE HAPPY?
A CERTAIN AGATHA CHRISTIE. SHE WRITES BESTSELLING DETECTIVE STORIES IN WHICH THE READER, A LA SHERLOCK HOLMES, CAN BOAST OF DOING THE POLICE'S JOB...
SPEAKING OF CASES AND MYSTERIES...
STILL NO NEWS FROM YOUR FIANCÉE, MY POOR EMMA?

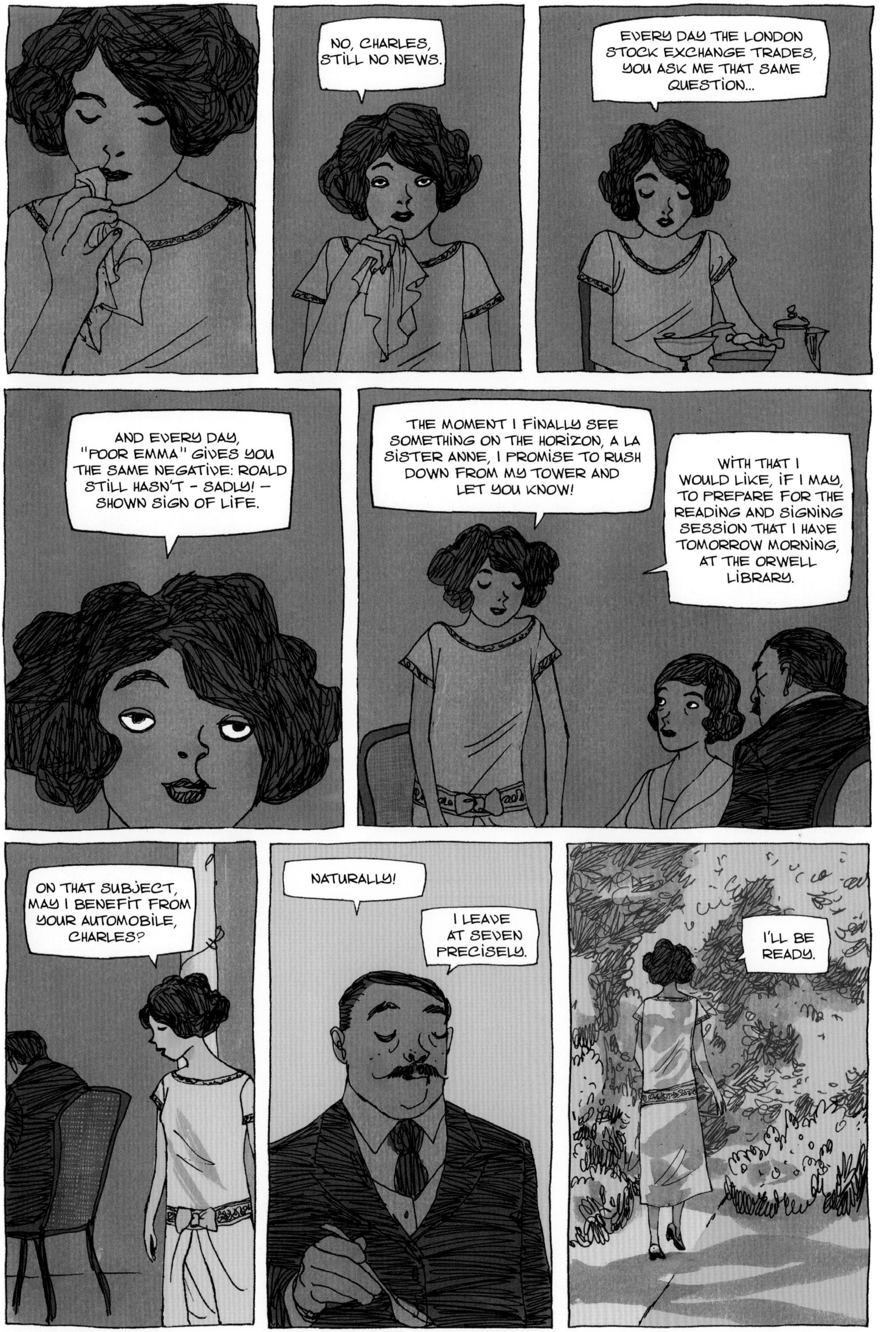
NO, CHARLES, STILL NO NEWS.
EVERY DAY THE LONDON STOCK EXCHANGE TRADES, YOU ASK ME THAT SAME QUESTION...
AND EVERY DAY, "POOR EMMA" GIVES YOU THE SAME NEGATIVE: ROALD STILL HASN'T - SADLY! - SHOWN SIGN OF LIFE.
THE MOMENT I FINALLY SEE SOMETHING ON THE HORIZON, A LA SISTER ANNE, I PROMISE TO RUSH DOWN FROM MY TOWER AND LET YOU KNOW!
WITH THAT I WOULD LIKE, IF I MAY, TO PREPARE FOR THE READING AND SIGNING SESSION THAT I HAVE TOMORROW MORNING, AT THE ORWELL LIBRARY.
ON THAT SUBJECT, MAY I BENEFIT FROM YOUR AUTOMOBILE, CHARLES?
NATURALLY!
I LEAVE AT SEVEN PRECISELY.
I'LL BE READY.

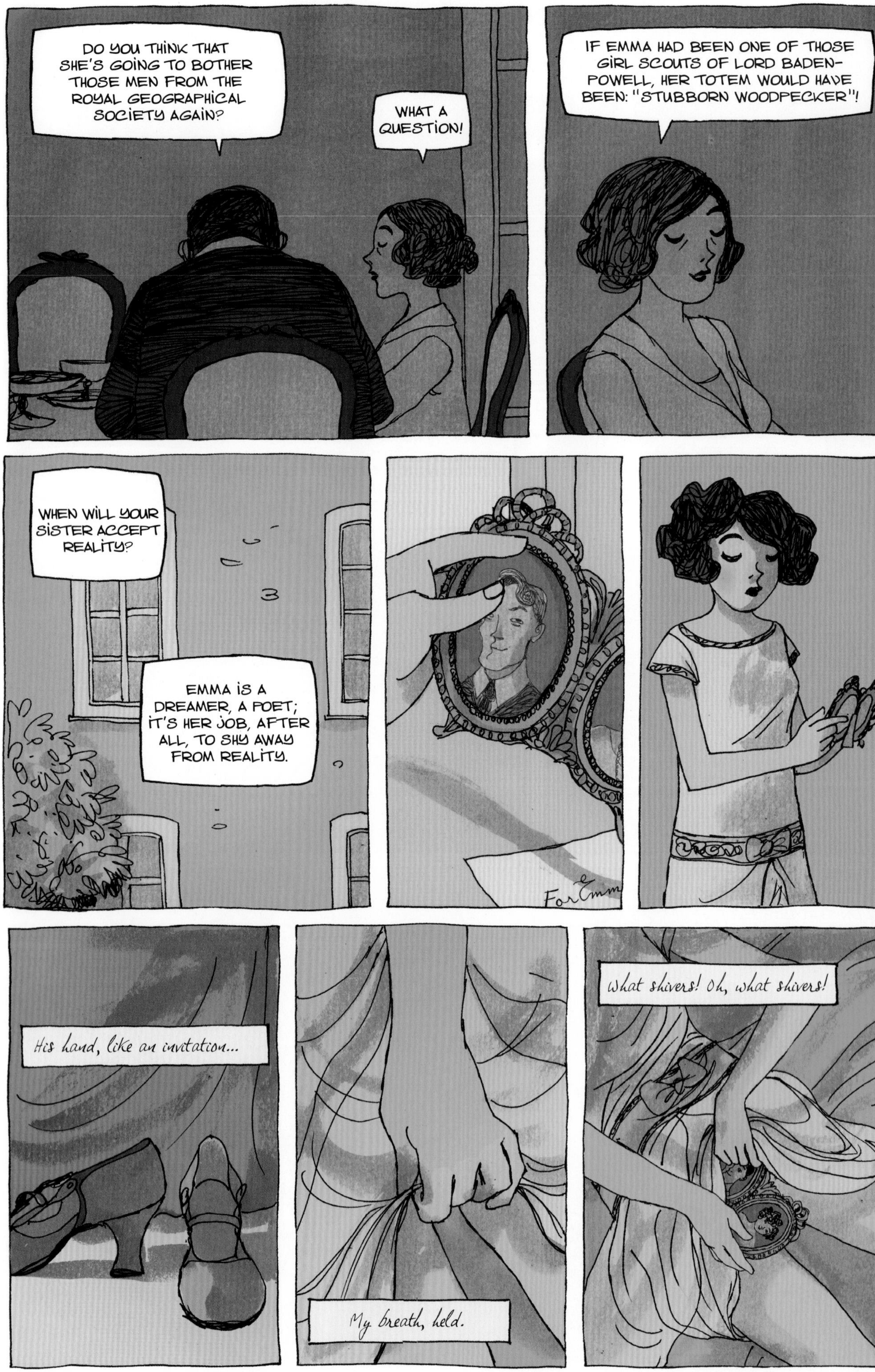

DO YOU THINK THAT SHE'S GOING TO BOTHER THOSE MEN FROM THE ROYAL GEOGRAPHICAL SOCIETY AGAIN?
WHAT A QUESTION!
IF EMMA HAD BEEN ONE OF THOSE GIRL SCOUTS OF LORD BADEN-POWELL, HER TOTEM WOULD HAVE BEEN: "STUBBORN WOODPECKER"!
WHEN WILL YOUR SISTER ACCEPT REALITY?
EMMA IS A DREAMER, A POET; IT'S HER JOB, AFTER ALL, TO SHY AWAY FROM REALITY.
For Emm
His hand, like an invitation...
My breath, held.
What shivers! Oh, what shivers!

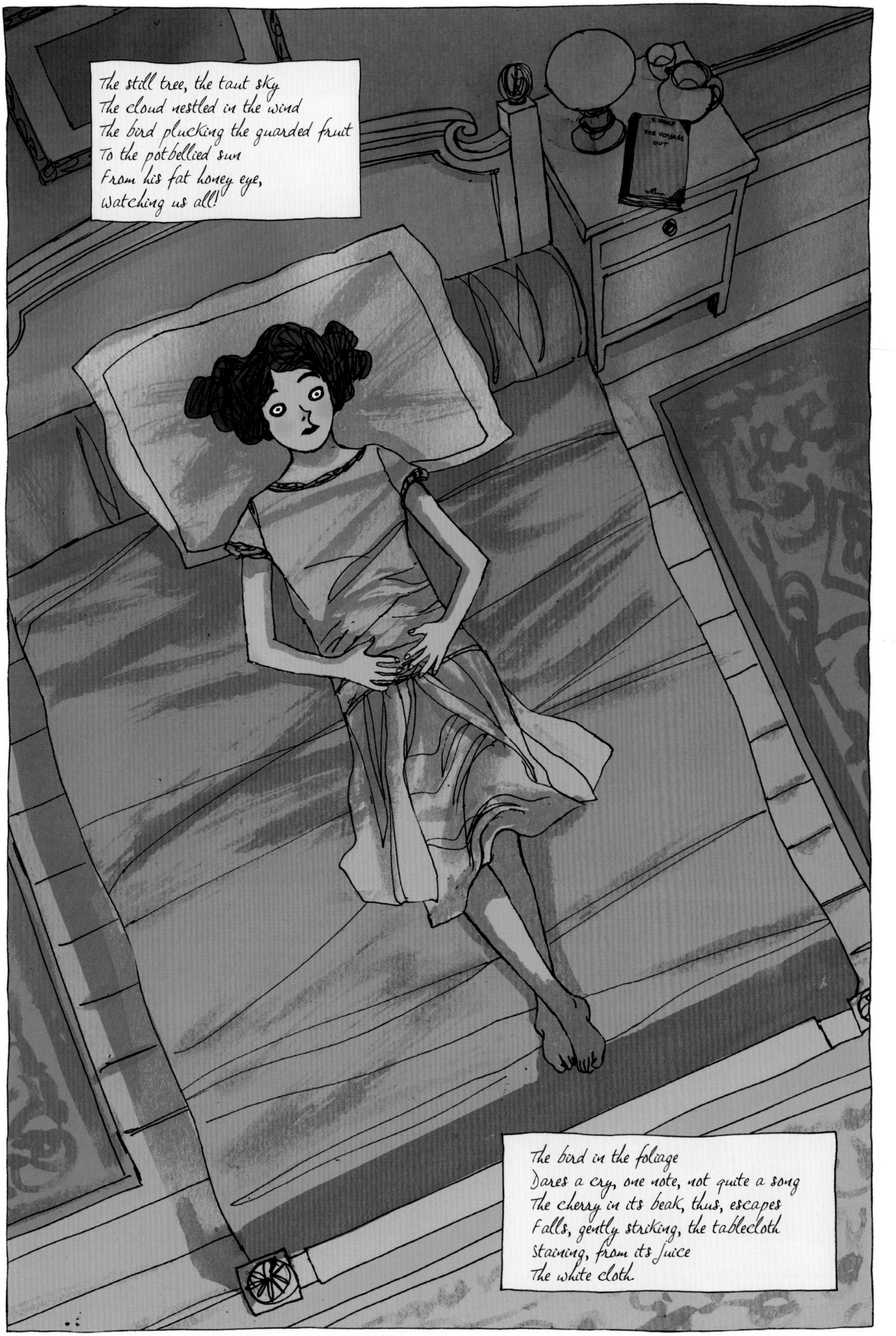
The still tree, the taut sky
The cloud nestled in the wind
The bird plucking the guarded fruit
To the potbellied sun
From his fat honey eye,
Watching us all!
V. WOOLF
THE VOYAGE OUT
The bird in the foliage
Dares a cry, one note, not quite a song
The cherry in its beak, thus, escapes
Falls, gently striking, the tablecloth
Staining, from its juice
The white cloth

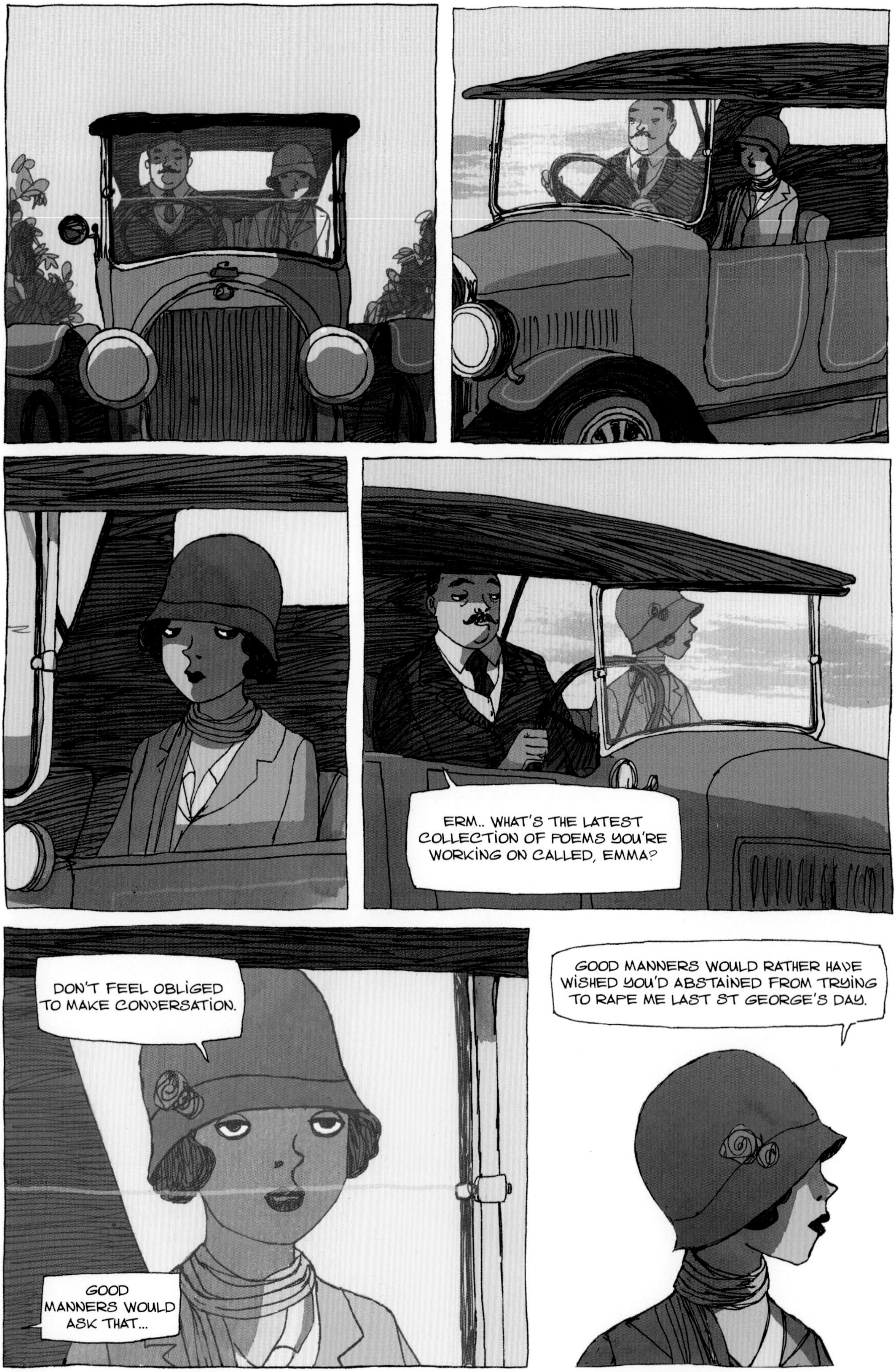
ERM.. WHAT'S THE LATEST COLLECTION OF POEMS YOU'RE WORKING ON CALLED, EMMA?
DON'T FEEL OBLIGED TO MAKE CONVERSATION.
GOOD MANNERS WOULD ASK THAT...
GOOD MANNERS WOULD RATHER HAVE WISHED YOU'D ABSTAINED FROM TRYING TO RAPE ME LAST ST GEORGE'S DAY.

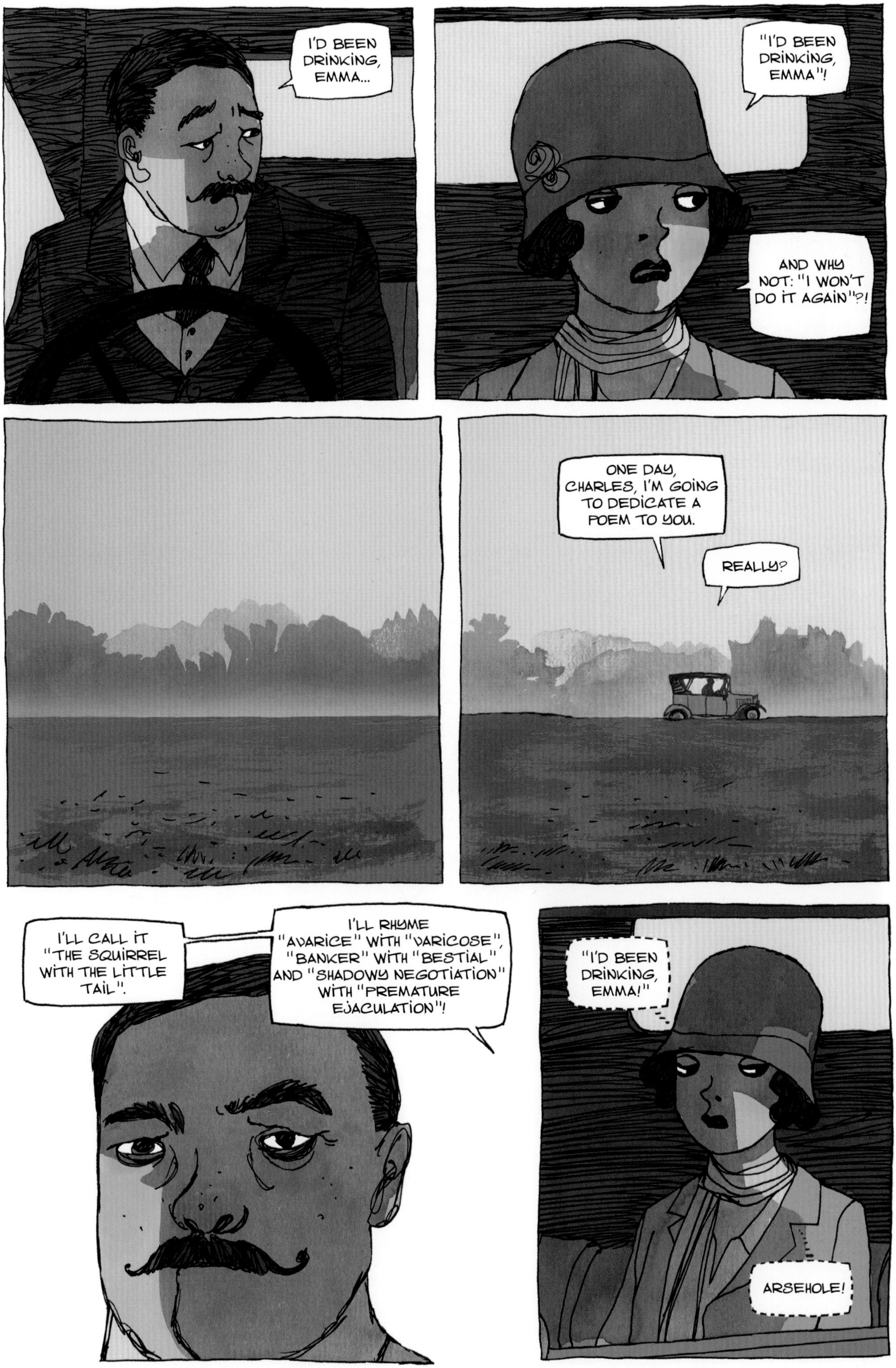
I'D BEEN DRINKING, EMMA...
"I'D BEEN DRINKING, EMMA"!
AND WHY NOT: "I WON'T DO IT AGAIN"?!
ONE DAY, CHARLES, I'M GOING TO DEDICATE A POEM TO YOU.
REALLY?
I'LL CALL IT "THE SQUIRREL WITH THE LITTLE TAIL".
I'LL RHYME "AVARICE" WITH "VARICOSE", "BANKER" WITH "BESTIAL" AND "SHADOWY NEGOTIATION" WITH "PREMATURE EJACULATION"!
"I'D BEEN DRINKING, EMMA!"
ARSEHOLE!

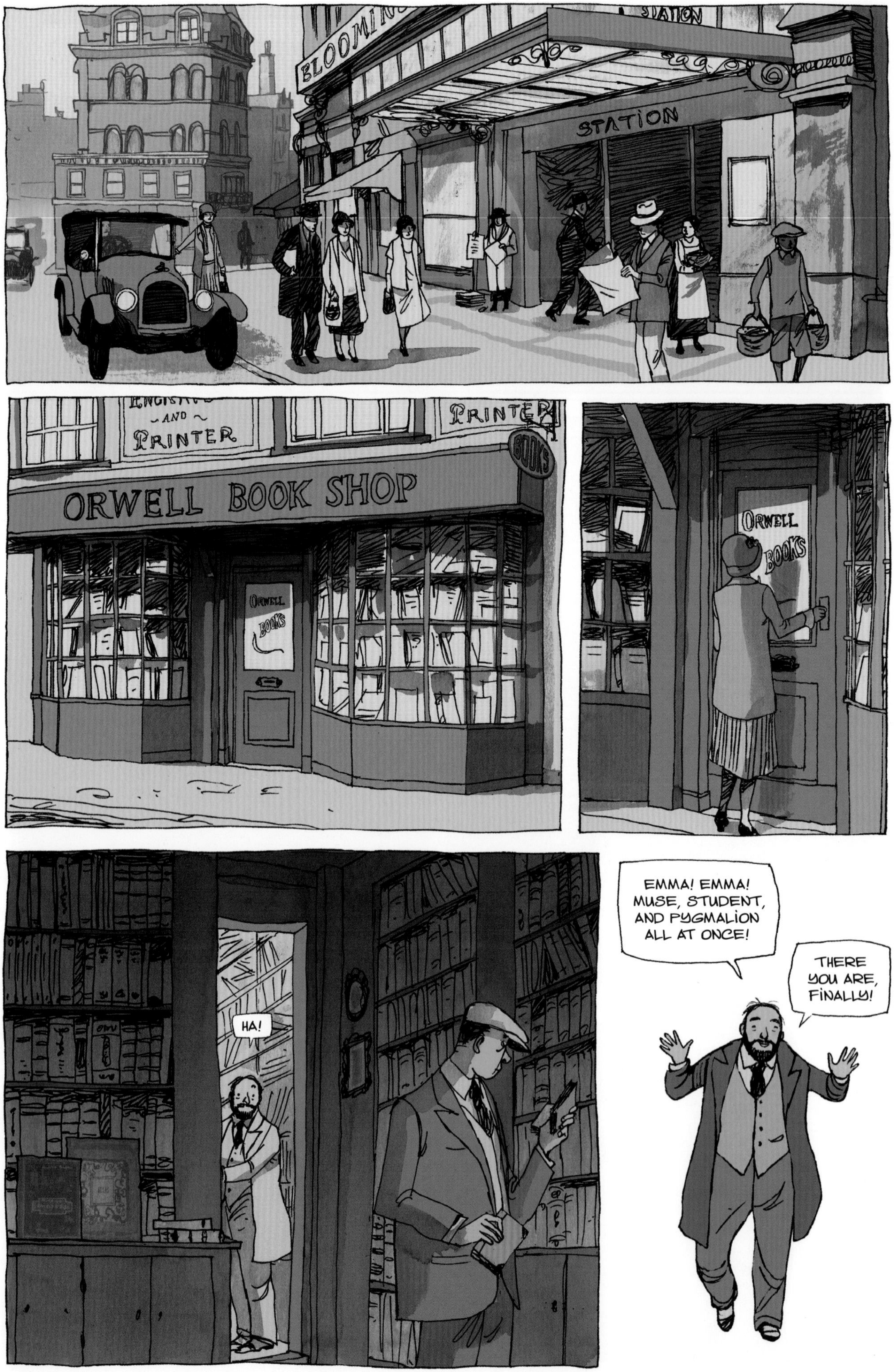
STATION
STATION
AND
PRINTER
PRINTER
BOOKS
ORWELL BOOK SHOP
ORWELL BOOKS
ORWELL BOOKS
HA!
EMMA! EMMA! MUSE, STUDENT, AND PYGMALION ALL AT ONCE!
THERE YOU ARE, FINALLY!

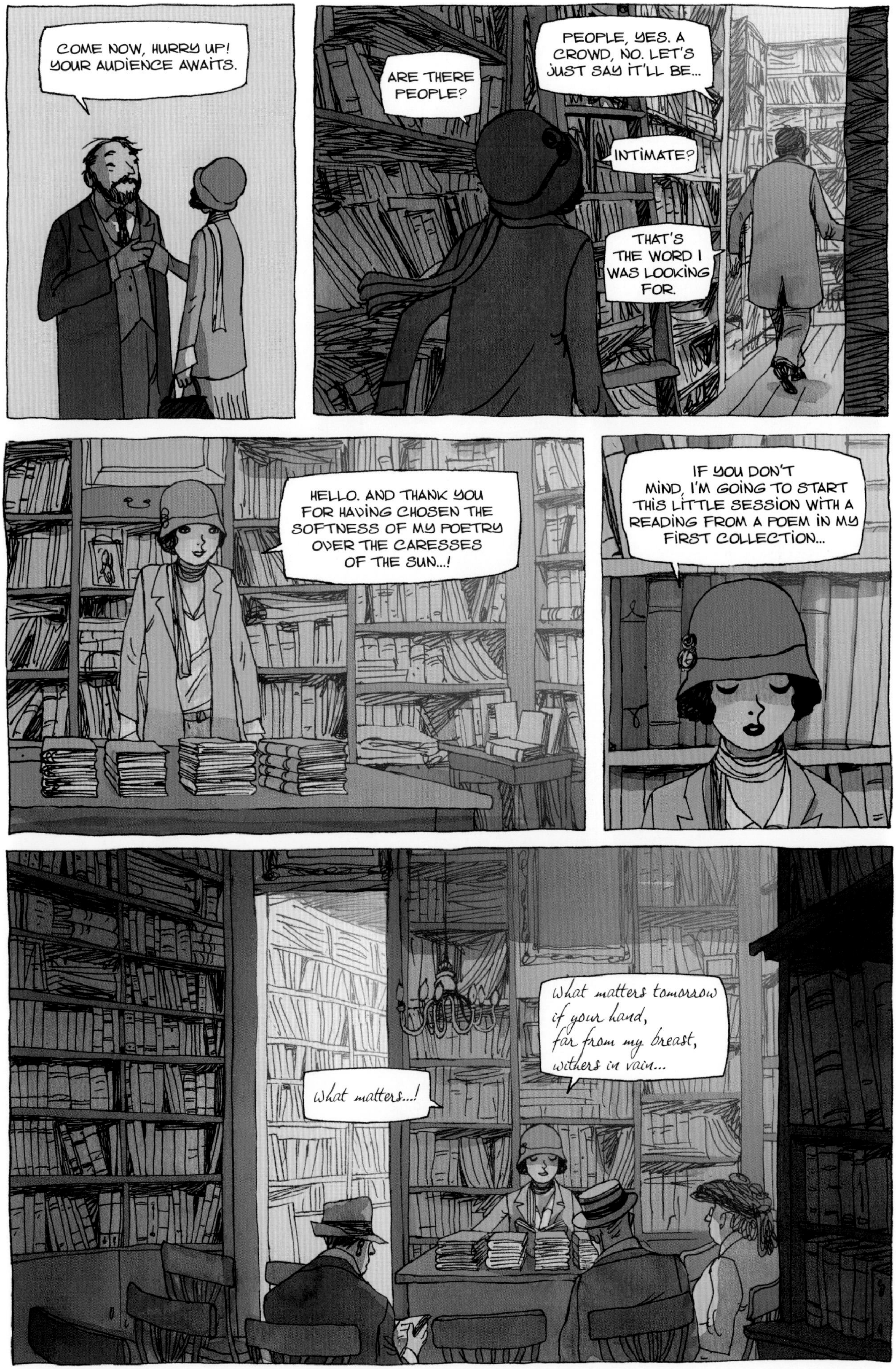
COME NOW, HURRY UP! YOUR AUDIENCE AWAITS.
ARE THERE PEOPLE?
PEOPLE, YES. A CROWD, NO. LET'S JUST SAY IT'LL BE...
INTIMATE?
THAT'S THE WORD I WAS LOOKING FOR.
HELLO. AND THANK YOU FOR HAVING CHOSEN THE SOFTNESS OF MY POETRY OVER THE CARESSES OF THE SUN...!
IF YOU DON'T MIND, I'M GOING TO START THIS LITTLE SESSION WITH A READING FROM A POEM IN MY FIRST COLLECTION...
What matters tomorrow if your hand, far from my breast, withers in vain...
What matters...!

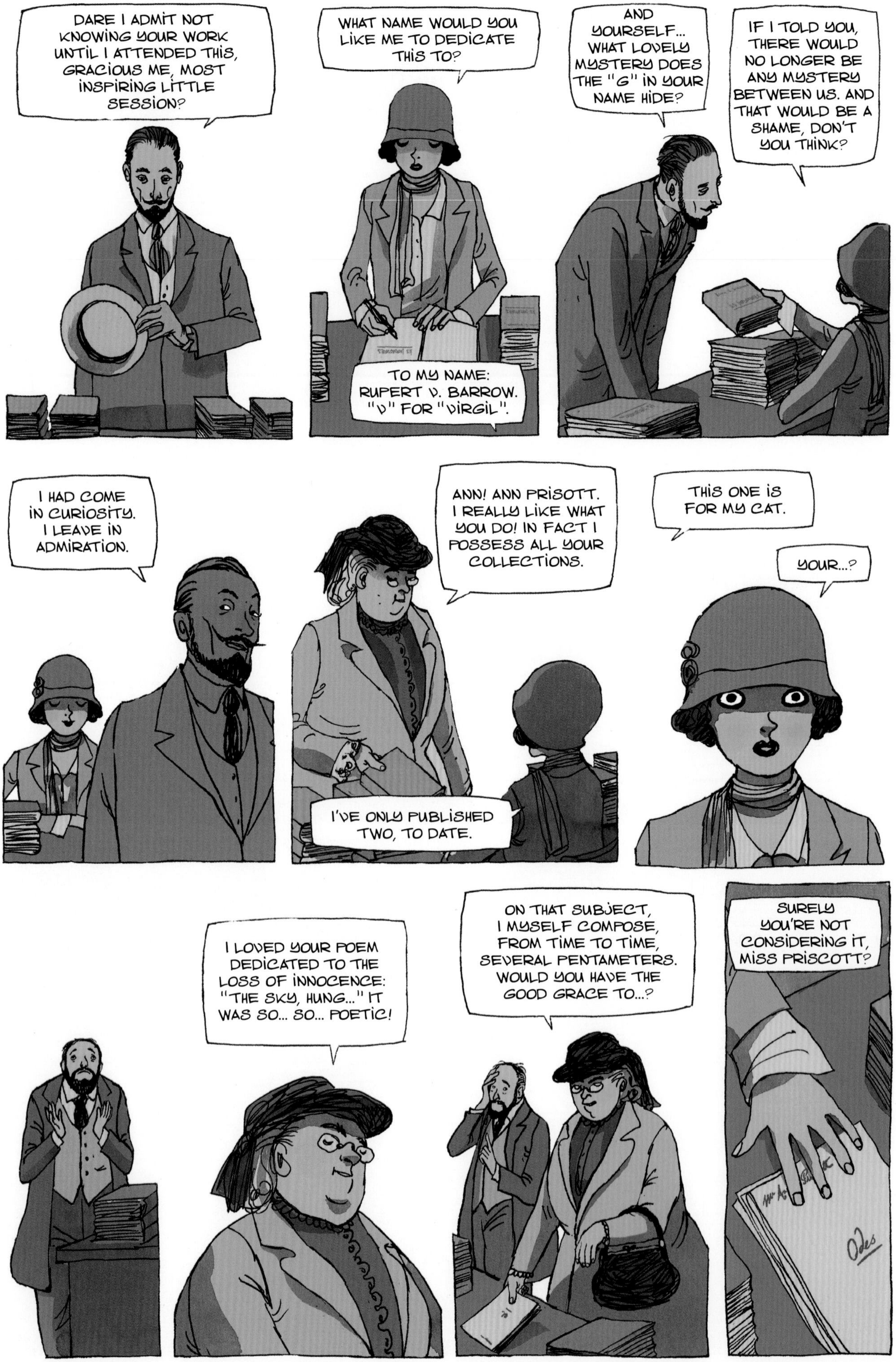
DARE I ADMIT NOT KNOWING YOUR WORK UNTIL I ATTENDED THIS, GRACIOUS ME, MOST INSPIRING LITTLE SESSION?
WHAT NAME WOULD YOU LIKE ME TO DEDICATE THIS TO?
TO MY NAME: RUPERT V. BARROW. "V" FOR "VIRGIL".
AND YOURSELF... WHAT LOVELY MYSTERY DOES THE "G" IN YOUR NAME HIDE?
IF I TOLD YOU, THERE WOULD NO LONGER BE ANY MYSTERY BETWEEN US. AND THAT WOULD BE A SHAME, DON'T YOU THINK?
I HAD COME IN CURIOSITY. I LEAVE IN ADMIRATION.
ANN! ANN PRISOTT. I REALLY LIKE WHAT YOU DO! IN FACT I POSSESS ALL YOUR COLLECTIONS.
I'VE ONLY PUBLISHED TWO, TO DATE.
THIS ONE IS FOR MY CAT.
YOUR...?
I LOVED YOUR POEM DEDICATED TO THE LOSS OF INNOCENCE: "THE SKY, HUNG..." IT WAS SO... SO... POETIC!
ON THAT SUBJECT, I MYSELF COMPOSE, FROM TIME TO TIME, SEVERAL PENTAMETERS. WOULD YOU HAVE THE GOOD GRACE TO...?
SURELY YOU'RE NOT CONSIDERING IT, MISS PRISCOTT?
Odes

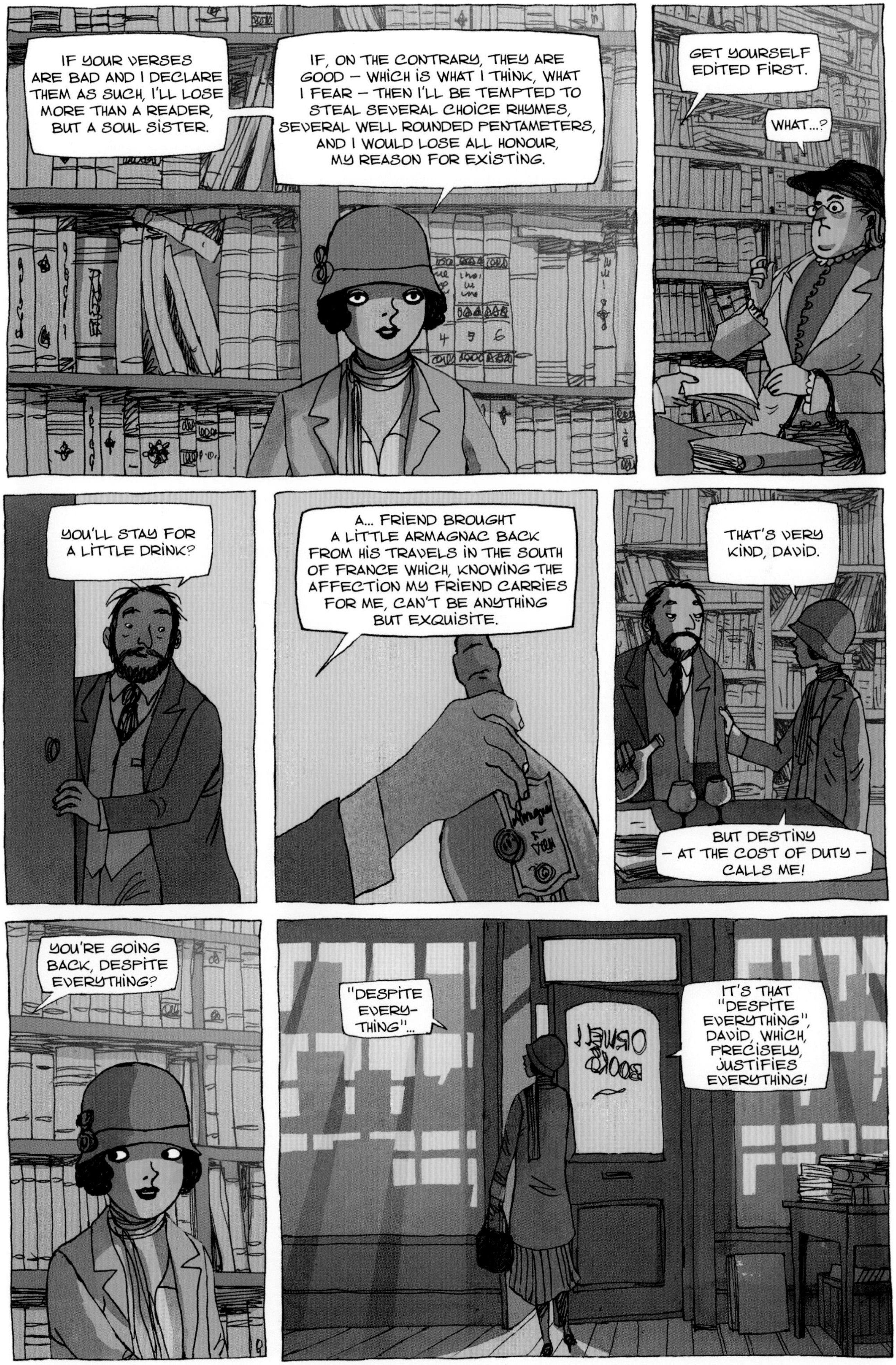
IF YOUR VERSES ARE BAD AND I DECLARE THEM AS SUCH, I'LL LOSE MORE THAN A READER, BUT A SOUL SISTER.
IF, ON THE CONTRARY, THEY ARE GOOD – WHICH IS WHAT I THINK, WHAT I FEAR – THEN I'LL BE TEMPTED TO STEAL SEVERAL CHOICE RHYMES, SEVERAL WELL ROUNDED PENTAMETERS, AND I WOULD LOSE ALL HONOUR, MY REASON FOR EXISTING.
GET YOURSELF EDITED FIRST.
WHAT...?
YOU'LL STAY FOR A LITTLE DRINK?
A... FRIEND BROUGHT A LITTLE ARMAGNAC BACK FROM HIS TRAVELS IN THE SOUTH OF FRANCE WHICH, KNOWING THE AFFECTION MY FRIEND CARRIES FOR ME, CAN'T BE ANYTHING BUT EXQUISITE.
THAT'S VERY KIND, DAVID.
BUT DESTINY – AT THE COST OF DUTY – CALLS ME!
YOU'RE GOING BACK, DESPITE EVERYTHING?
"DESPITE EVERY-THING"...
IT'S THAT "DESPITE EVERYTHING", DAVID, WHICH, PRECISELY, JUSTIFIES EVERYTHING!

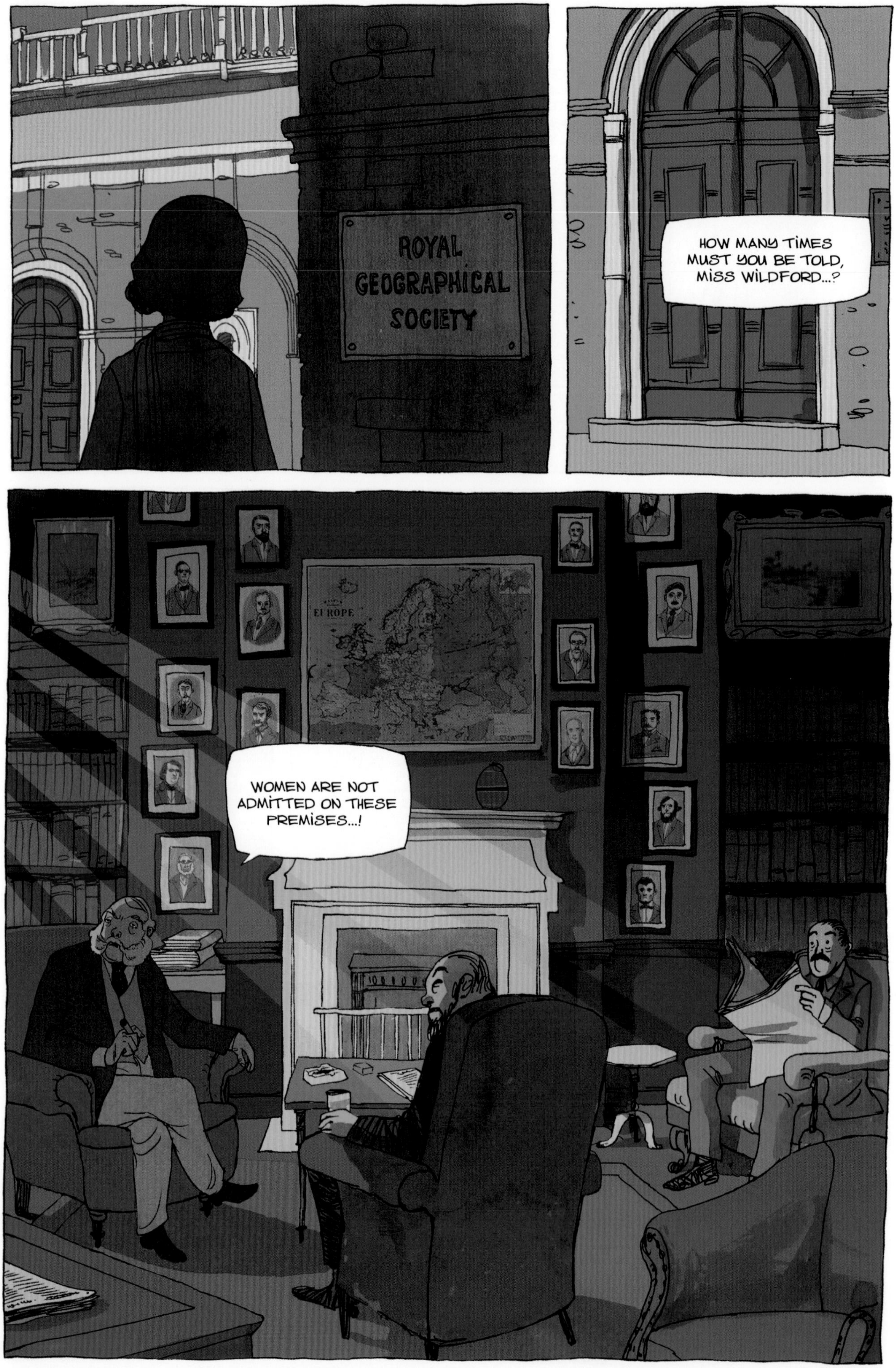
ROYAL GEOGRAPHICAL SOCIETY
HOW MANY TIMES MUST YOU BE TOLD, MISS WILDFORD...?
EUROPE
WOMEN ARE NOT ADMITTED ON THESE PREMISES...!

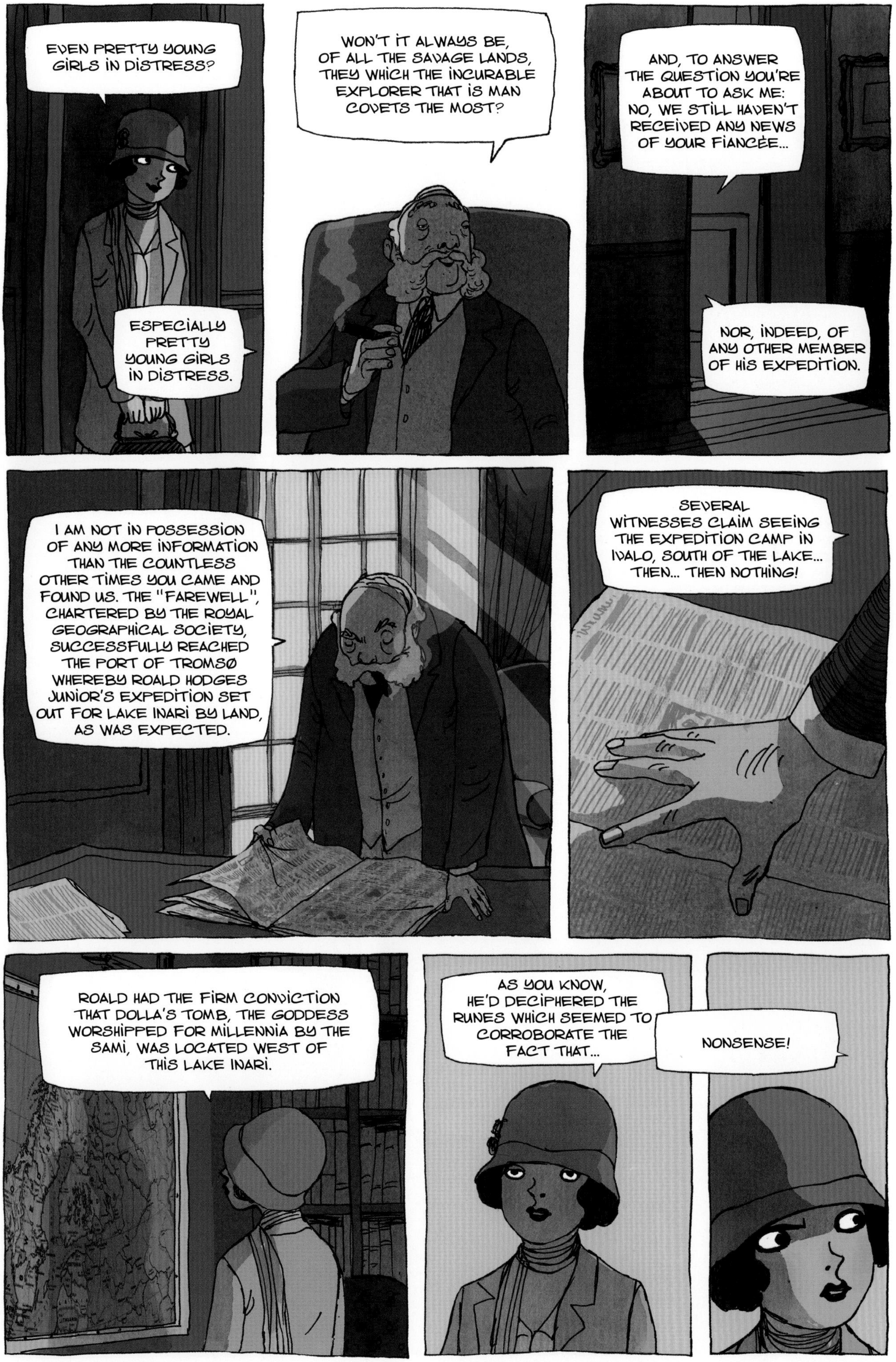
EVEN PRETTY YOUNG GIRLS IN DISTRESS?
ESPECIALLY PRETTY YOUNG GIRLS IN DISTRESS.
WON'T IT ALWAYS BE, OF ALL THE SAVAGE LANDS, THEY WHICH THE INCURABLE EXPLORER THAT IS MAN COVETS THE MOST?
AND, TO ANSWER THE QUESTION YOU'RE ABOUT TO ASK ME: NO, WE STILL HAVEN'T RECEIVED ANY NEWS OF YOUR FIANCÉE...
NOR, INDEED, OF ANY OTHER MEMBER OF HIS EXPEDITION.
I AM NOT IN POSSESSION OF ANY MORE INFORMATION THAN THE COUNTLESS OTHER TIMES YOU CAME AND FOUND US. THE "FAREWELL", CHARTERED BY THE ROYAL GEOGRAPHICAL SOCIETY, SUCCESSFULLY REACHED THE PORT OF TROMSØ WHEREBY ROALD HODGES JUNIOR'S EXPEDITION SET OUT FOR LAKE INARI BY LAND, AS WAS EXPECTED.
SEVERAL WITNESSES CLAIM SEEING THE EXPEDITION CAMP IN IVALO, SOUTH OF THE LAKE... THEN... THEN NOTHING!
ROALD HAD THE FIRM CONVICTION THAT DOLLA'S TOMB, THE GODDESS WORSHIPPED FOR MILLENNIA BY THE SAMI, WAS LOCATED WEST OF THIS LAKE INARI.
AS YOU KNOW, HE'D DECIPHERED THE RUNES WHICH SEEMED TO CORROBORATE THE FACT THAT...
NONSENSE!

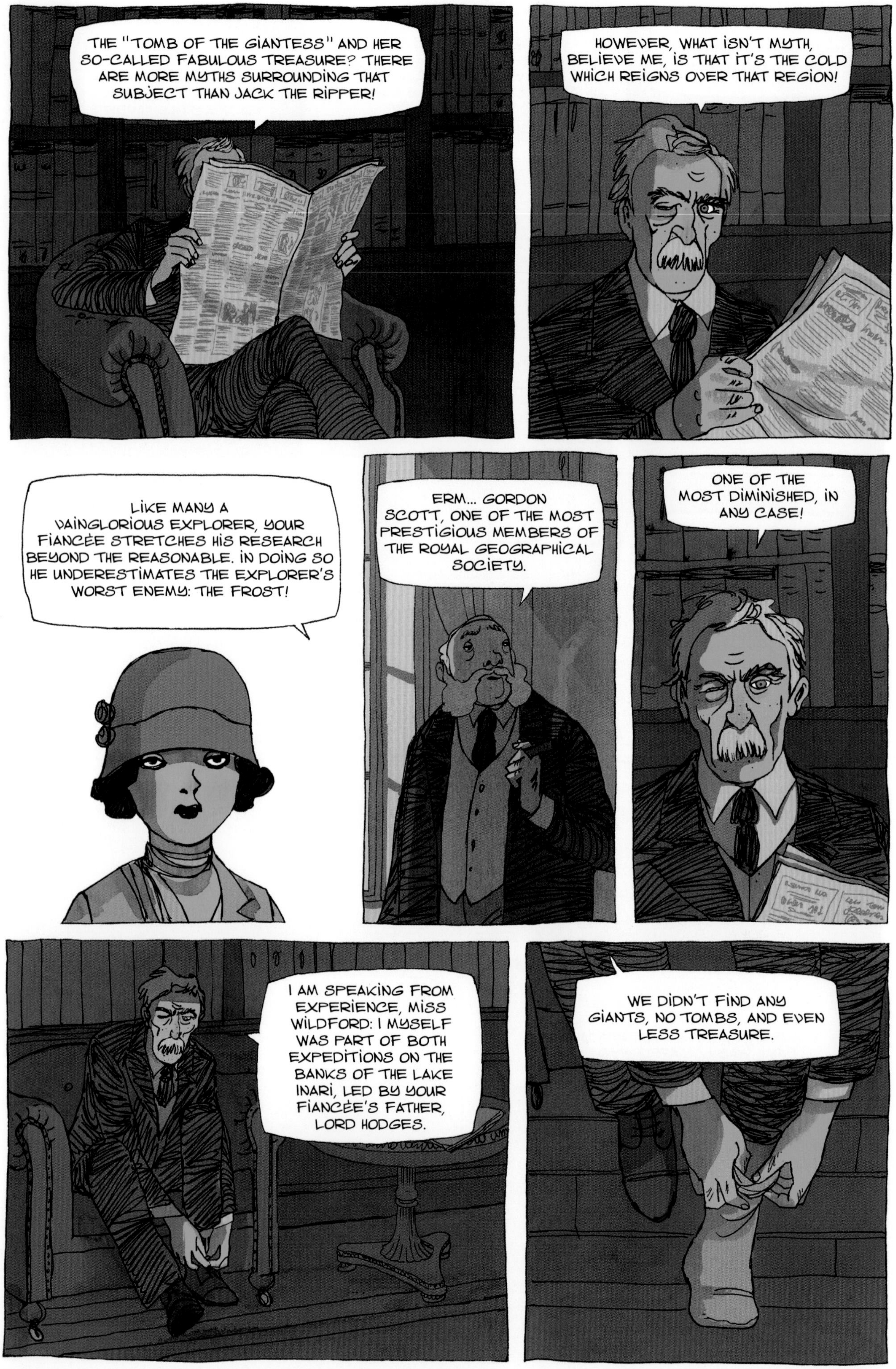
THE "TOMB OF THE GIANTESS" AND HER SO-CALLED FABULOUS TREASURE? THERE ARE MORE MYTHS SURROUNDING THAT SUBJECT THAN JACK THE RIPPER!
HOWEVER, WHAT ISN'T MYTH, BELIEVE ME, IS THAT IT'S THE COLD WHICH REIGNS OVER THAT REGION!
LIKE MANY A VAINGLORIOUS EXPLORER, YOUR FIANCÉE STRETCHES HIS RESEARCH BEYOND THE REASONABLE. IN DOING SO HE UNDERESTIMATES THE EXPLORER'S WORST ENEMY: THE FROST!
ERM... GORDON SCOTT, ONE OF THE MOST PRESTIGIOUS MEMBERS OF THE ROYAL GEOGRAPHICAL SOCIETY.
ONE OF THE MOST DIMINISHED, IN ANY CASE!
I AM SPEAKING FROM EXPERIENCE, MISS WILDFORD: I MYSELF WAS PART OF BOTH EXPEDITIONS ON THE BANKS OF THE LAKE INARI, LED BY YOUR FIANCÉE'S FATHER, LORD HODGES.
WE DIDN'T FIND ANY GIANTS, NO TOMBS, AND EVEN LESS TREASURE.

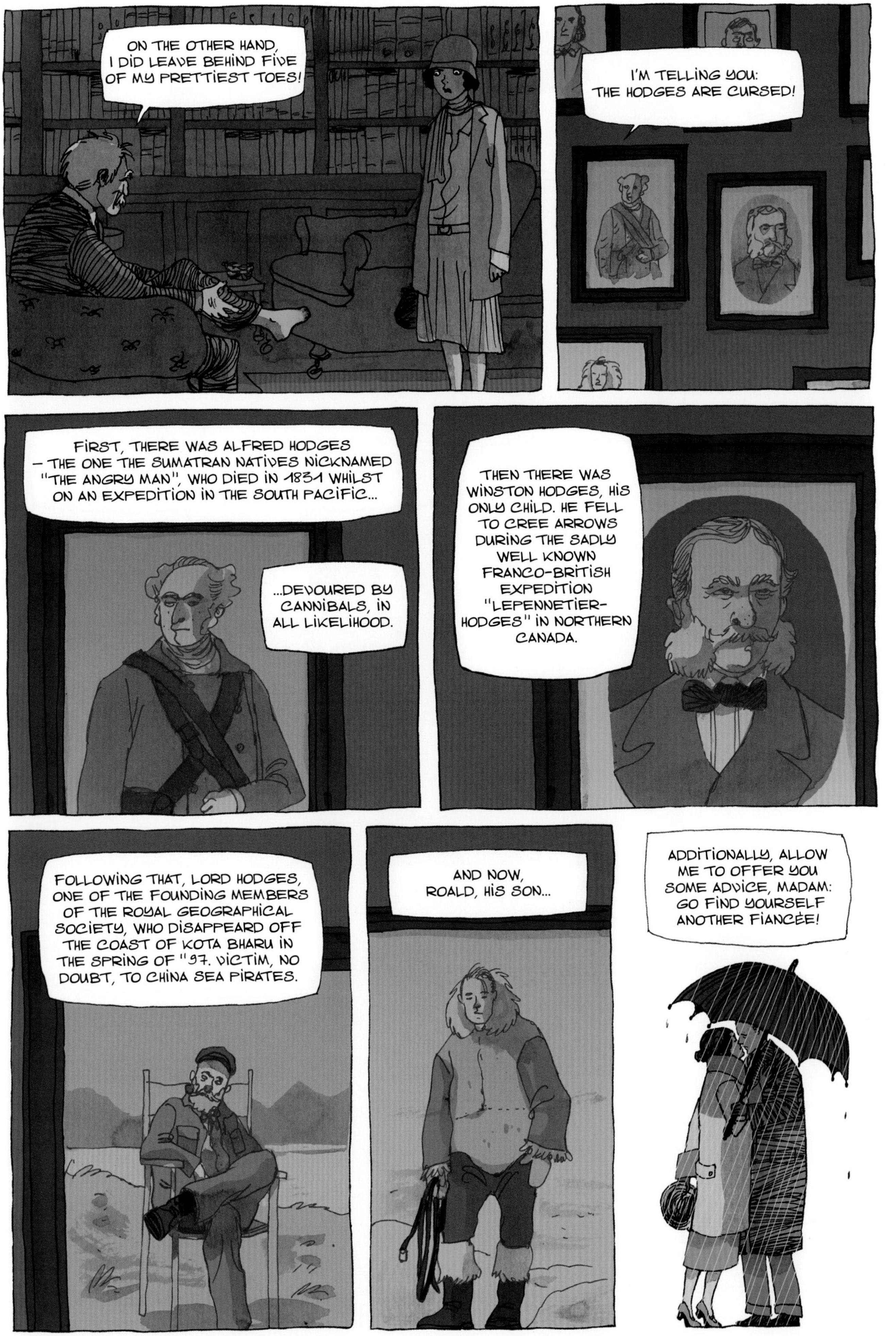
ON THE OTHER HAND, I DID LEAVE BEHIND FIVE OF MY PRETTIEST TOES!
I'M TELLING YOU: THE HODGES ARE CURSED!
FIRST, THERE WAS ALFRED HODGES – THE ONE THE SUMATRAN NATIVES NICKNAMED "THE ANGRY MAN", WHO DIED IN 1831 WHILST ON AN EXPEDITION IN THE SOUTH PACIFIC...
...DEVOURED BY CANNIBALS, IN ALL LIKELIHOOD.
THEN THERE WAS WINSTON HODGES, HIS ONLY CHILD. HE FELL TO CREE ARROWS DURING THE SADLY WELL KNOWN FRANCO-BRITISH EXPEDITION "LEPENNETIER-HODGES" IN NORTHERN CANADA.
FOLLOWING THAT, LORD HODGES, ONE OF THE FOUNDING MEMBERS OF THE ROYAL GEOGRAPHICAL SOCIETY, WHO DISAPPEARD OFF THE COAST OF KOTA BHARU IN THE SPRING OF "97. VICTIM, NO DOUBT, TO CHINA SEA PIRATES.
AND NOW, ROALD, HIS SON...
ADDITIONALLY, ALLOW ME TO OFFER YOU SOME ADVICE, MADAM: GO FIND YOURSELF ANOTHER FIANCÉE!

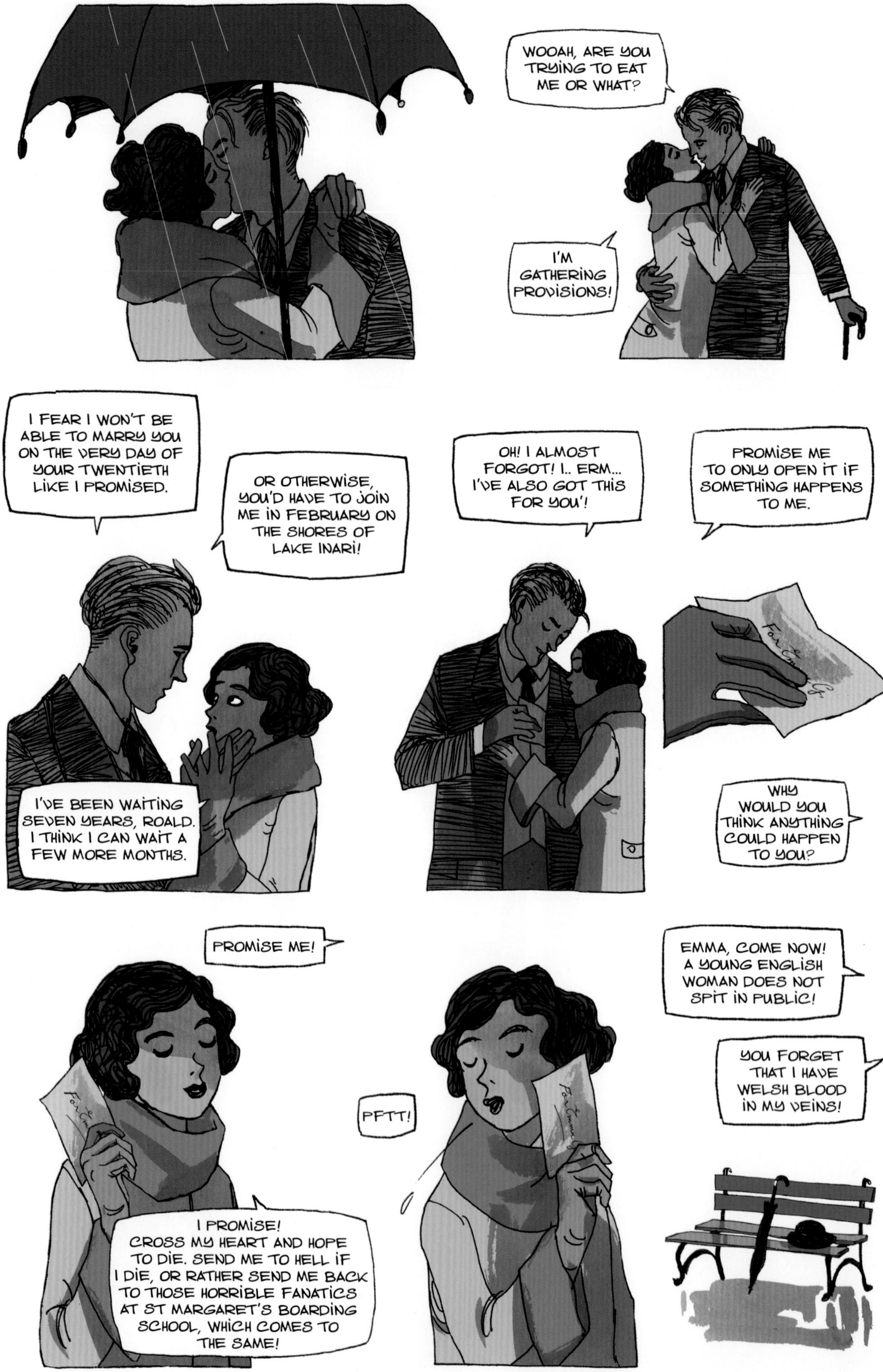
WOOAH, ARE YOU TRYING TO EAT ME OR WHAT?
I'M GATHERING PROVISIONS!
I FEAR I WON'T BE ABLE TO MARRY YOU ON THE VERY DAY OF YOUR TWENTIETH LIKE I PROMISED.
OR OTHERWISE, YOU'D HAVE TO JOIN ME IN FEBRUARY ON THE SHORES OF LAKE INARI!
I'VE BEEN WAITING SEVEN YEARS, ROALD. I THINK I CAN WAIT A FEW MORE MONTHS.
OH! I ALMOST FORGOT! I.. ERM... I'VE ALSO GOT THIS FOR YOU'!
PROMISE ME TO ONLY OPEN IT IF SOMETHING HAPPENS TO ME.
WHY WOULD YOU THINK ANYTHING COULD HAPPEN TO YOU?
PROMISE ME!
I PROMISE! CROSS MY HEART AND HOPE TO DIE. SEND ME TO HELL IF I DIE, OR RATHER SEND ME BACK TO THOSE HORRIBLE FANATICS AT ST MARGARET'S BOARDING SCHOOL, WHICH COMES TO THE SAME!
PFTT!
EMMA, COME NOW! A YOUNG ENGLISH WOMAN DOES NOT SPIT IN PUBLIC!
YOU FORGET THAT I HAVE WELSH BLOOD IN MY VEINS!

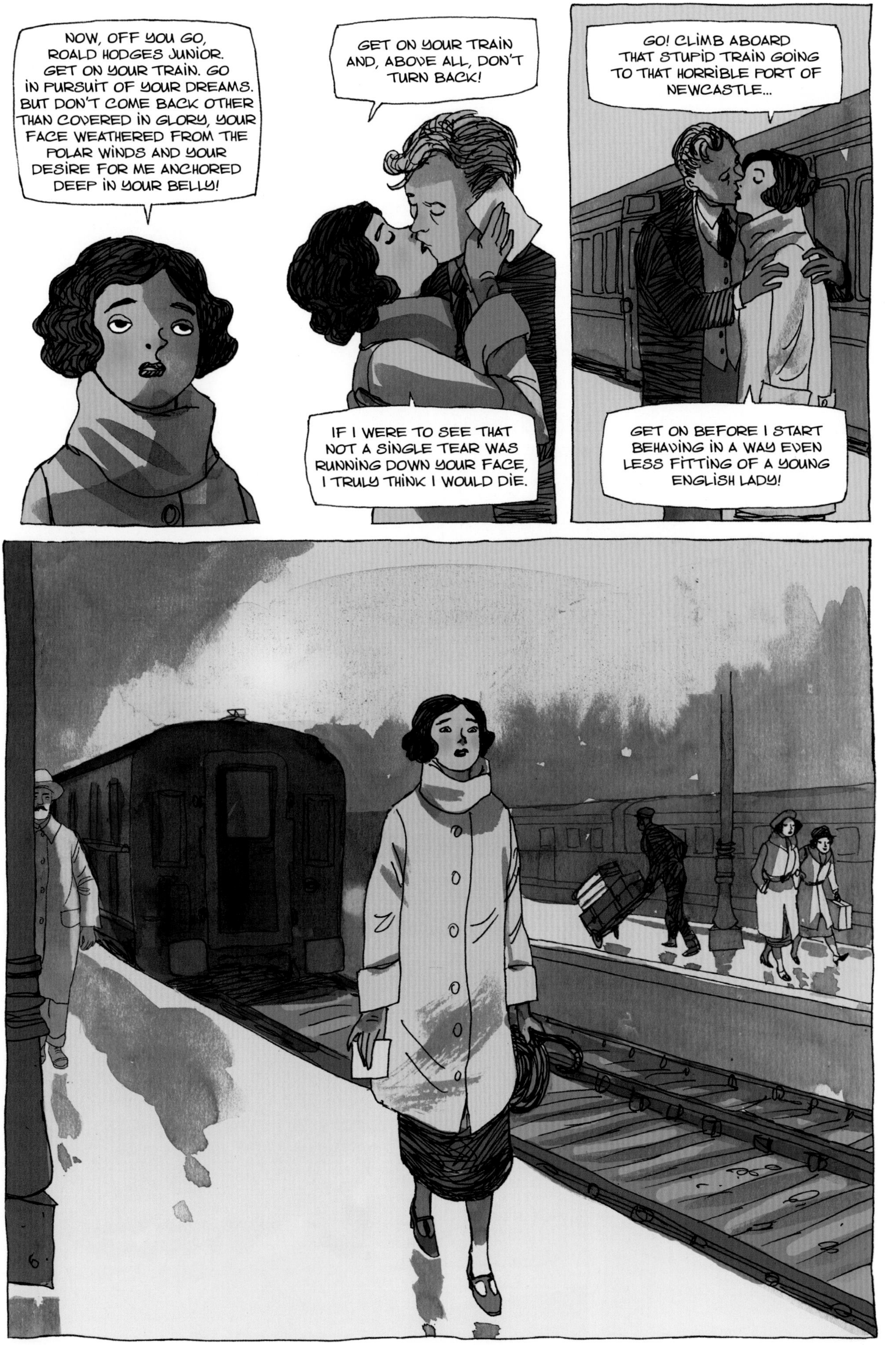
NOW, OFF YOU GO, ROALD HODGES JUNIOR. GET ON YOUR TRAIN. GO IN PURSUIT OF YOUR DREAMS. BUT DON'T COME BACK OTHER THAN COVERED IN GLORY, YOUR FACE WEATHERED FROM THE POLAR WINDS AND YOUR DESIRE FOR ME ANCHORED DEEP IN YOUR BELLY!
GET ON YOUR TRAIN AND, ABOVE ALL, DON'T TURN BACK!
IF I WERE TO SEE THAT NOT A SINGLE TEAR WAS RUNNING DOWN YOUR FACE, I TRULY THINK I WOULD DIE.
GO! CLIMB ABOARD THAT STUPID TRAIN GOING TO THAT HORRIBLE PORT OF NEWCASTLE...
GET ON BEFORE I START BEHAVING IN A WAY EVEN LESS FITTING OF A YOUNG ENGLISH LADY!

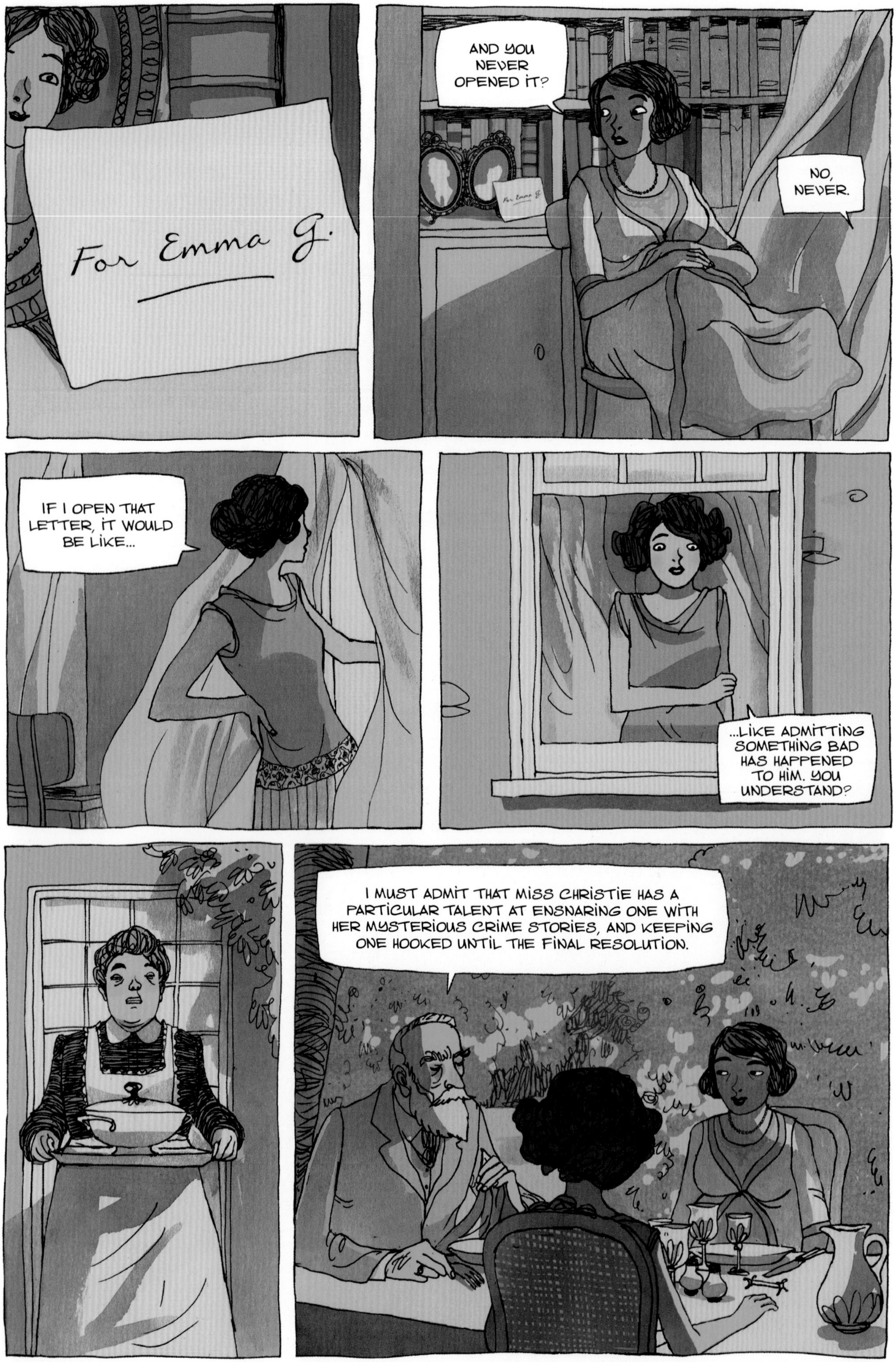
For Emma G.
AND YOU NEVER OPENED IT?
For Emma G.
NO, NEVER.
IF I OPEN THAT LETTER, IT WOULD BE LIKE...
...LIKE ADMITTING SOMETHING BAD HAS HAPPENED TO HIM. YOU UNDERSTAND?
I MUST ADMIT THAT MISS CHRISTIE HAS A PARTICULAR TALENT AT ENSNARING ONE WITH HER MYSTERIOUS CRIME STORIES, AND KEEPING ONE HOOKED UNTIL THE FINAL RESOLUTION.

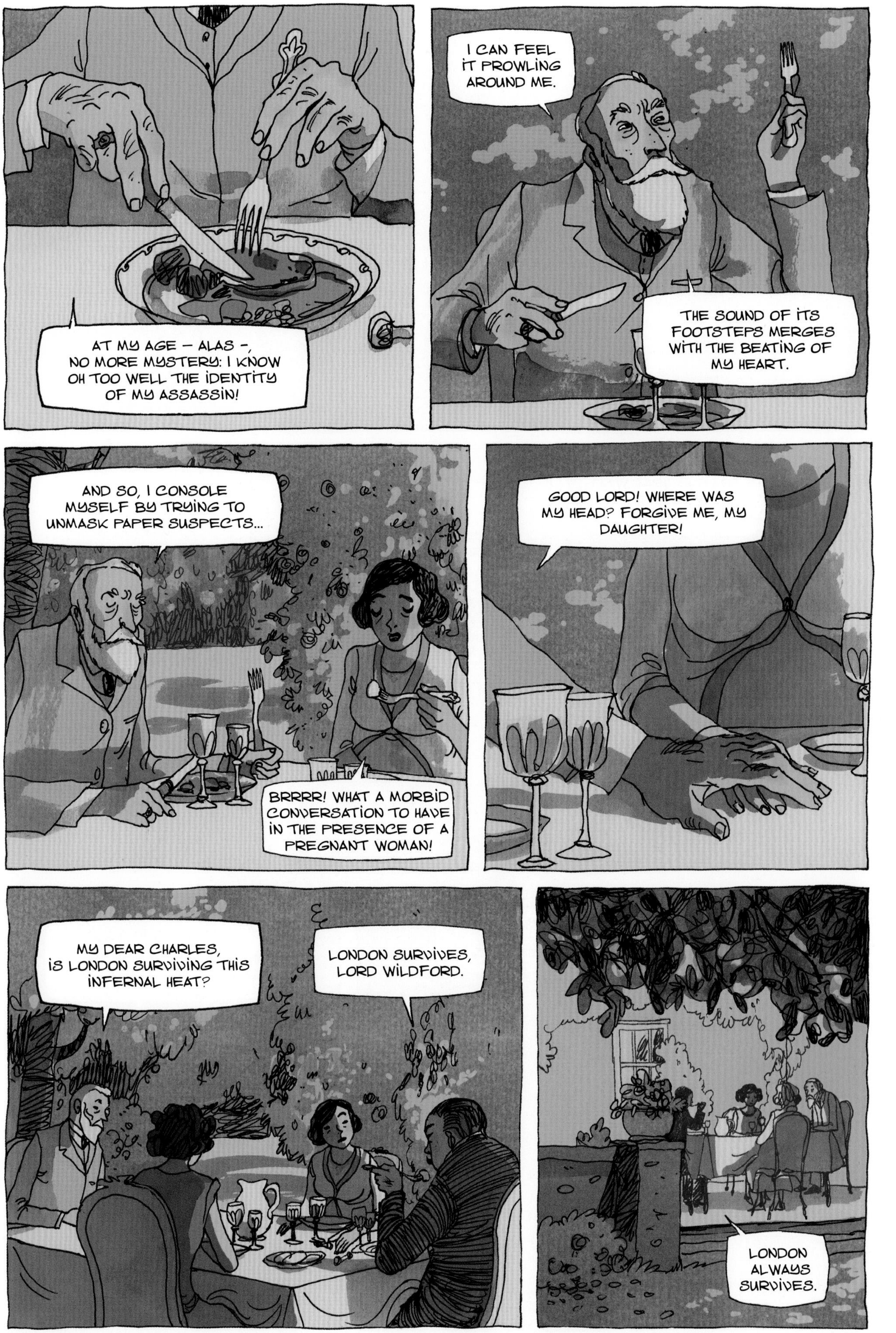
AT MY AGE — ALAS —, NO MORE MYSTERY: I KNOW OH TOO WELL THE IDENTITY OF MY ASSASSIN!
I CAN FEEL IT PROWLING AROUND ME.
THE SOUND OF ITS FOOTSTEPS MERGES WITH THE BEATING OF MY HEART.
AND SO, I CONSOLE MYSELF BY TRYING TO UNMASK PAPER SUSPECTS...
BRRRR! WHAT A MORBID CONVERSATION TO HAVE IN THE PRESENCE OF A PREGNANT WOMAN!
GOOD LORD! WHERE WAS MY HEAD? FORGIVE ME, MY DAUGHTER!
MY DEAR CHARLES, IS LONDON SURVIVING THIS INFERNAL HEAT?
LONDON SURVIVES, LORD WILDFORD.
LONDON ALWAYS SURVIVES.

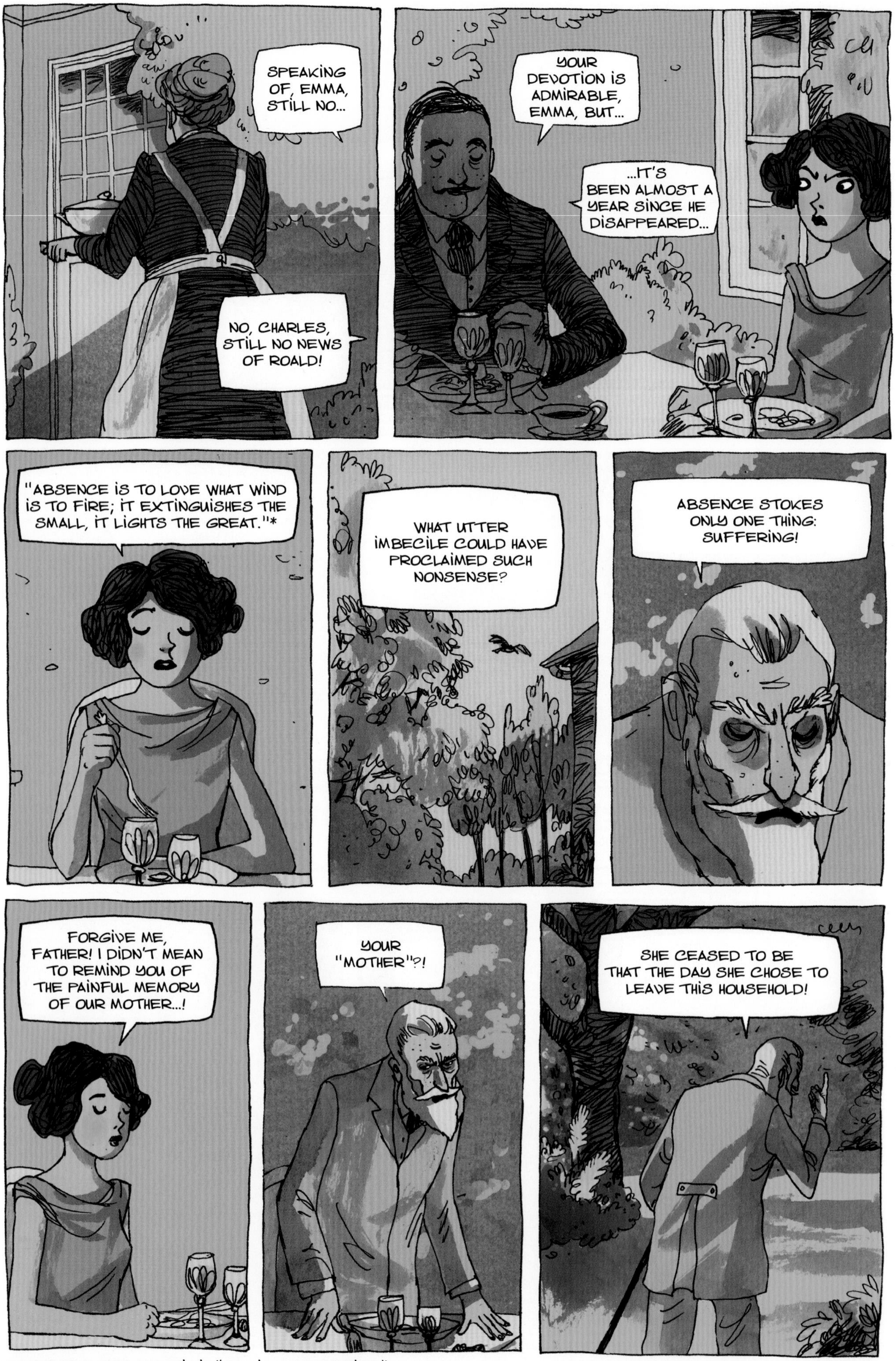
SPEAKING OF, EMMA, STILL NO...
NO, CHARLES, STILL NO NEWS OF ROALD!
YOUR DEVOTION IS ADMIRABLE, EMMA, BUT...
...IT'S BEEN ALMOST A YEAR SINCE HE DISAPPEARED...
"ABSENCE IS TO LOVE WHAT WIND IS TO FIRE; IT EXTINGUISHES THE SMALL, IT LIGHTS THE GREAT."*
WHAT UTTER IMBECILE COULD HAVE PROCLAIMED SUCH NONSENSE?
ABSENCE STOKES ONLY ONE THING: SUFFERING!
FORGIVE ME, FATHER! I DIDN'T MEAN TO REMIND YOU OF THE PAINFUL MEMORY OF OUR MOTHER...!
YOUR "MOTHER"?!
SHE CEASED TO BE THAT THE DAY SHE CHOSE TO LEAVE THIS HOUSEHOLD!

* ROGER DE BUSSY-RABUTIN IN "GALLIC LOVE STORIES."

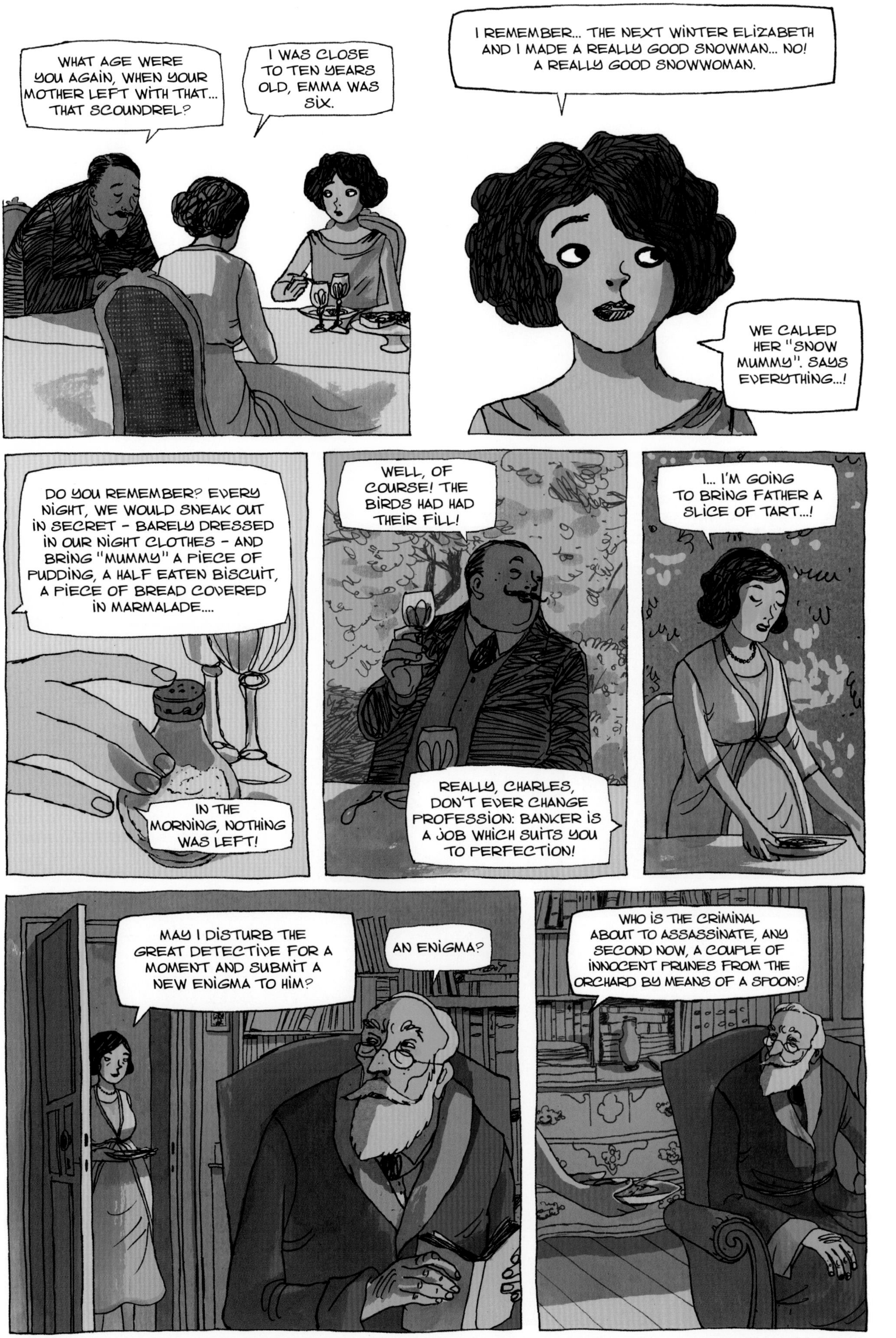
WHAT AGE WERE YOU AGAIN, WHEN YOUR MOTHER LEFT WITH THAT... THAT SCOUNDREL?
I WAS CLOSE TO TEN YEARS OLD, EMMA WAS SIX.
I REMEMBER... THE NEXT WINTER ELIZABETH AND I MADE A REALLY GOOD SNOWMAN... NO! A REALLY GOOD SNOWWOMAN.
WE CALLED HER "SNOW MUMMY". SAYS EVERYTHING...!
DO YOU REMEMBER? EVERY NIGHT, WE WOULD SNEAK OUT IN SECRET - BARELY DRESSED IN OUR NIGHT CLOTHES - AND BRING "MUMMY" A PIECE OF PUDDING, A HALF EATEN BISCUIT, A PIECE OF BREAD COVERED IN MARMALADE....
IN THE MORNING, NOTHING WAS LEFT!
WELL, OF COURSE! THE BIRDS HAD HAD THEIR FILL!
REALLY, CHARLES, DON'T EVER CHANGE PROFESSION: BANKER IS A JOB WHICH SUITS YOU TO PERFECTION!
I... I'M GOING TO BRING FATHER A SLICE OF TART...!
MAY I DISTURB THE GREAT DETECTIVE FOR A MOMENT AND SUBMIT A NEW ENIGMA TO HIM?
AN ENIGMA?
WHO IS THE CRIMINAL ABOUT TO ASSASSINATE, ANY SECOND NOW, A COUPLE OF INNOCENT PRUNES FROM THE ORCHARD BY MEANS OF A SPOON?

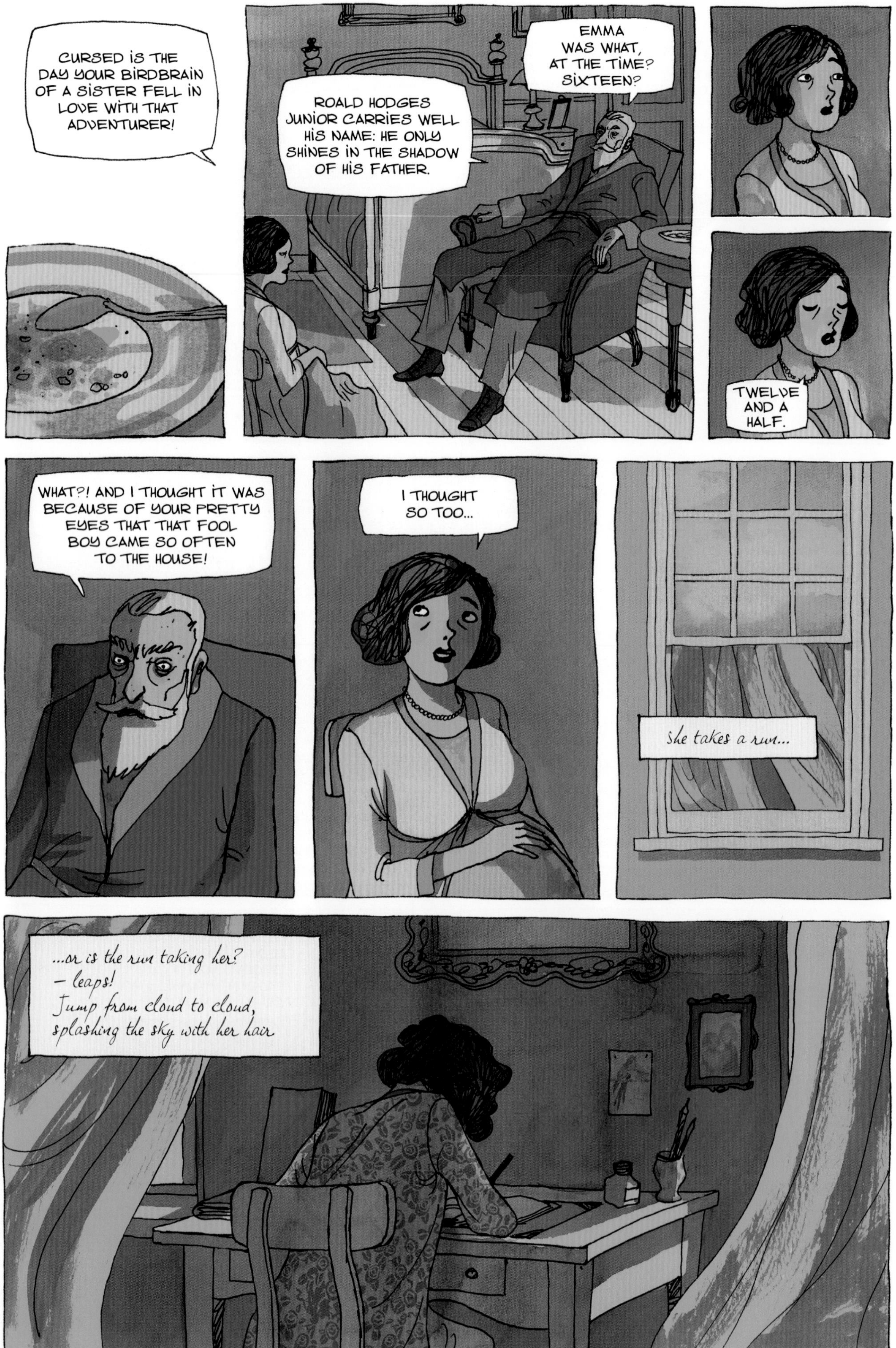
CURSED IS THE DAY YOUR BIRDBRAIN OF A SISTER FELL IN LOVE WITH THAT ADVENTURER!
ROALD HODGES JUNIOR CARRIES WELL HIS NAME: HE ONLY SHINES IN THE SHADOW OF HIS FATHER.
EMMA WAS WHAT, AT THE TIME? SIXTEEN?
TWELVE AND A HALF.
WHAT?! AND I THOUGHT IT WAS BECAUSE OF YOUR PRETTY EYES THAT THAT FOOL BOY CAME SO OFTEN TO THE HOUSE!
I THOUGHT SO TOO...
She takes a run...
...or is the run taking her?
– leaps!
Jump from cloud to cloud,
splashing the sky with her hair

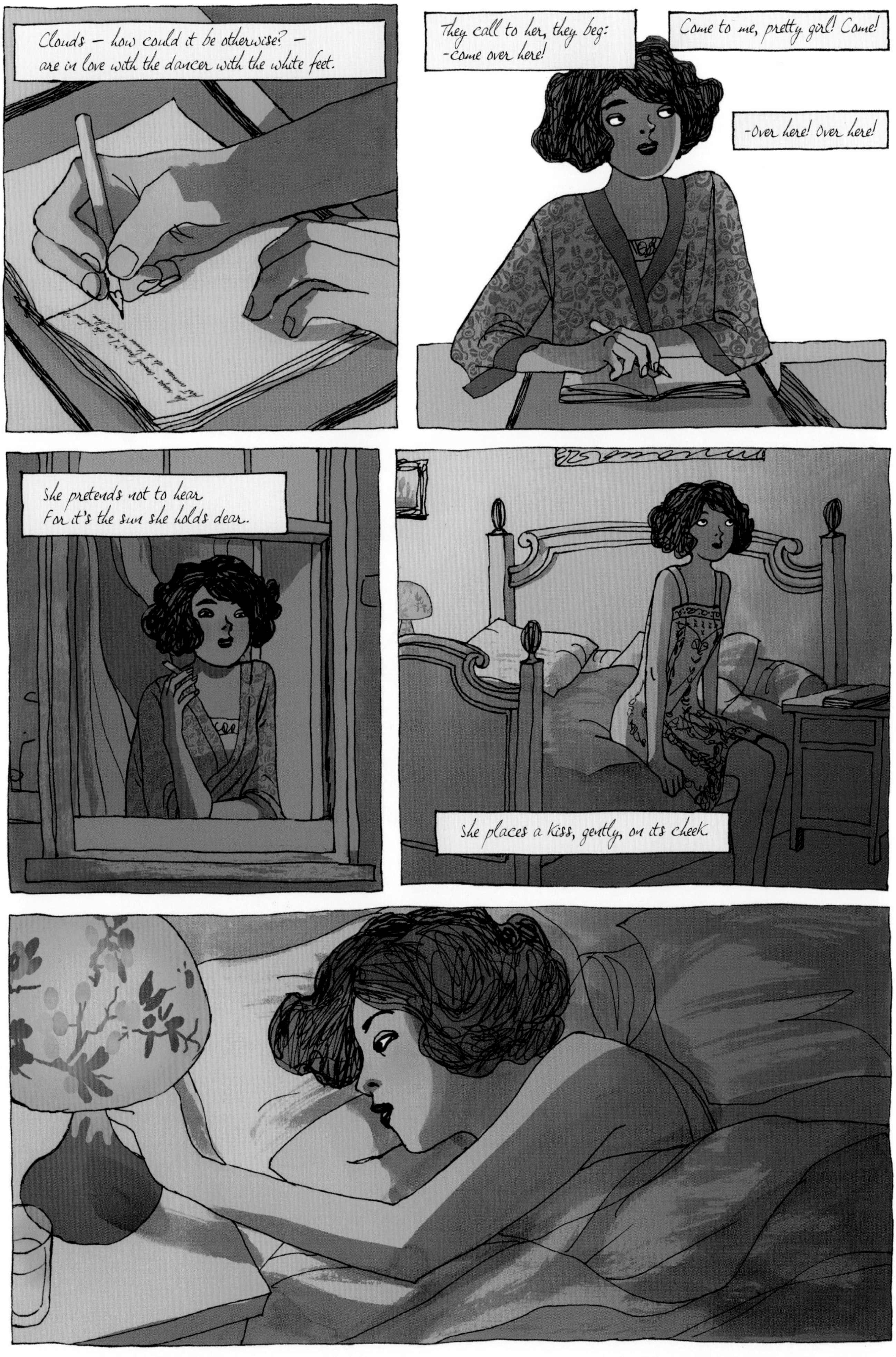
Clouds – how could it be otherwise? –
are in love with the dancer with the white feet.
They call to her, they beg:
-Come over here!
Come to me, pretty girl! Come!
-Over here! Over here!
She pretends not to hear
For it's the sun she holds dear.
She places a kiss, gently, on its cheek

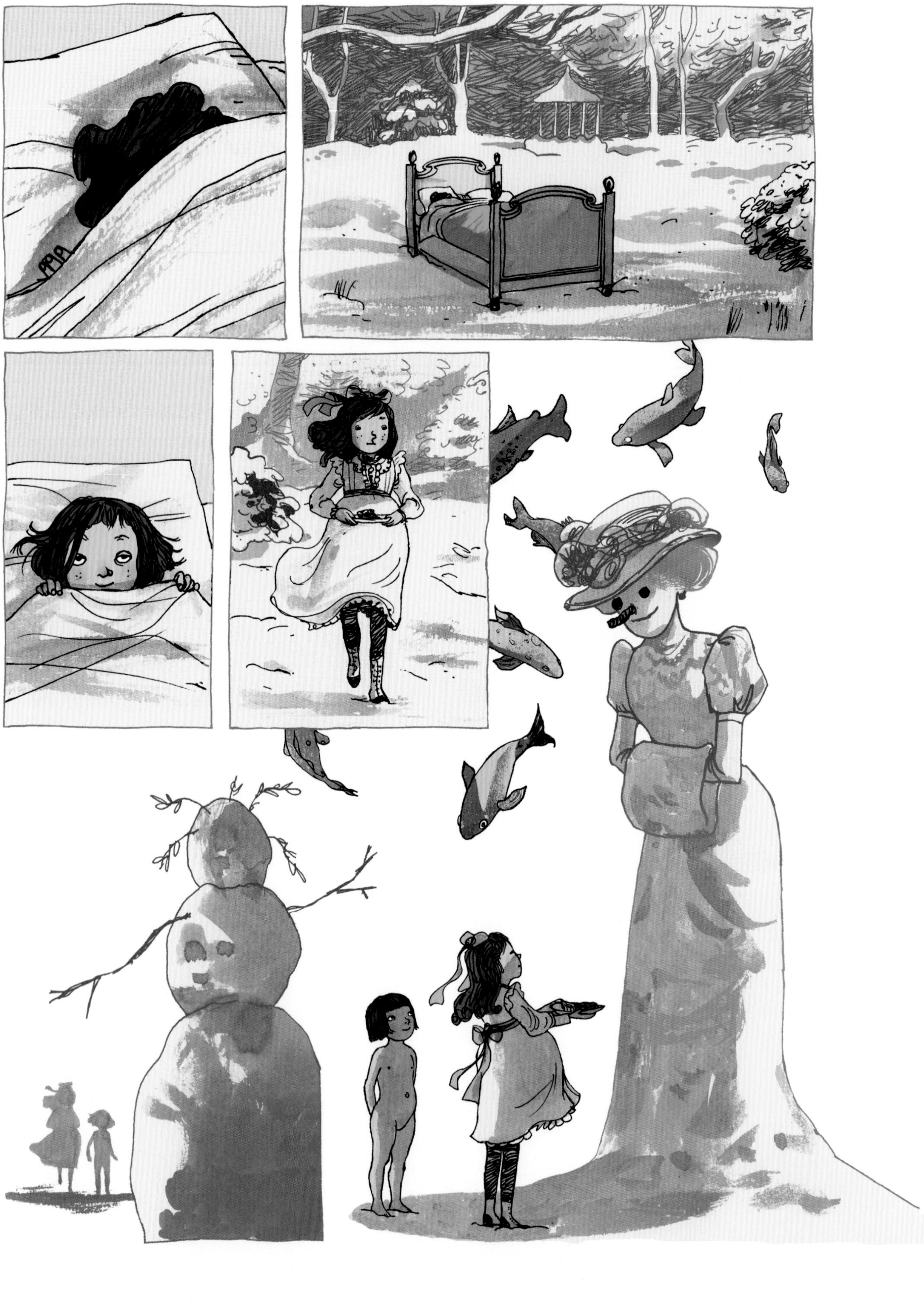

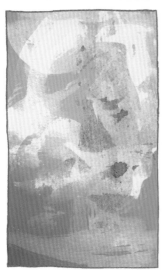

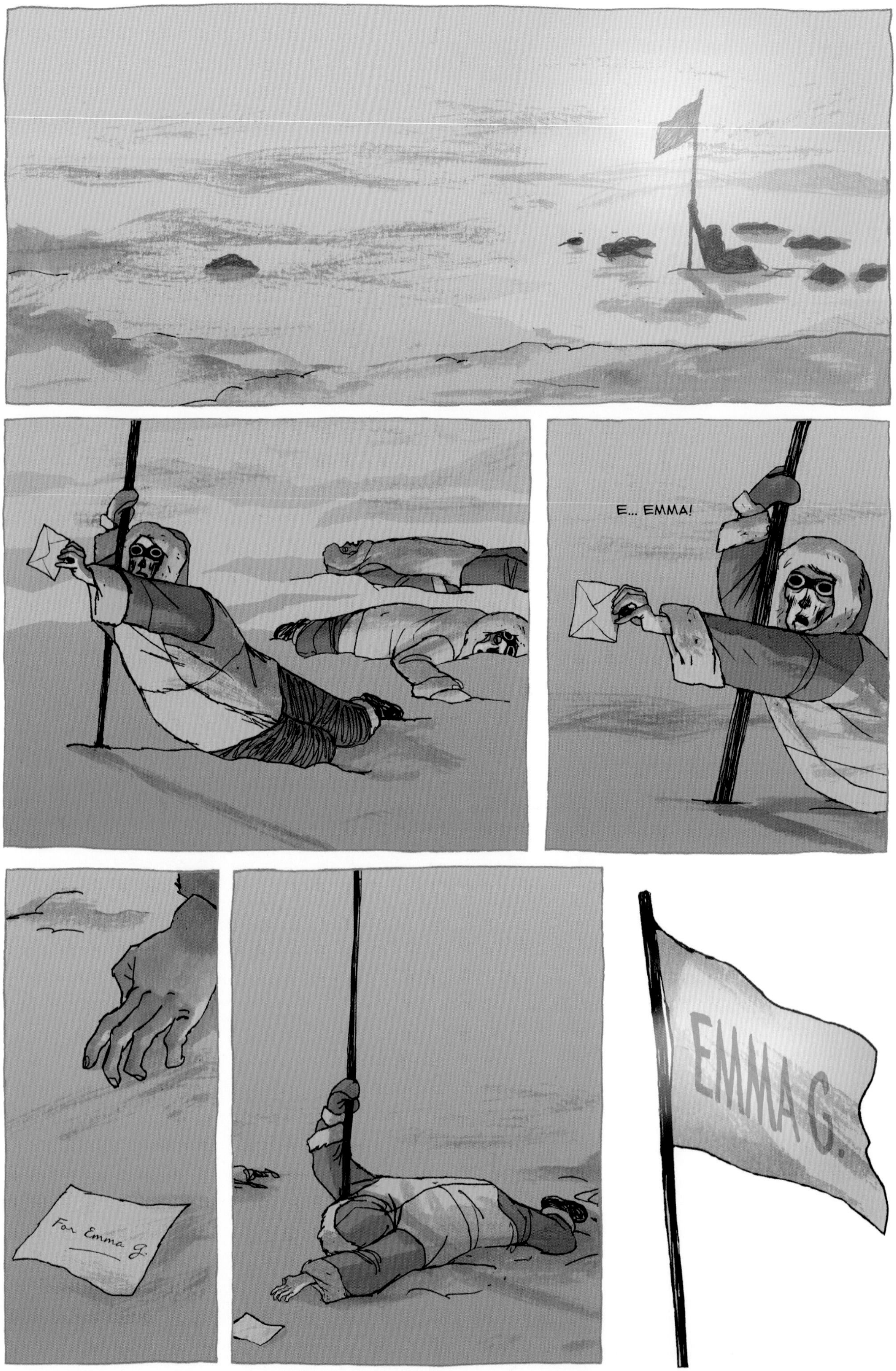
E... EMMA!
For Emma G.
EMMA G.

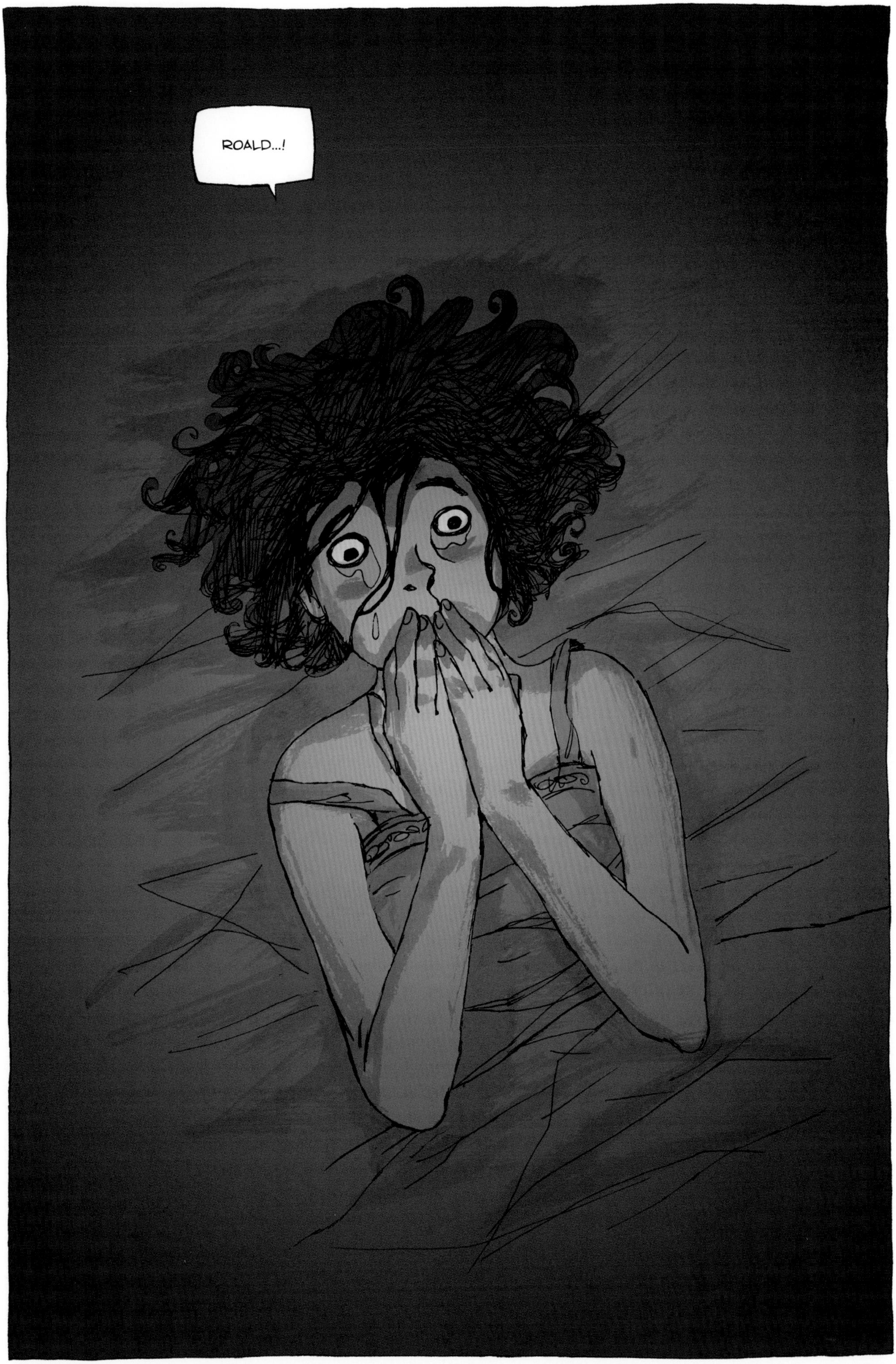
ROALD...!

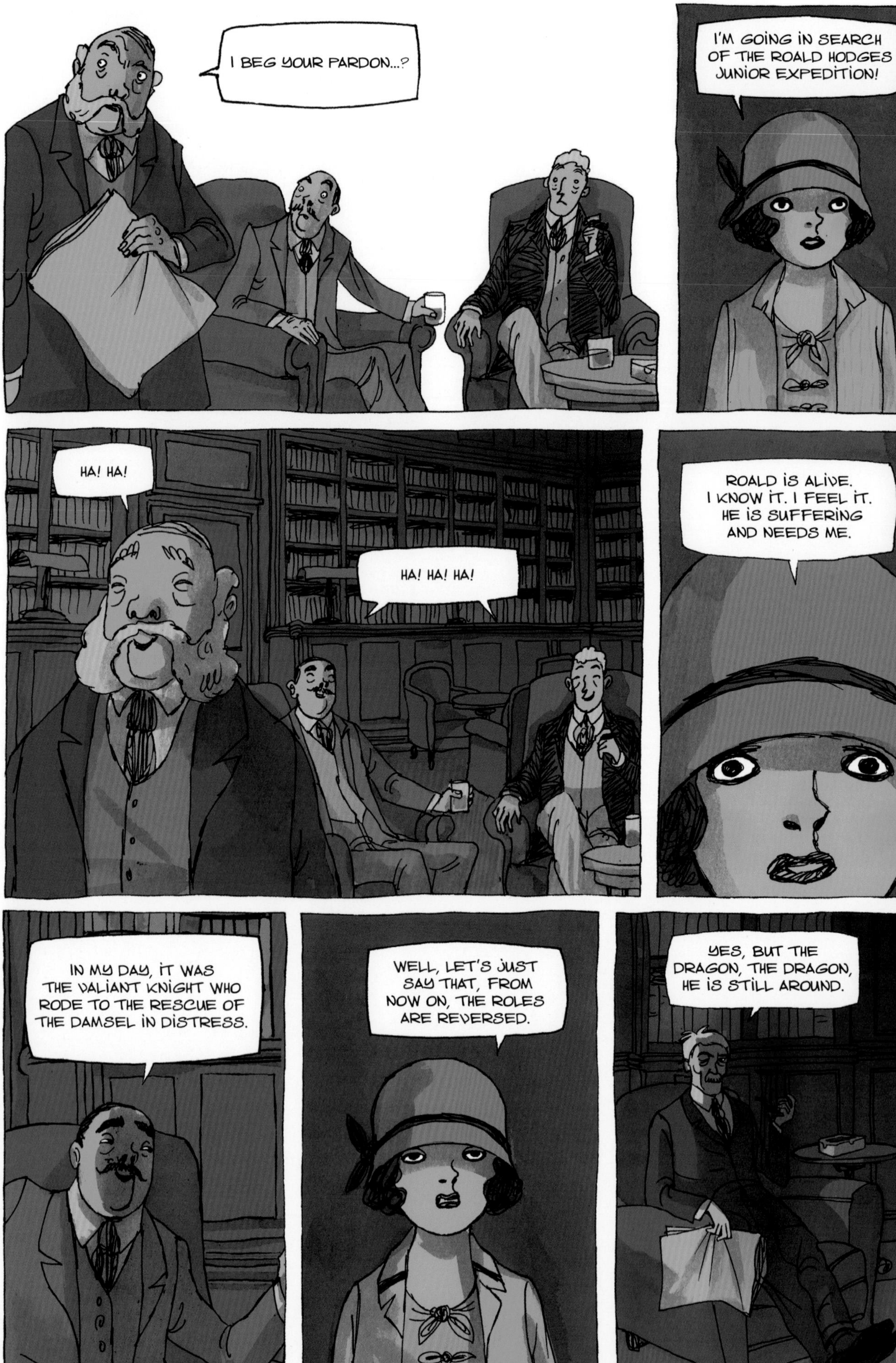
I BEG YOUR PARDON...?
I'M GOING IN SEARCH OF THE ROALD HODGES JUNIOR EXPEDITION!
HA! HA!
HA! HA! HA!
ROALD IS ALIVE. I KNOW IT. I FEEL IT. HE IS SUFFERING AND NEEDS ME.
IN MY DAY, IT WAS THE VALIANT KNIGHT WHO RODE TO THE RESCUE OF THE DAMSEL IN DISTRESS.
WELL, LET'S JUST SAY THAT, FROM NOW ON, THE ROLES ARE REVERSED.
YES, BUT THE DRAGON, THE DRAGON, HE IS STILL AROUND.

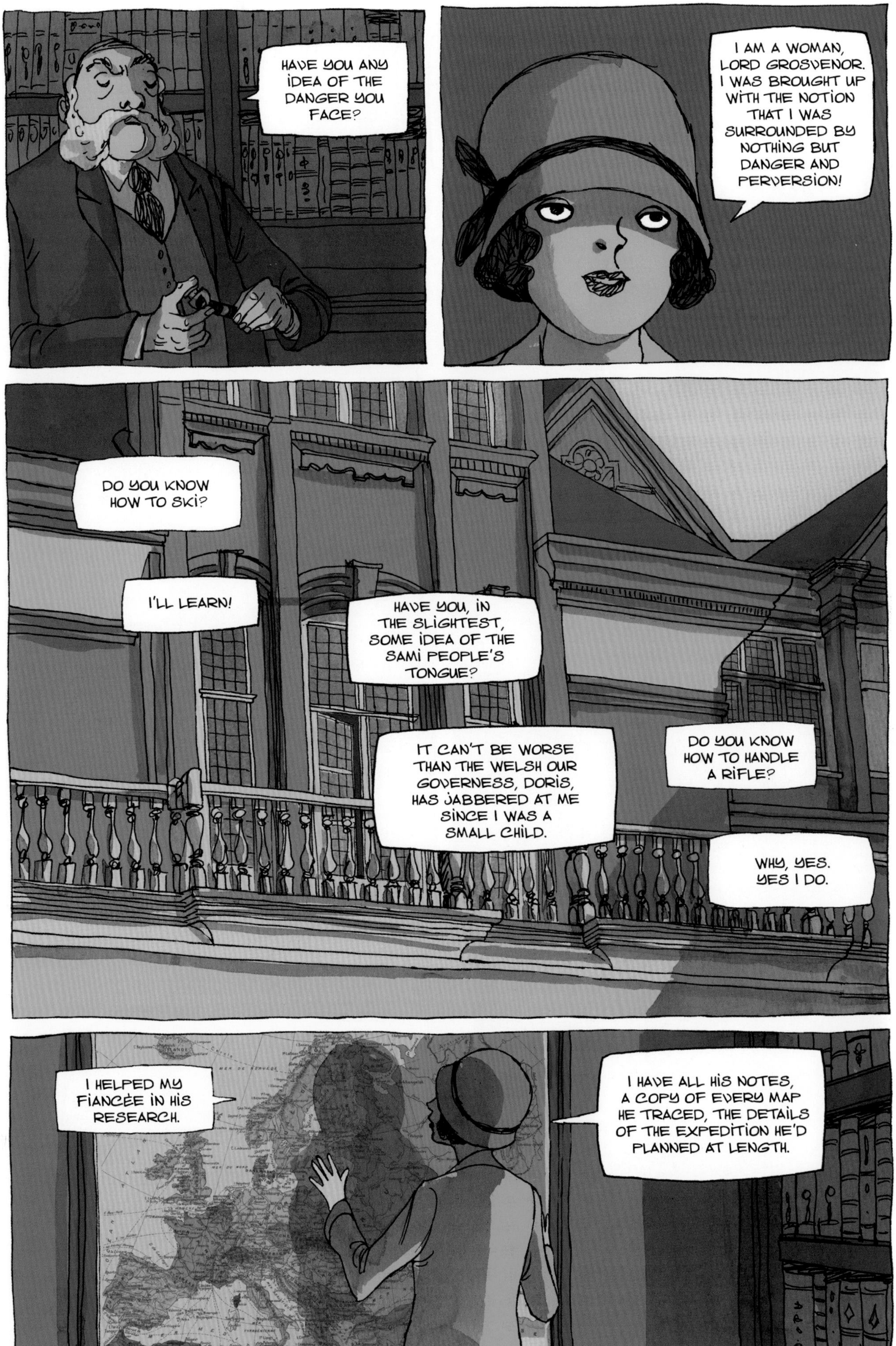
HAVE YOU ANY IDEA OF THE DANGER YOU FACE?
I AM A WOMAN, LORD GROSVENOR. I WAS BROUGHT UP WITH THE NOTION THAT I WAS SURROUNDED BY NOTHING BUT DANGER AND PERVERSION!
DO YOU KNOW HOW TO SKI?
I'LL LEARN!
HAVE YOU, IN THE SLIGHTEST, SOME IDEA OF THE SAMI PEOPLE'S TONGUE?
IT CAN'T BE WORSE THAN THE WELSH OUR GOVERNESS, DORIS, HAS JABBERED AT ME SINCE I WAS A SMALL CHILD.
DO YOU KNOW HOW TO HANDLE A RIFLE?
WHY, YES. YES I DO.
I HELPED MY FIANCÉE IN HIS RESEARCH.
I HAVE ALL HIS NOTES, A COPY OF EVERY MAP HE TRACED, THE DETAILS OF THE EXPEDITION HE'D PLANNED AT LENGTH.

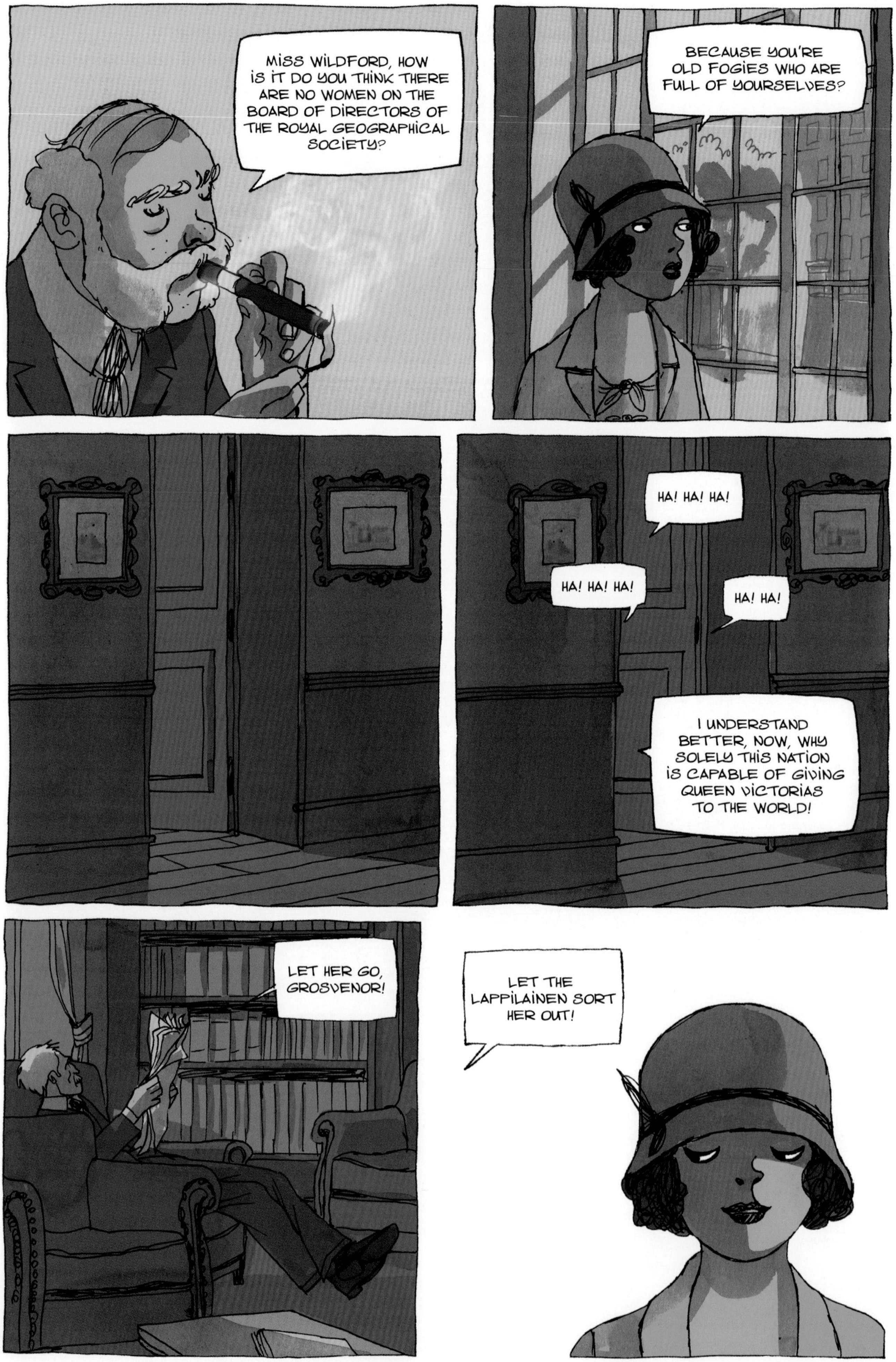
MISS WILDFORD, HOW IS IT DO YOU THINK THERE ARE NO WOMEN ON THE BOARD OF DIRECTORS OF THE ROYAL GEOGRAPHICAL SOCIETY?
BECAUSE YOU'RE OLD FOGIES WHO ARE FULL OF YOURSELVES?
HA! HA! HA!
HA! HA! HA!
HA! HA!
I UNDERSTAND BETTER, NOW, WHY SOLELY THIS NATION IS CAPABLE OF GIVING QUEEN VICTORIAS TO THE WORLD!
LET HER GO, GROSVENOR!
LET THE LAPPILAINEN SORT HER OUT!

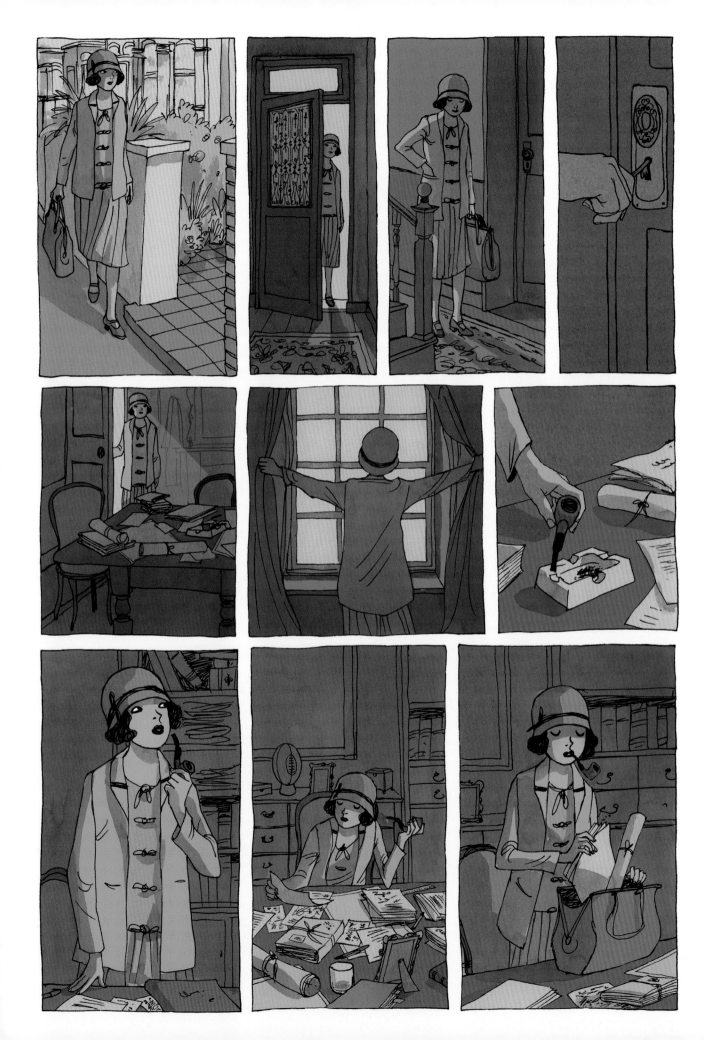

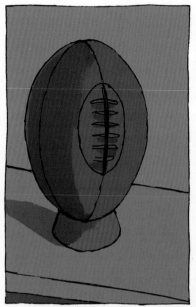

MADNESS!
IT'S MADNESS!

IT'S NOT YOU
THAT I'M LEAVING,
FATHER. IT'S HIM I'M
GOING TO FIND.

THAT'S NOT A
WORLD AWAY FROM
WHAT YOUR MOTHER
STRUCK ME WITH WHEN
SHE WENT OFF WITH
THAT GARDENER.

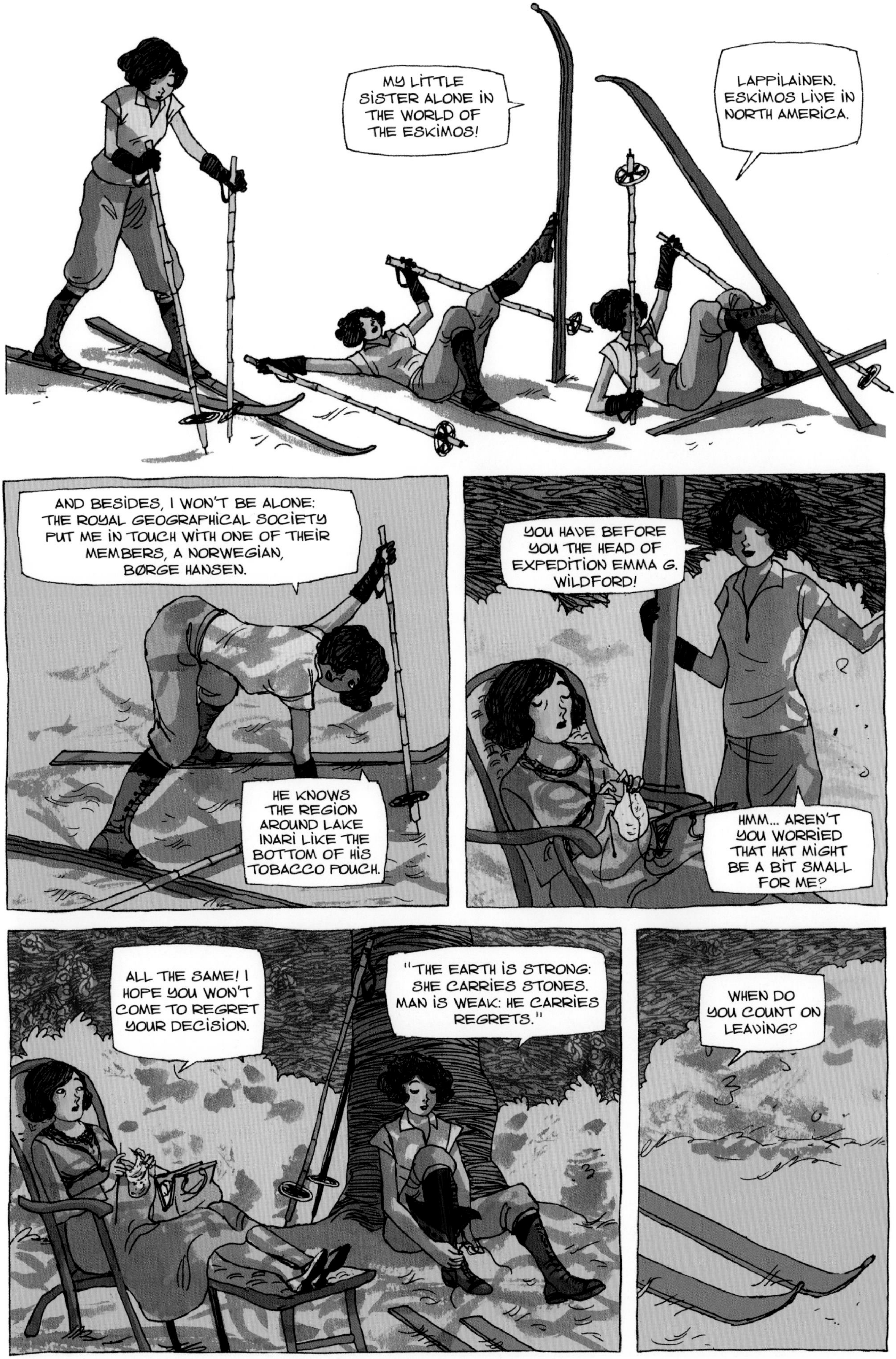
MY LITTLE SISTER ALONE IN THE WORLD OF THE ESKIMOS!
LAPPILAINEN. ESKIMOS LIVE IN NORTH AMERICA.
AND BESIDES, I WON'T BE ALONE: THE ROYAL GEOGRAPHICAL SOCIETY PUT ME IN TOUCH WITH ONE OF THEIR MEMBERS, A NORWEGIAN, BØRGE HANSEN.
HE KNOWS THE REGION AROUND LAKE INARI LIKE THE BOTTOM OF HIS TOBACCO POUCH.
YOU HAVE BEFORE YOU THE HEAD OF EXPEDITION EMMA G. WILDFORD!
HMM... AREN'T YOU WORRIED THAT HAT MIGHT BE A BIT SMALL FOR ME?
ALL THE SAME! I HOPE YOU WON'T COME TO REGRET YOUR DECISION.
"THE EARTH IS STRONG: SHE CARRIES STONES. MAN IS WEAK: HE CARRIES REGRETS."
WHEN DO YOU COUNT ON LEAVING?

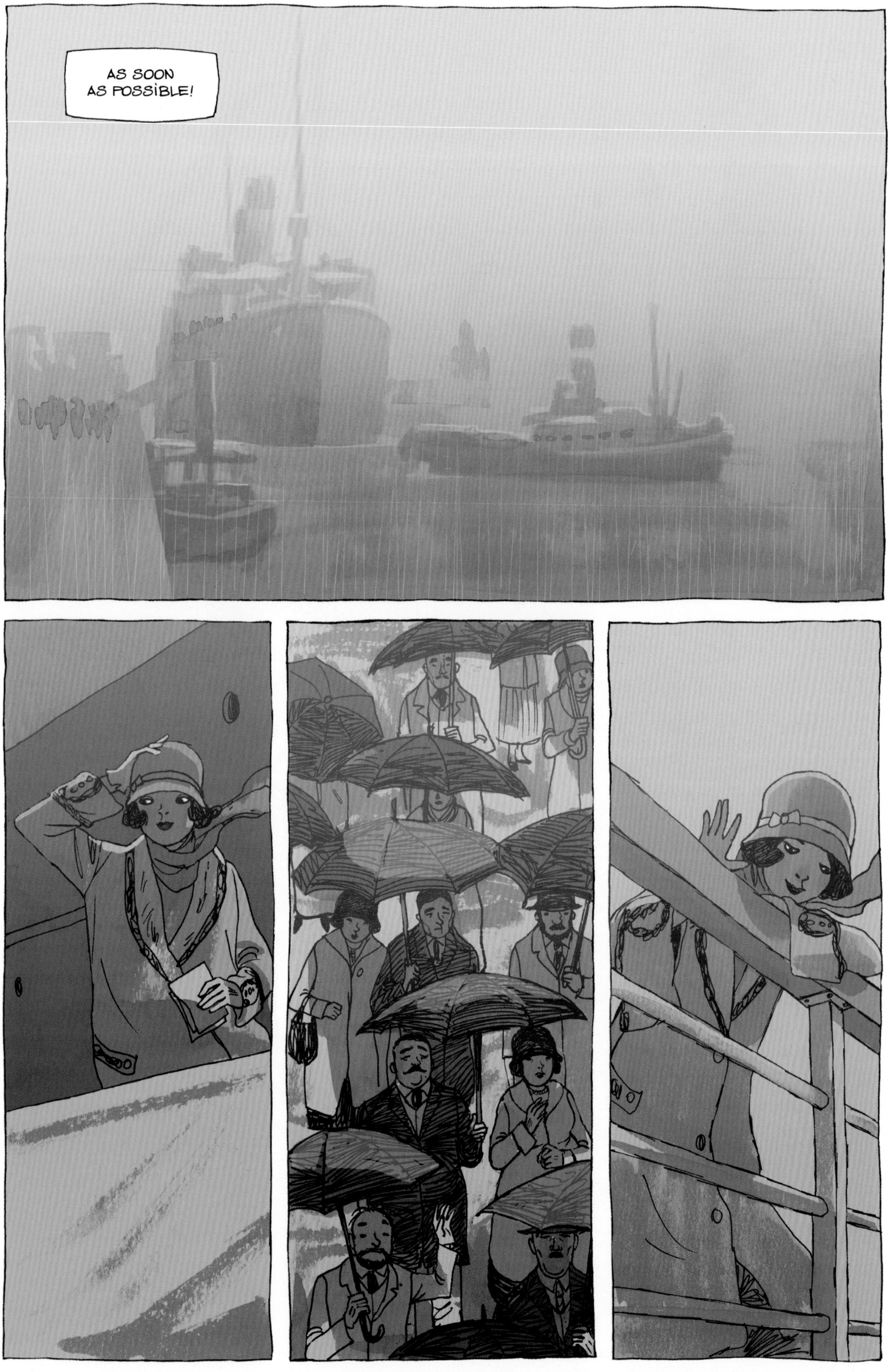
AS SOON
AS POSSIBLE!

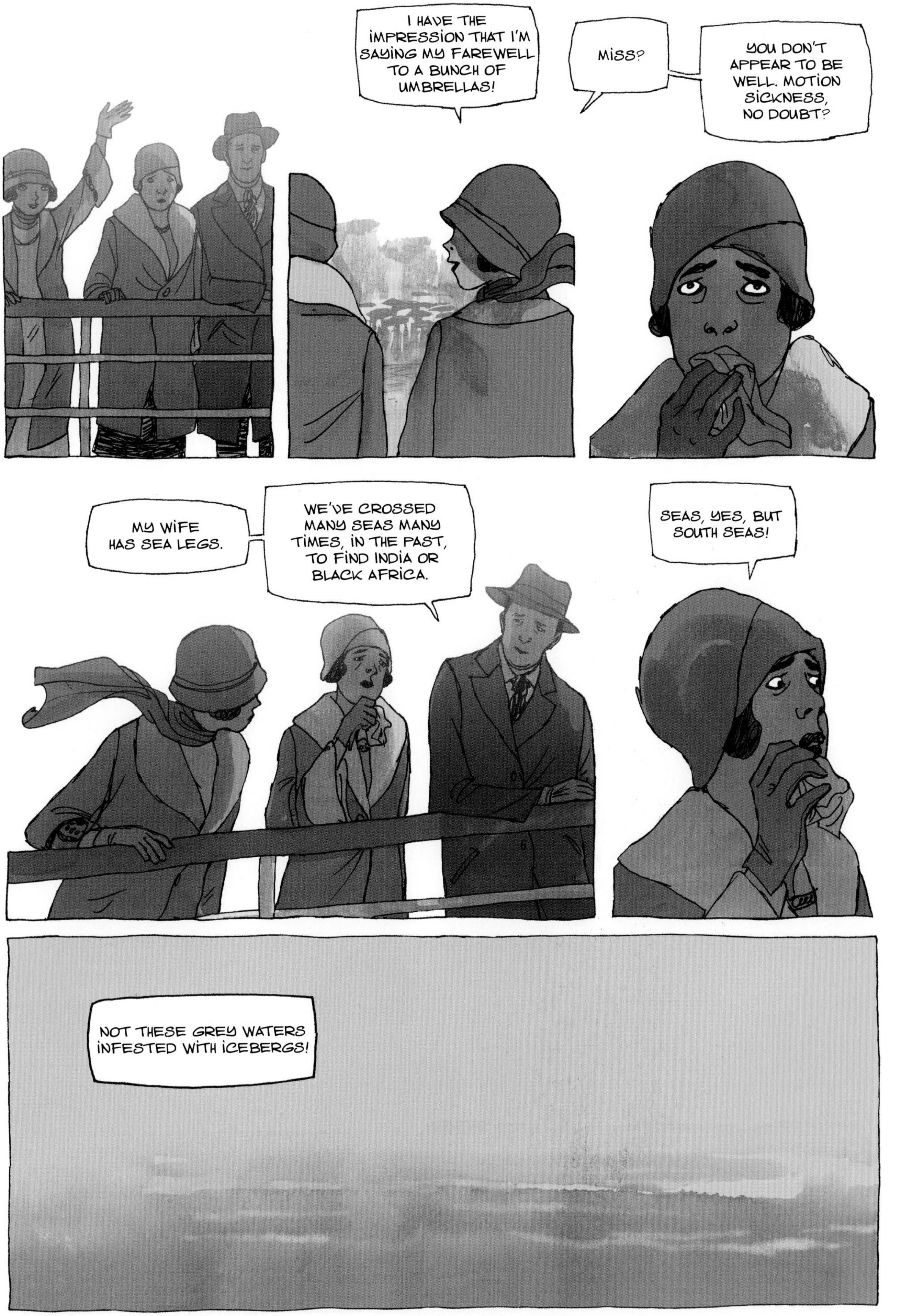
I HAVE THE IMPRESSION THAT I'M SAYING MY FAREWELL TO A BUNCH OF UMBRELLAS!
MISS?
YOU DON'T APPEAR TO BE WELL. MOTION SICKNESS, NO DOUBT?
MY WIFE HAS SEA LEGS.
WE'VE CROSSED MANY SEAS MANY TIMES, IN THE PAST, TO FIND INDIA OR BLACK AFRICA.
SEAS, YES, BUT SOUTH SEAS!
NOT THESE GREY WATERS INFESTED WITH ICEBERGS!

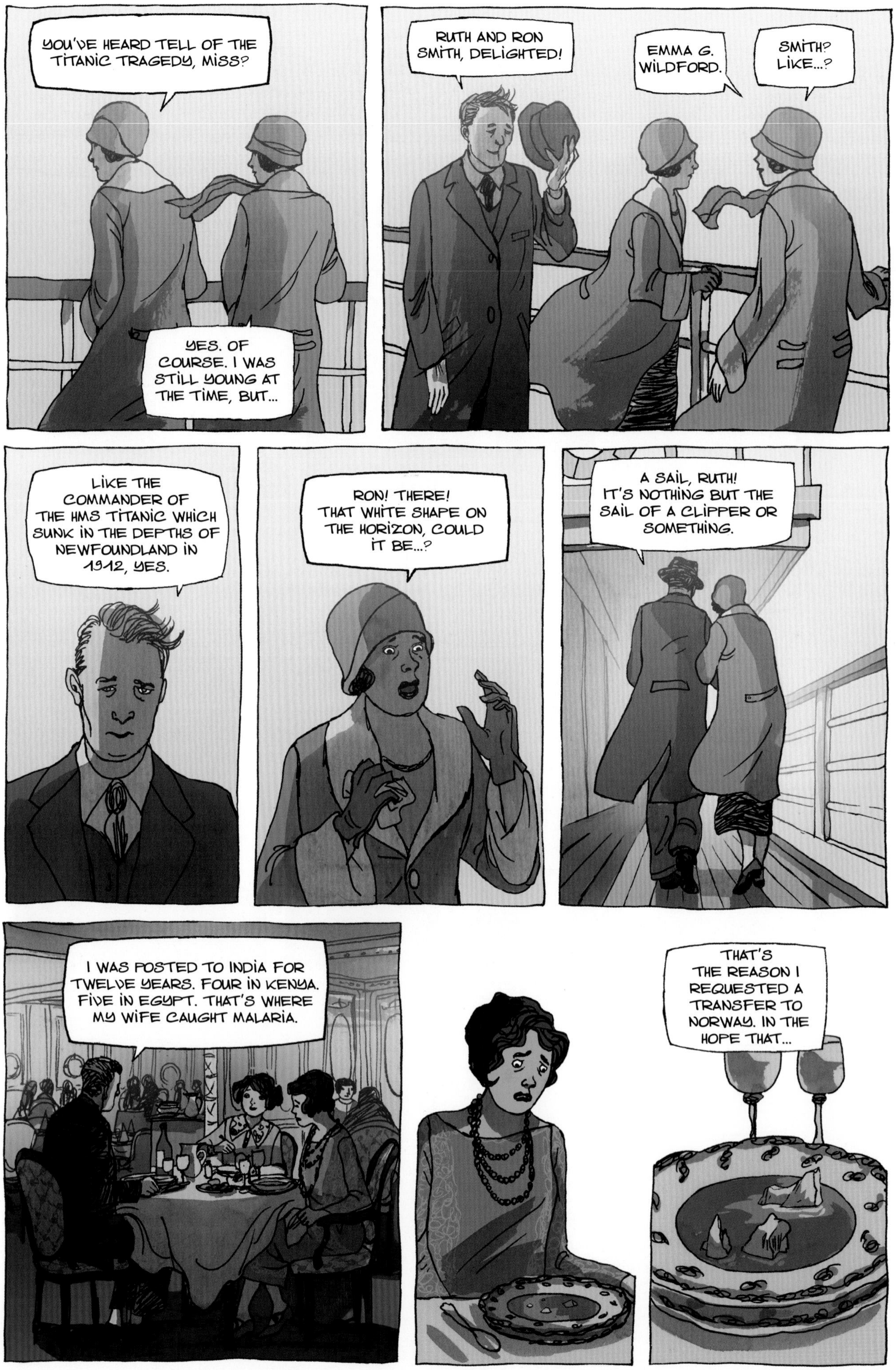
YOU'VE HEARD TELL OF THE TITANIC TRAGEDY, MISS?
YES. OF COURSE. I WAS STILL YOUNG AT THE TIME, BUT...
RUTH AND RON SMITH, DELIGHTED!
EMMA G. WILDFORD.
SMITH? LIKE...?
LIKE THE COMMANDER OF THE HMS TITANIC WHICH SUNK IN THE DEPTHS OF NEWFOUNDLAND IN 1912, YES.
RON! THERE! THAT WHITE SHAPE ON THE HORIZON, COULD IT BE...?
A SAIL, RUTH! IT'S NOTHING BUT THE SAIL OF A CLIPPER OR SOMETHING.
I WAS POSTED TO INDIA FOR TWELVE YEARS. FOUR IN KENYA. FIVE IN EGYPT. THAT'S WHERE MY WIFE CAUGHT MALARIA.
THAT'S THE REASON I REQUESTED A TRANSFER TO NORWAY. IN THE HOPE THAT...

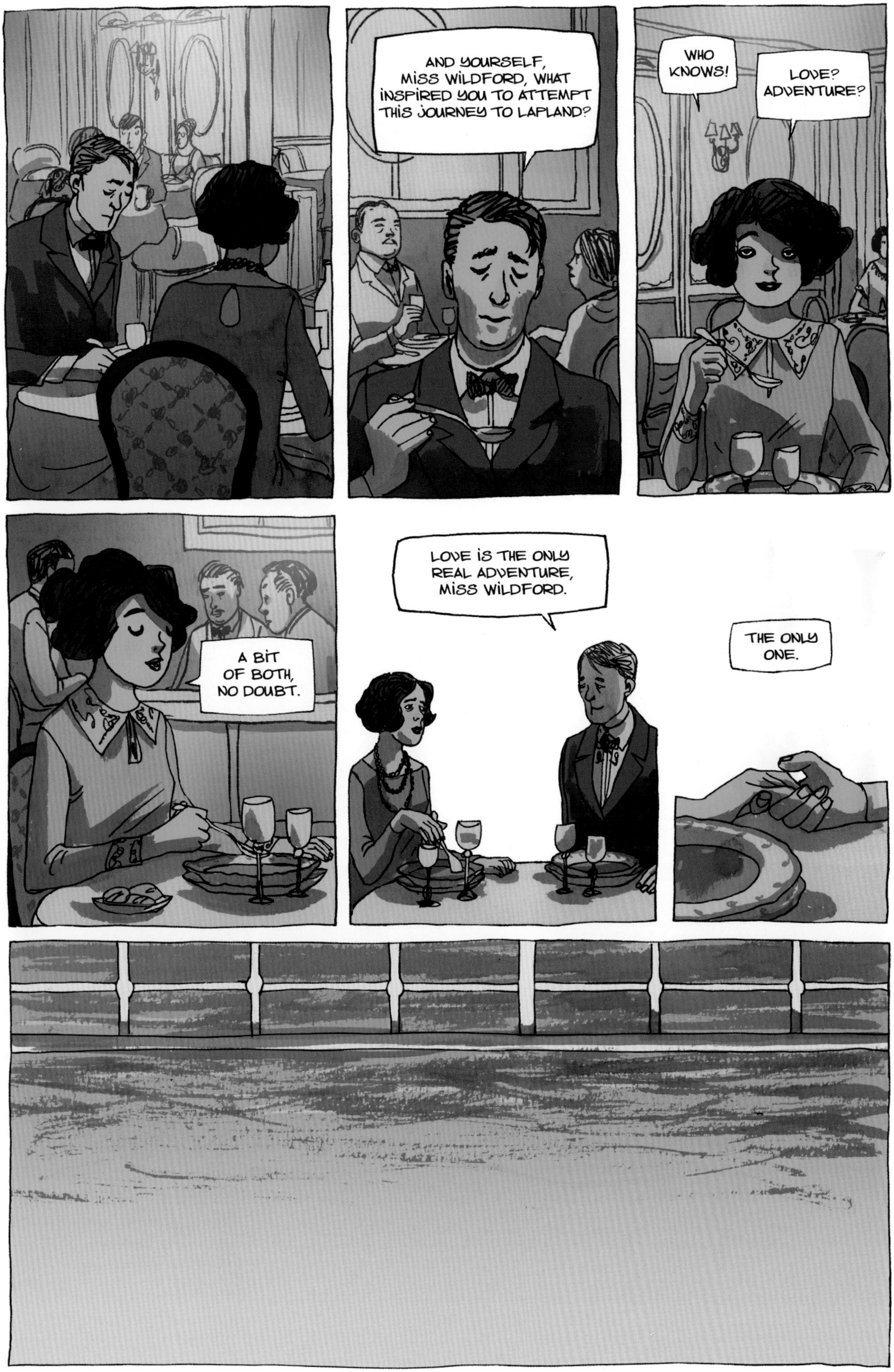
AND YOURSELF, MISS WILDFORD, WHAT INSPIRED YOU TO ATTEMPT THIS JOURNEY TO LAPLAND?
WHO KNOWS!
LOVE? ADVENTURE?
A BIT OF BOTH, NO DOUBT.
LOVE IS THE ONLY REAL ADVENTURE, MISS WILDFORD.
THE ONLY ONE.

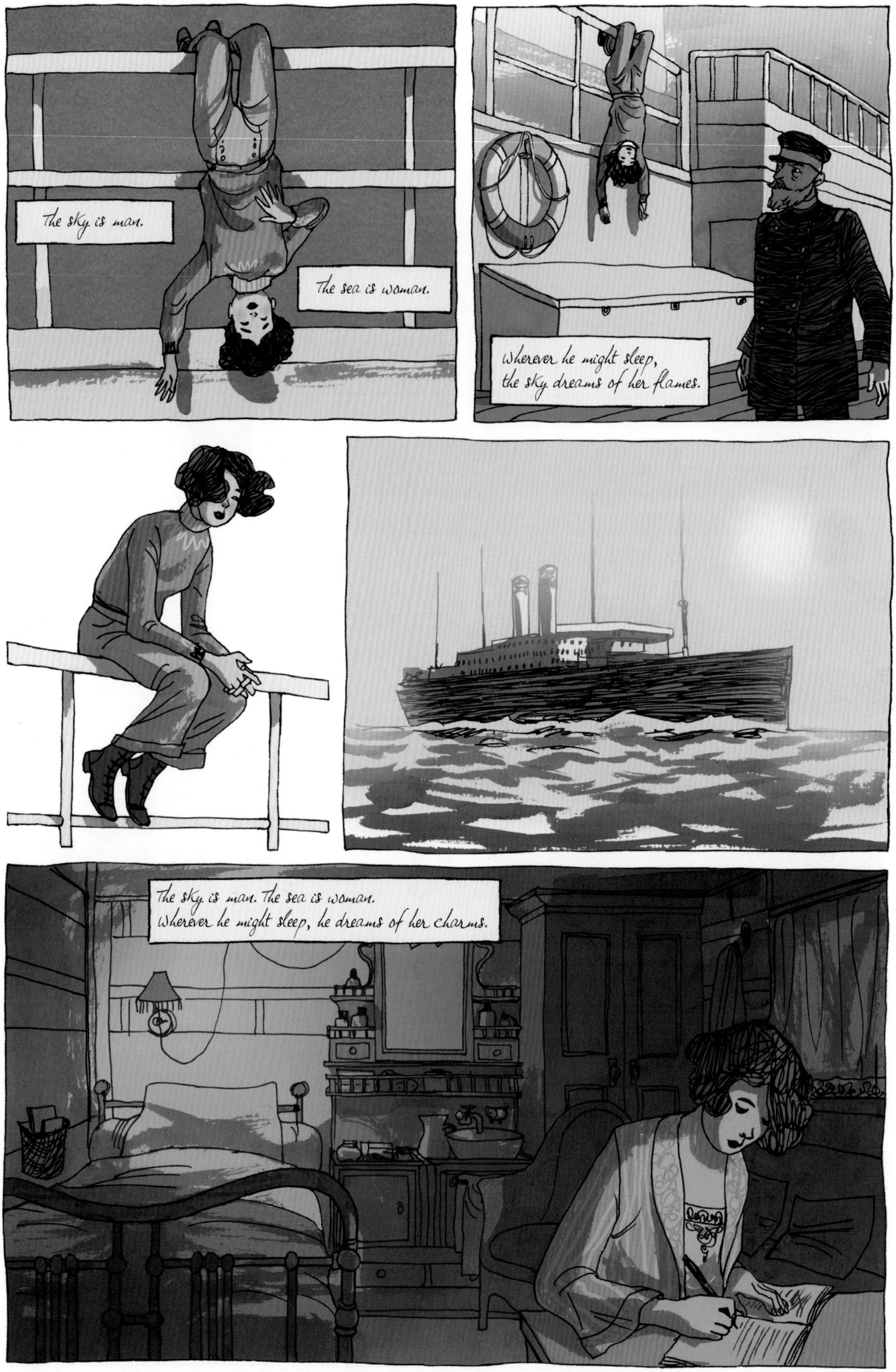
The sky is man.
The sea is woman.
Wherever he might sleep, the sky dreams of her flames.
The sky is man. The sea is woman. Wherever he might sleep, he dreams of her charms.

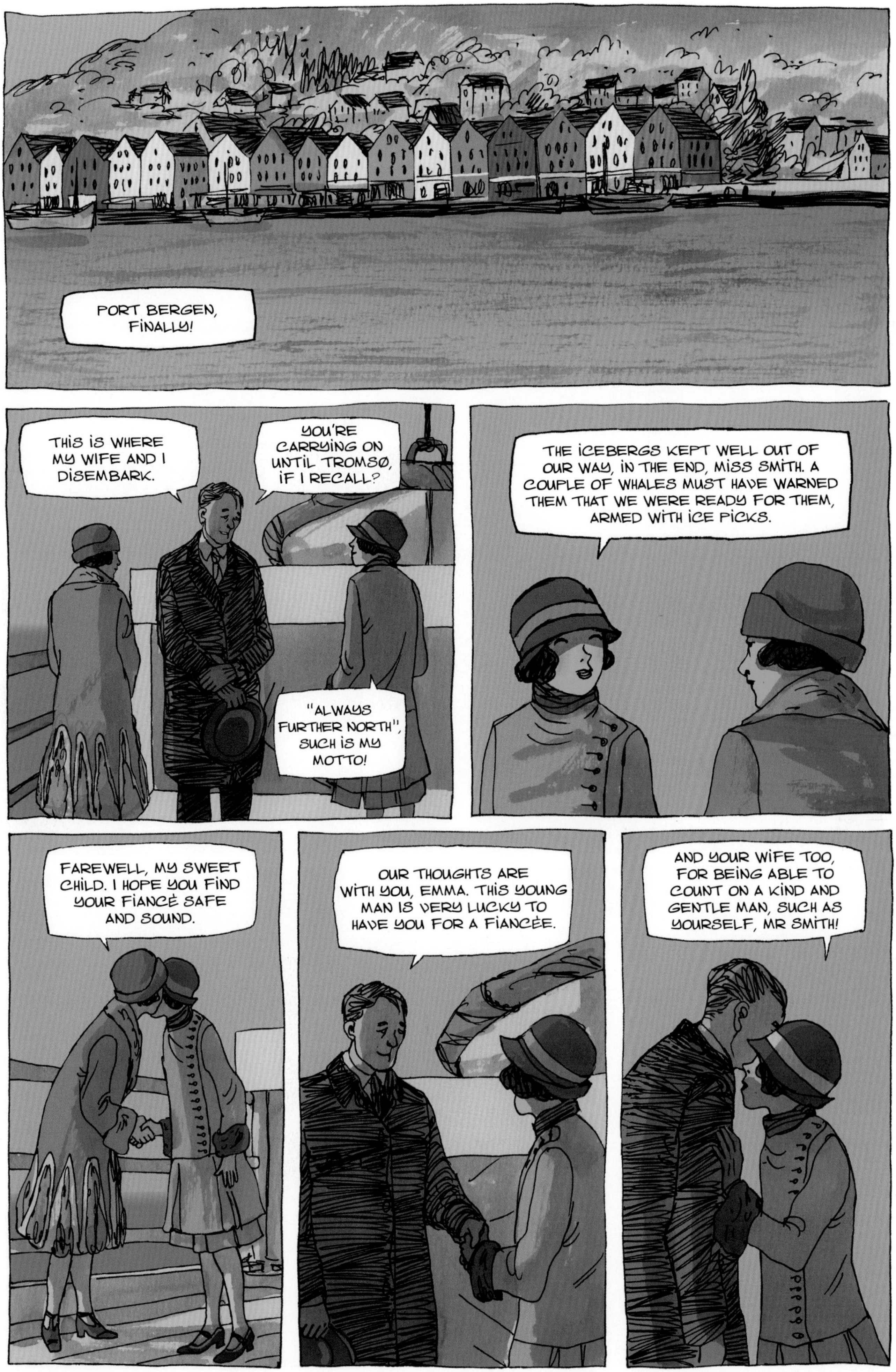

PORT BERGEN, FINALLY!
THIS IS WHERE MY WIFE AND I DISEMBARK.
YOU'RE CARRYING ON UNTIL TROMSØ, IF I RECALL?
"ALWAYS FURTHER NORTH", SUCH IS MY MOTTO!
THE ICEBERGS KEPT WELL OUT OF OUR WAY, IN THE END, MISS SMITH. A COUPLE OF WHALES MUST HAVE WARNED THEM THAT WE WERE READY FOR THEM, ARMED WITH ICE PICKS.
FAREWELL, MY SWEET CHILD. I HOPE YOU FIND YOUR FIANCÉ SAFE AND SOUND.
OUR THOUGHTS ARE WITH YOU, EMMA. THIS YOUNG MAN IS VERY LUCKY TO HAVE YOU FOR A FIANCÉE.
AND YOUR WIFE TOO, FOR BEING ABLE TO COUNT ON A KIND AND GENTLE MAN, SUCH AS YOURSELF, MR SMITH!

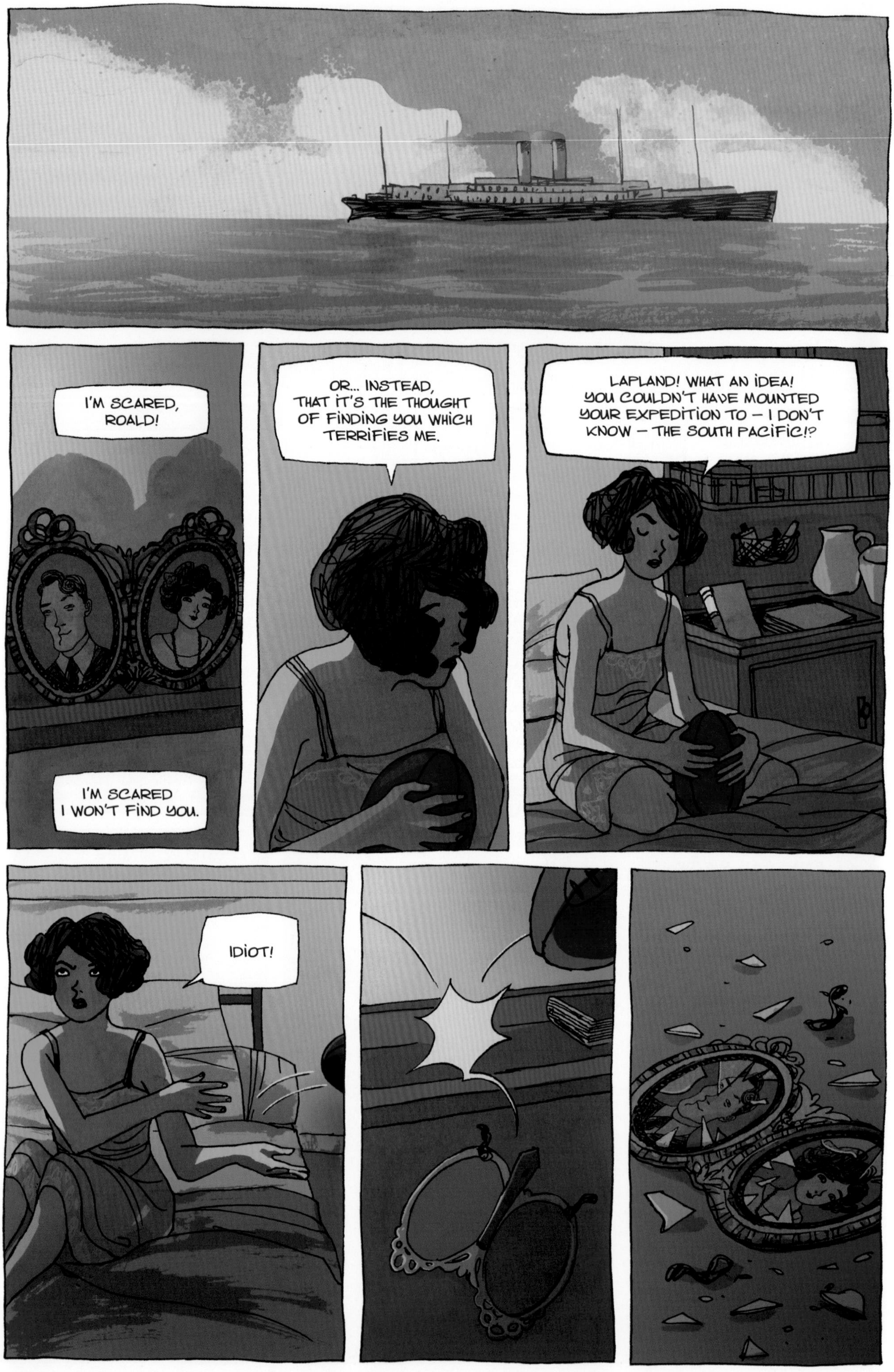

I'M SCARED, ROALD!
I'M SCARED I WON'T FIND YOU.
OR... INSTEAD, THAT IT'S THE THOUGHT OF FINDING YOU WHICH TERRIFIES ME.
LAPLAND! WHAT AN IDEA! YOU COULDN'T HAVE MOUNTED YOUR EXPEDITION TO – I DON'T KNOW – THE SOUTH PACIFIC!?
IDIOT!

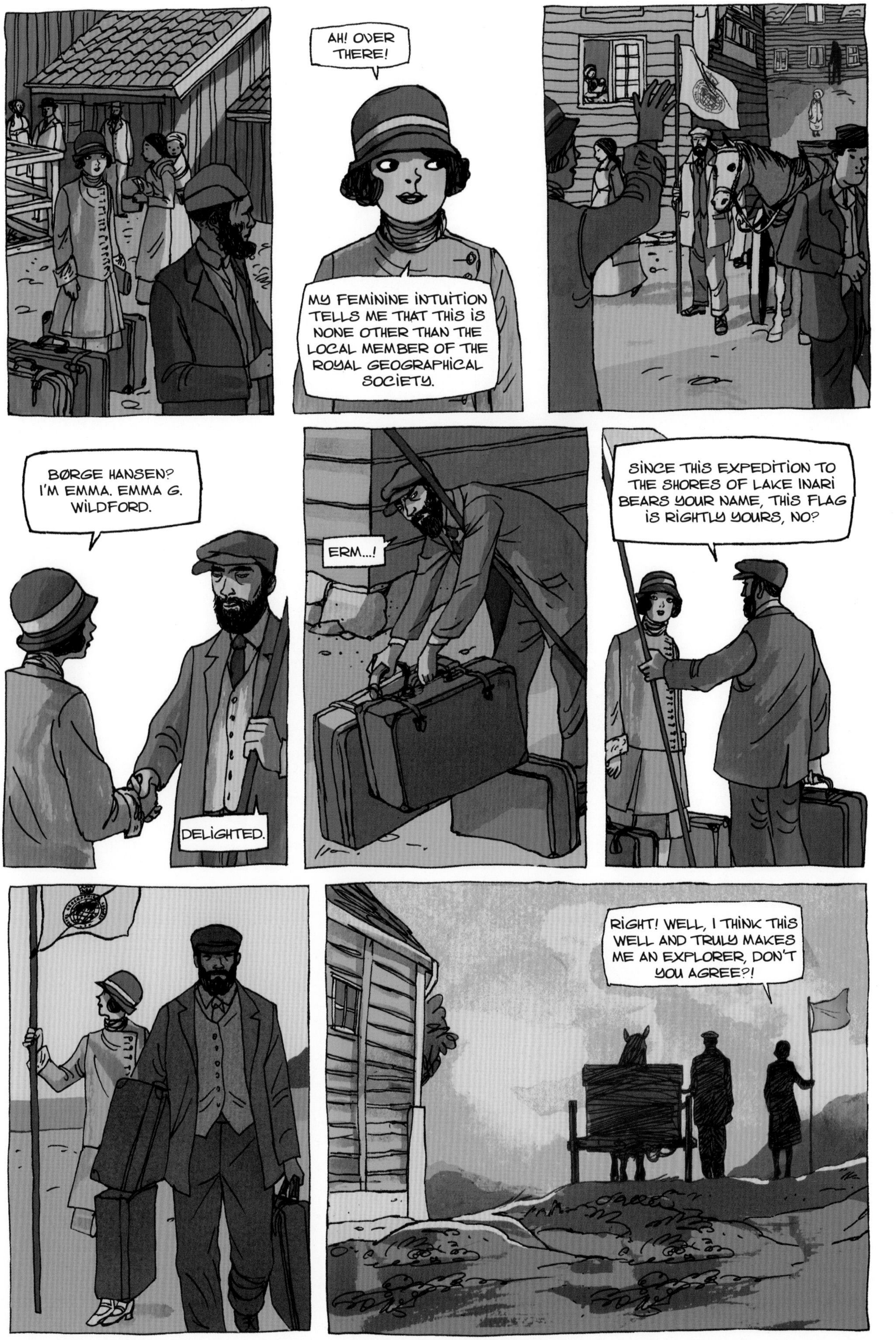
AH! OVER THERE!
MY FEMININE INTUITION TELLS ME THAT THIS IS NONE OTHER THAN THE LOCAL MEMBER OF THE ROYAL GEOGRAPHICAL SOCIETY.
BØRGE HANSEN? I'M EMMA. EMMA G. WILDFORD.
DELIGHTED.
ERM...!
SINCE THIS EXPEDITION TO THE SHORES OF LAKE INARI BEARS YOUR NAME, THIS FLAG IS RIGHTLY YOURS, NO?
RIGHT! WELL, I THINK THIS WELL AND TRULY MAKES ME AN EXPLORER, DON'T YOU AGREE?!

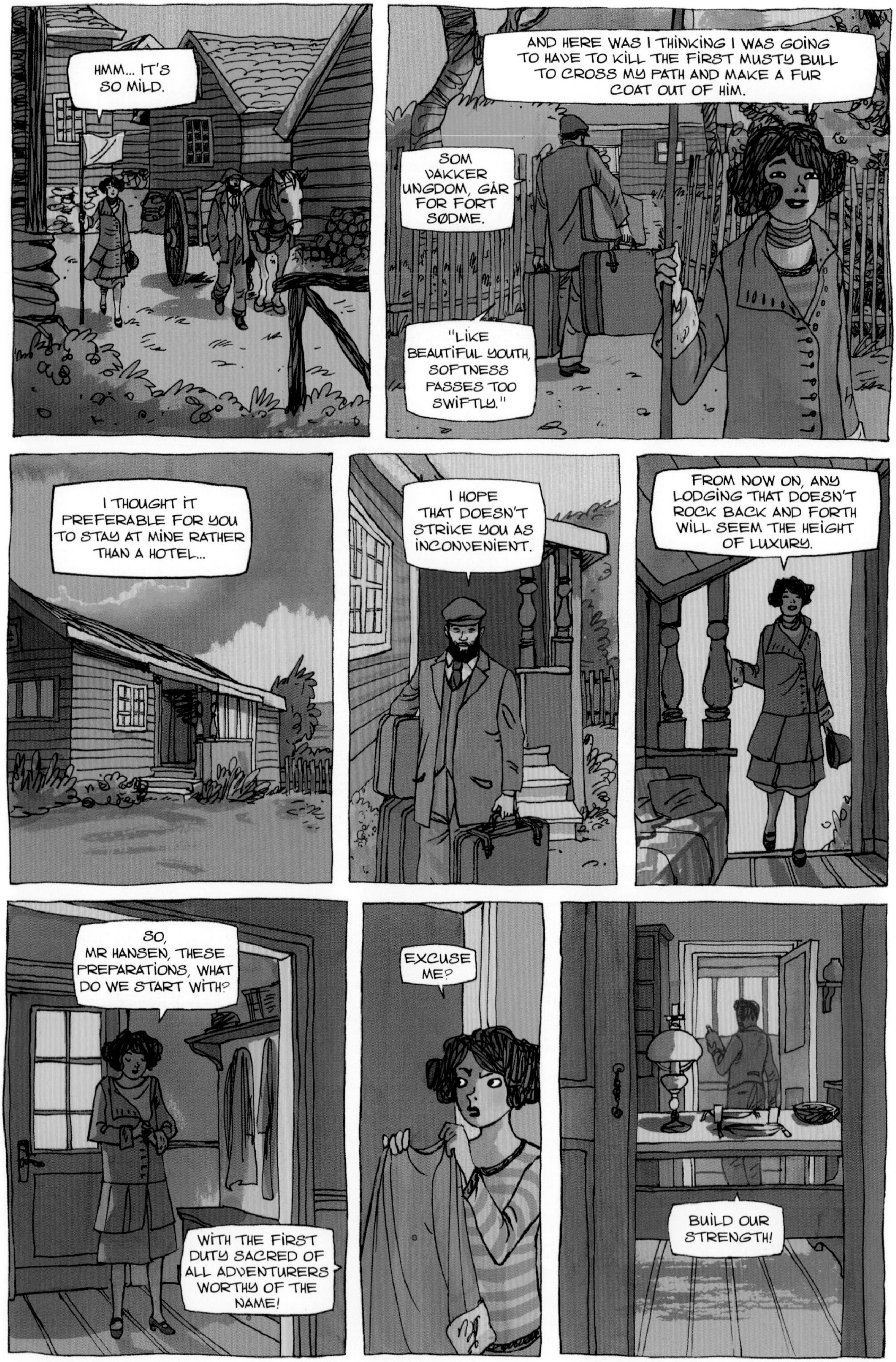
HMM... IT'S SO MILD.
AND HERE WAS I THINKING I WAS GOING TO HAVE TO KILL THE FIRST MUSTY BULL TO CROSS MY PATH AND MAKE A FUR COAT OUT OF HIM.
SOM VAKKER UNGDOM, GÅR FOR FORT SØDME.
"LIKE BEAUTIFUL YOUTH, SOFTNESS PASSES TOO SWIFTLY."
I THOUGHT IT PREFERABLE FOR YOU TO STAY AT MINE RATHER THAN A HOTEL...
I HOPE THAT DOESN'T STRIKE YOU AS INCONVENIENT.
FROM NOW ON, ANY LODGING THAT DOESN'T ROCK BACK AND FORTH WILL SEEM THE HEIGHT OF LUXURY.
SO, MR HANSEN, THESE PREPARATIONS, WHAT DO WE START WITH?
WITH THE FIRST DUTY SACRED OF ALL ADVENTURERS WORTHY OF THE NAME!
EXCUSE ME?
BUILD OUR STRENGTH!

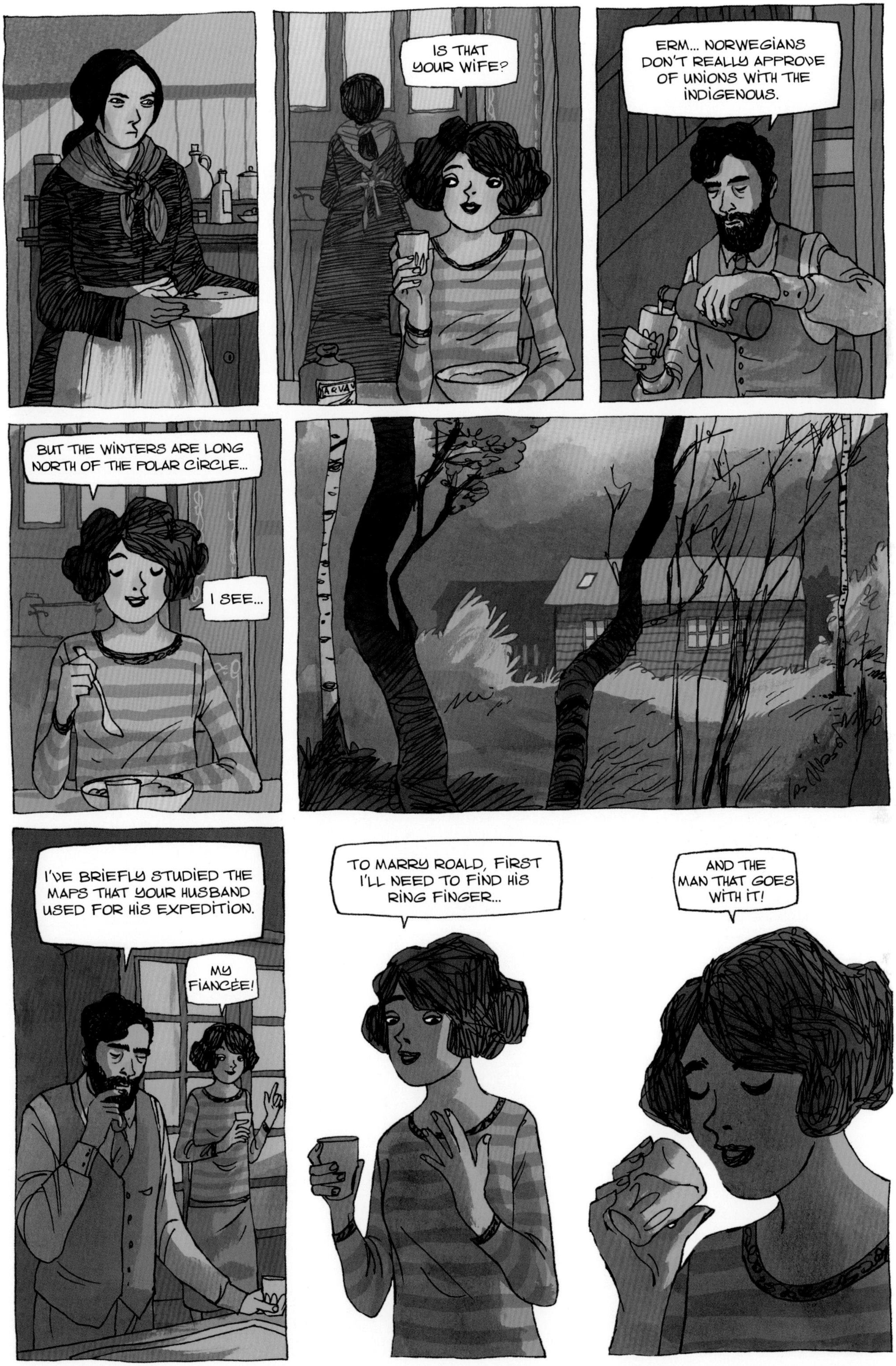
IS THAT YOUR WIFE?
ERM... NORWEGIANS DON'T REALLY APPROVE OF UNIONS WITH THE INDIGENOUS.
BUT THE WINTERS ARE LONG NORTH OF THE POLAR CIRCLE...
I SEE...
I'VE BRIEFLY STUDIED THE MAPS THAT YOUR HUSBAND USED FOR HIS EXPEDITION.
MY FIANCÉE!
TO MARRY ROALD, FIRST I'LL NEED TO FIND HIS RING FINGER...
AND THE MAN THAT GOES WITH IT!

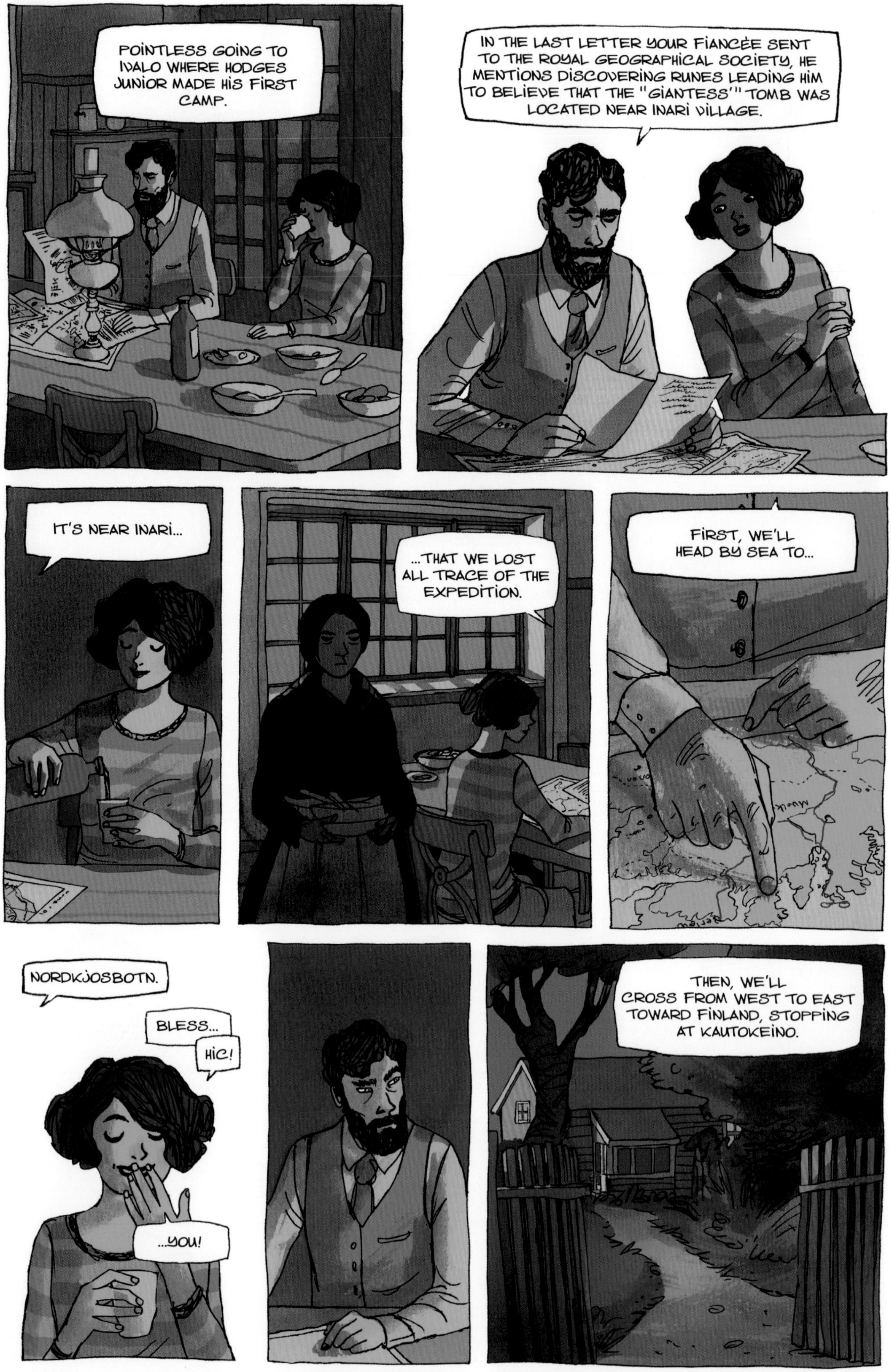

POINTLESS GOING TO IVALO WHERE HODGES JUNIOR MADE HIS FIRST CAMP.
IN THE LAST LETTER YOUR FIANCÉE SENT TO THE ROYAL GEOGRAPHICAL SOCIETY, HE MENTIONS DISCOVERING RUNES LEADING HIM TO BELIEVE THAT THE "GIANTESS'" TOMB WAS LOCATED NEAR INARI VILLAGE.
IT'S NEAR INARI...
...THAT WE LOST ALL TRACE OF THE EXPEDITION.
FIRST, WE'LL HEAD BY SEA TO...
NORDKJOSBOTN.
BLESS...
HIC!
...YOU!
THEN, WE'LL CROSS FROM WEST TO EAST TOWARD FINLAND, STOPPING AT KAUTOKEINO.

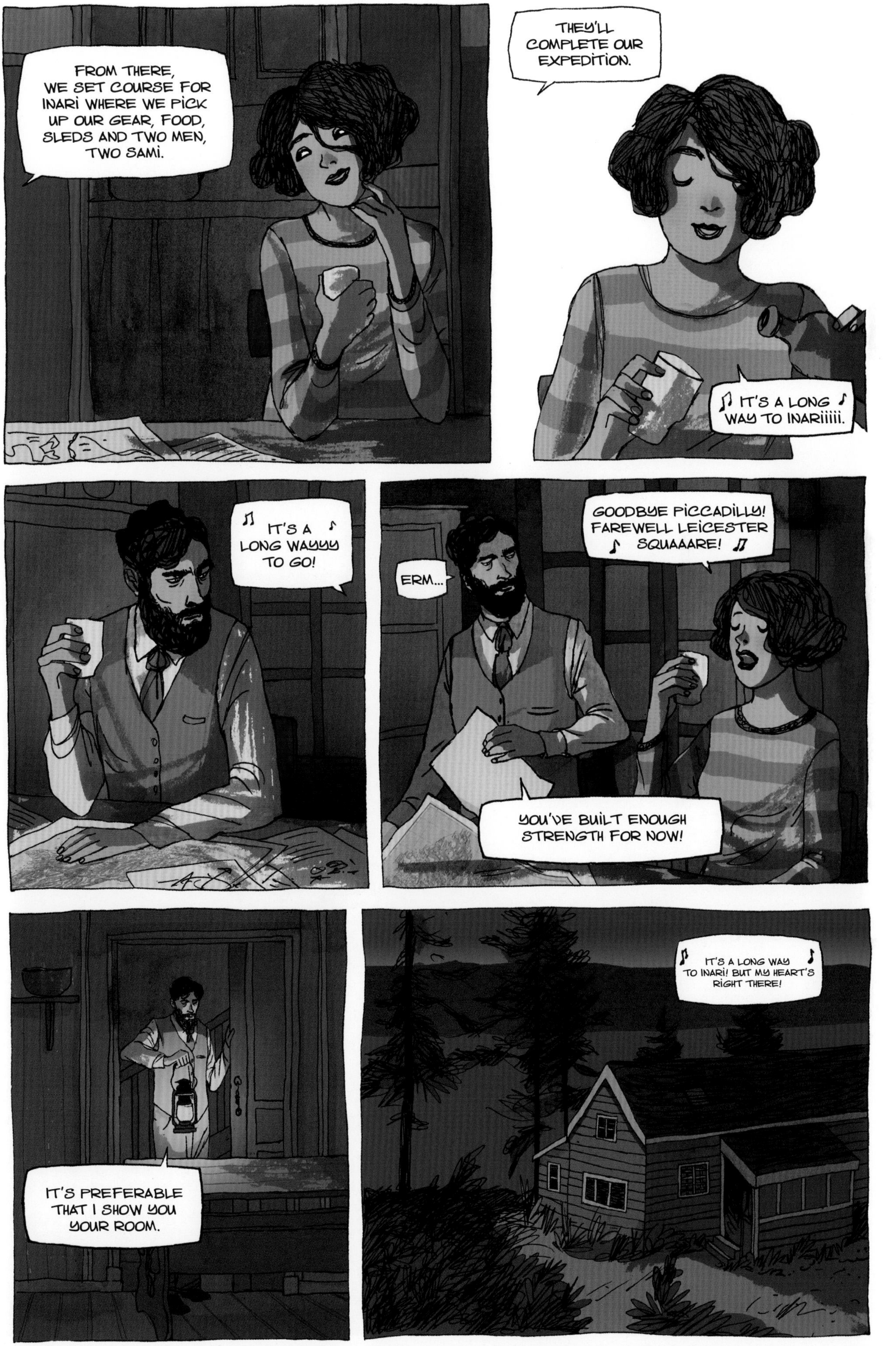
FROM THERE, WE SET COURSE FOR INARI WHERE WE PICK UP OUR GEAR, FOOD, SLEDS AND TWO MEN, TWO SAMI.
THEY'LL COMPLETE OUR EXPEDITION.
♫ IT'S A LONG ♪ WAY TO INARIiiiii.
♫ IT'S A ♪ LONG WAYYY TO GO!
GOODBYE PICCADILLY! FAREWELL LEICESTER ♪ SQUAAARE! ♫
ERM...
YOU'VE BUILT ENOUGH STRENGTH FOR NOW!
IT'S PREFERABLE THAT I SHOW YOU YOUR ROOM.
♫ IT'S A LONG WAY ♪ TO INARI! BUT MY HEART'S RIGHT THERE!

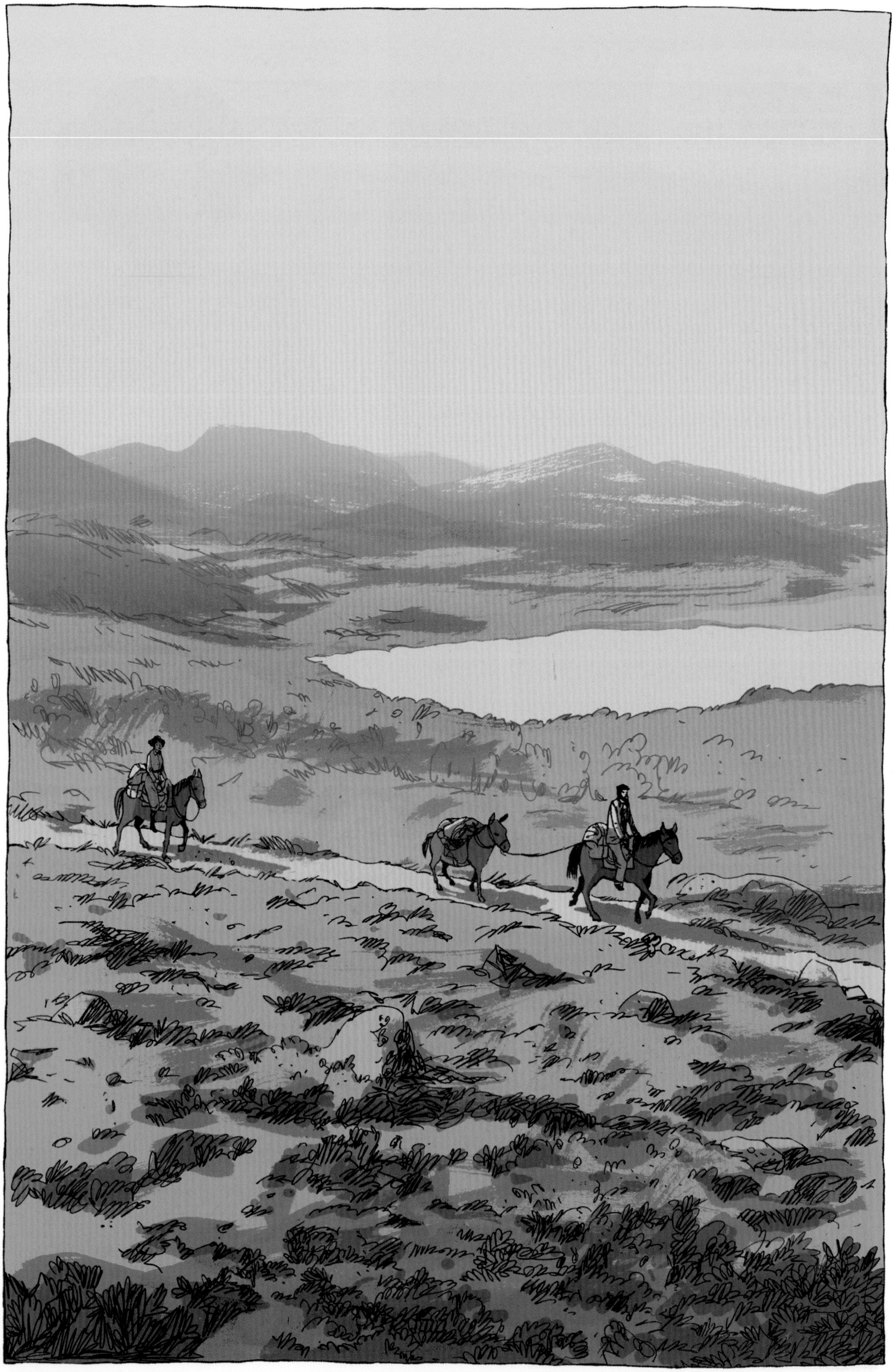

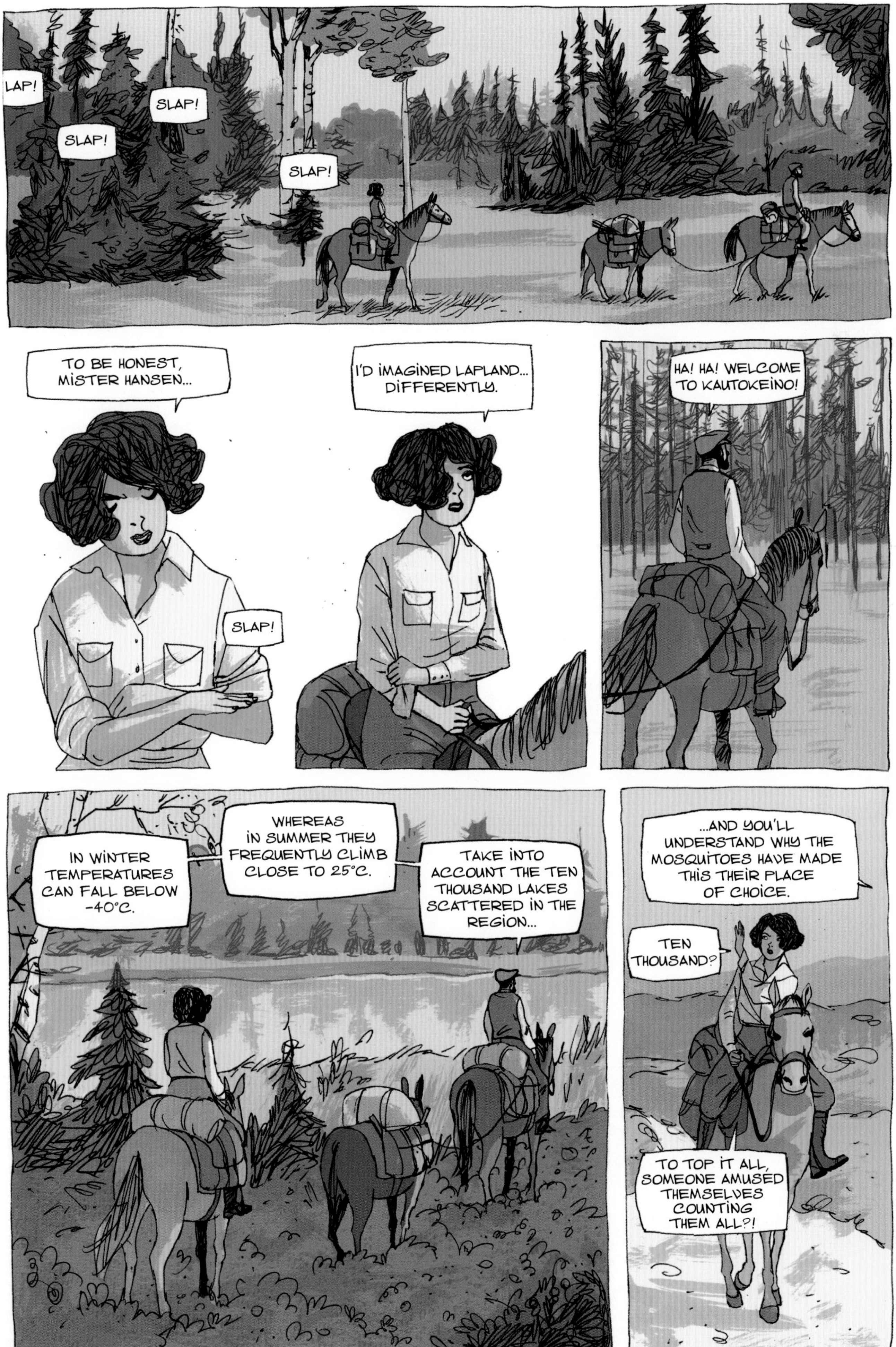
LAP!
SLAP!
SLAP!
SLAP!
TO BE HONEST, MISTER HANSEN...
SLAP!
I'D IMAGINED LAPLAND... DIFFERENTLY.
HA! HA! WELCOME TO KAUTOKEINO!
IN WINTER TEMPERATURES CAN FALL BELOW -40°C.
WHEREAS IN SUMMER THEY FREQUENTLY CLIMB CLOSE TO 25°C.
TAKE INTO ACCOUNT THE TEN THOUSAND LAKES SCATTERED IN THE REGION...
...AND YOU'LL UNDERSTAND WHY THE MOSQUITOES HAVE MADE THIS THEIR PLACE OF CHOICE.
TEN THOUSAND?
TO TOP IT ALL, SOMEONE AMUSED THEMSELVES COUNTING THEM ALL?!

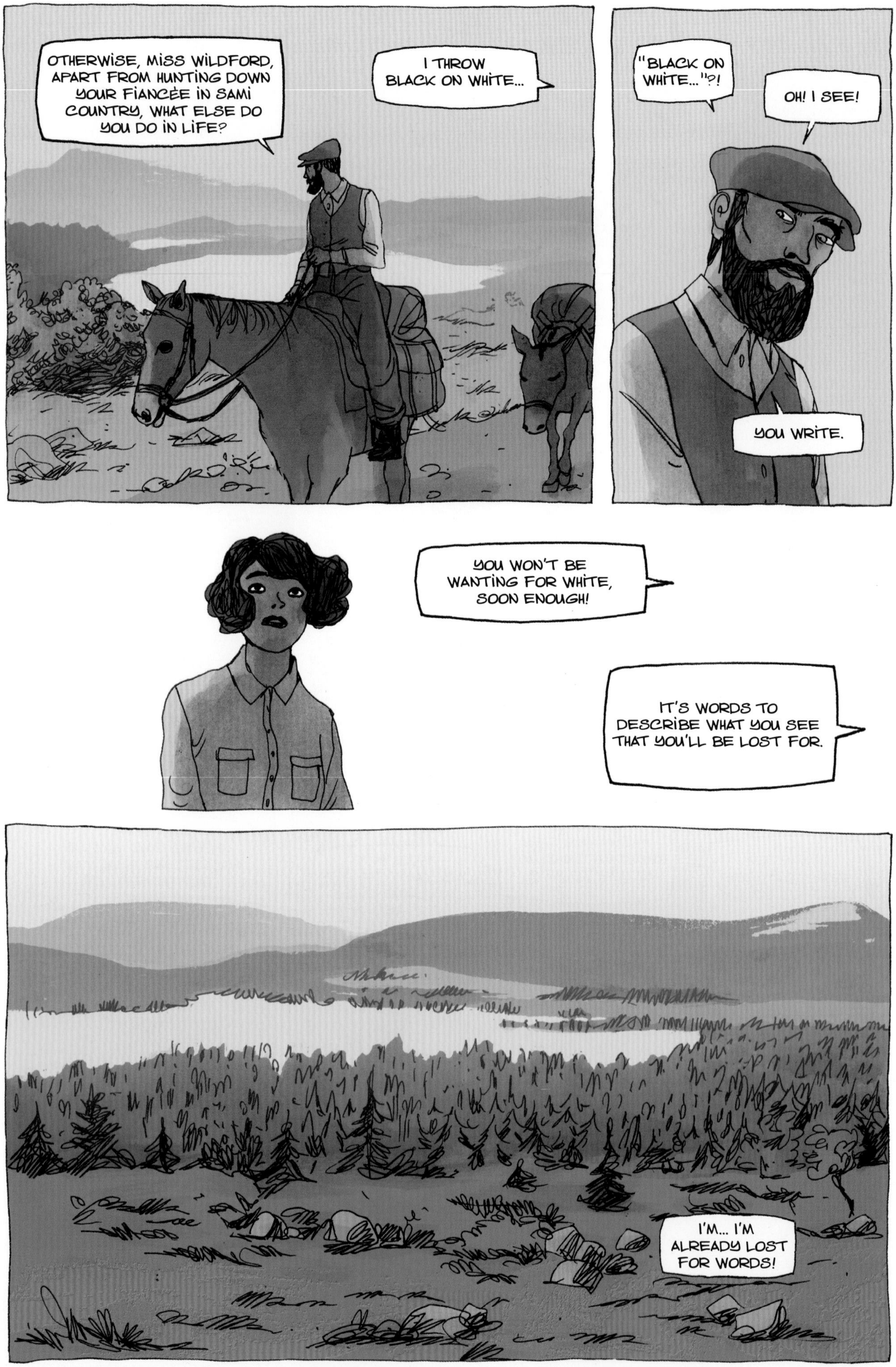
OTHERWISE, MISS WILDFORD, APART FROM HUNTING DOWN YOUR FIANCÉE IN SAMI COUNTRY, WHAT ELSE DO YOU DO IN LIFE?
I THROW BLACK ON WHITE...
"BLACK ON WHITE..."?!
OH! I SEE!
YOU WRITE.
YOU WON'T BE WANTING FOR WHITE, SOON ENOUGH!
IT'S WORDS TO DESCRIBE WHAT YOU SEE THAT YOU'LL BE LOST FOR.
I'M... I'M ALREADY LOST FOR WORDS!

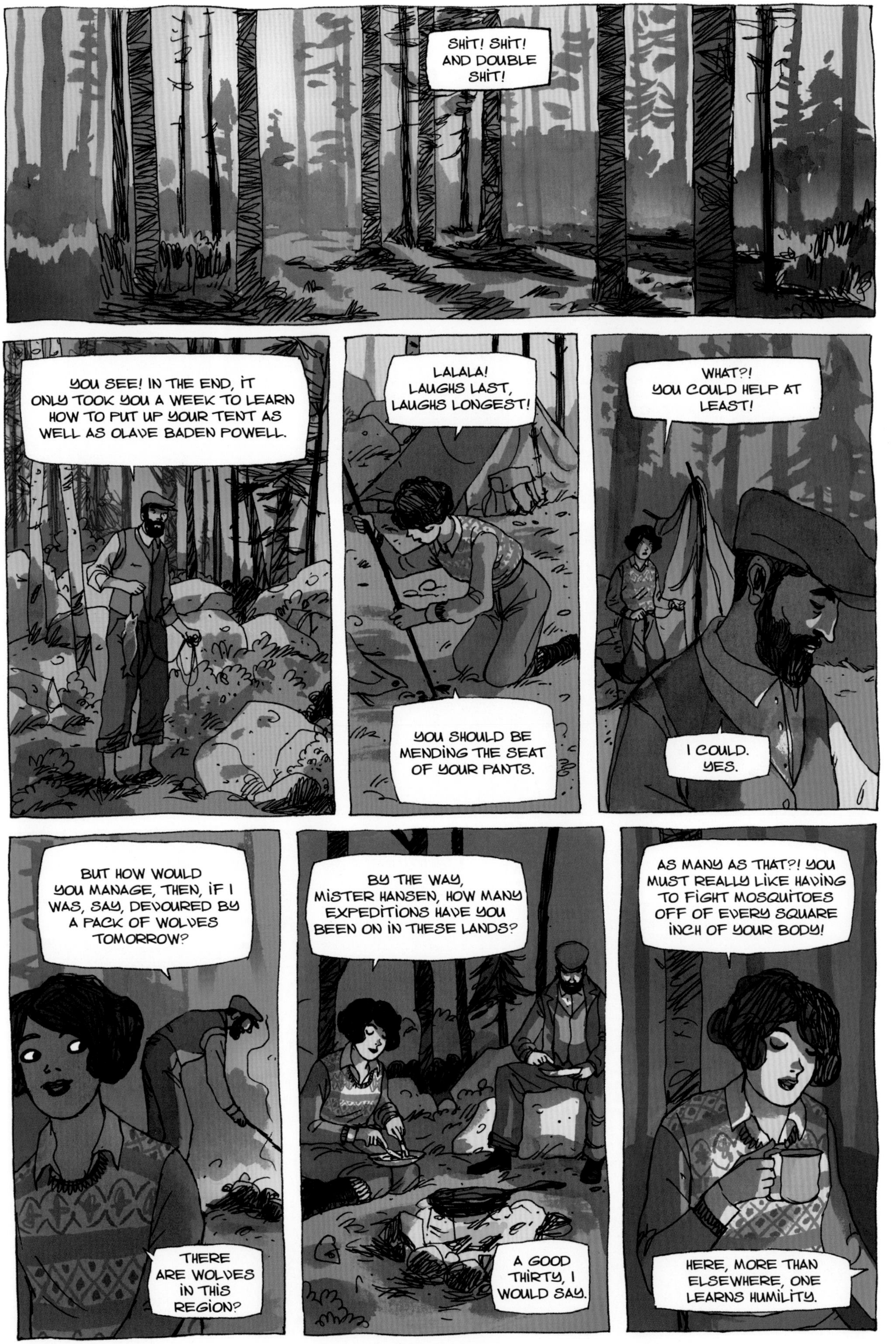
SHIT! SHIT! AND DOUBLE SHIT!
YOU SEE! IN THE END, IT ONLY TOOK YOU A WEEK TO LEARN HOW TO PUT UP YOUR TENT AS WELL AS OLAVE BADEN POWELL.
LALALA! LAUGHS LAST, LAUGHS LONGEST!
YOU SHOULD BE MENDING THE SEAT OF YOUR PANTS.
WHAT?! YOU COULD HELP AT LEAST!
I COULD. YES.
BUT HOW WOULD YOU MANAGE, THEN, IF I WAS, SAY, DEVOURED BY A PACK OF WOLVES TOMORROW?
THERE ARE WOLVES IN THIS REGION?
BY THE WAY, MISTER HANSEN, HOW MANY EXPEDITIONS HAVE YOU BEEN ON IN THESE LANDS?
A GOOD THIRTY, I WOULD SAY.
AS MANY AS THAT?! YOU MUST REALLY LIKE HAVING TO FIGHT MOSQUITOES OFF OF EVERY SQUARE INCH OF YOUR BODY!
HERE, MORE THAN ELSEWHERE, ONE LEARNS HUMILITY.

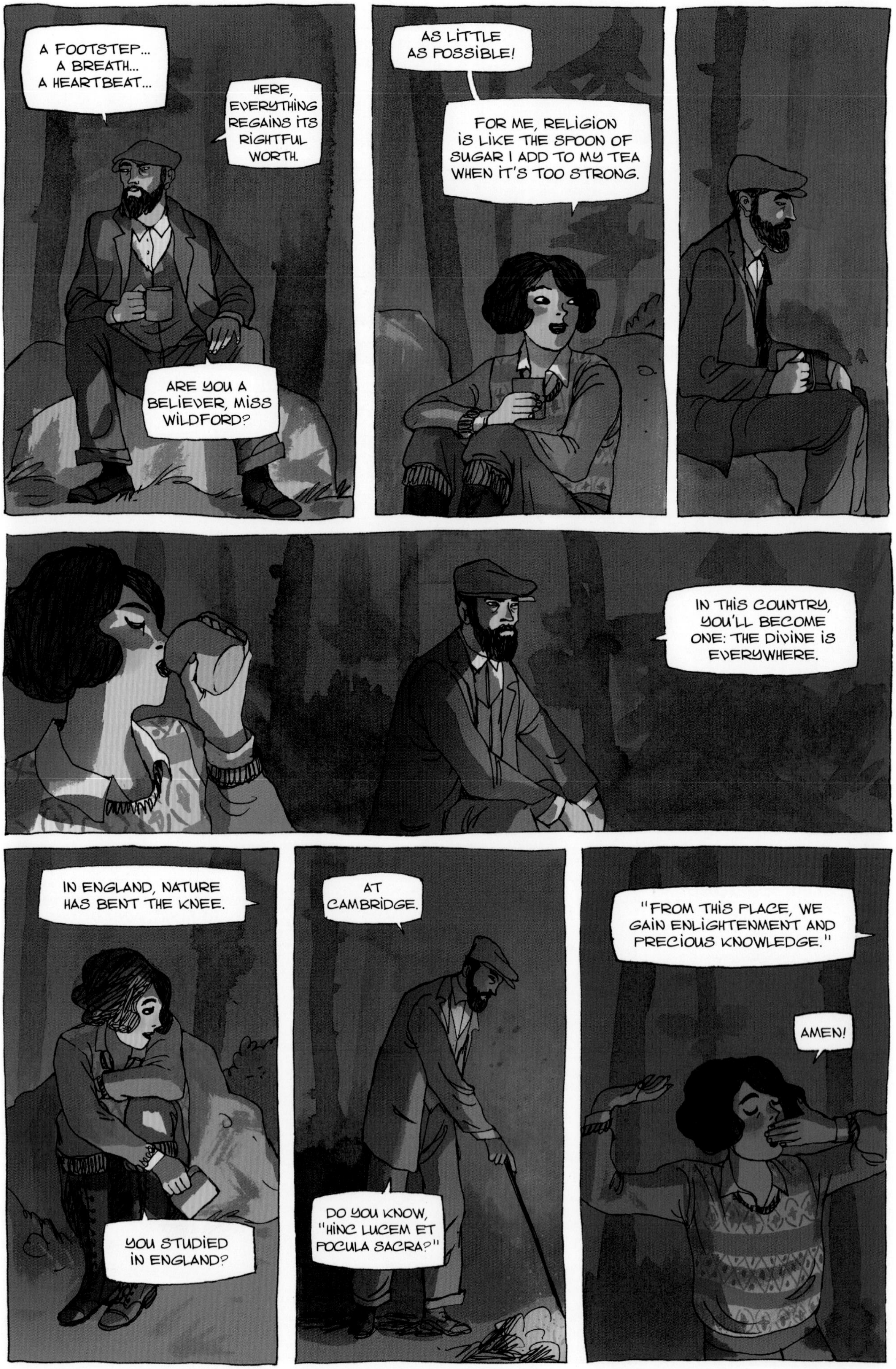
A FOOTSTEP... A BREATH... A HEARTBEAT...
HERE, EVERYTHING REGAINS ITS RIGHTFUL WORTH.
ARE YOU A BELIEVER, MISS WILDFORD?
AS LITTLE AS POSSIBLE!
FOR ME, RELIGION IS LIKE THE SPOON OF SUGAR I ADD TO MY TEA WHEN IT'S TOO STRONG.
IN THIS COUNTRY, YOU'LL BECOME ONE: THE DIVINE IS EVERYWHERE.
IN ENGLAND, NATURE HAS BENT THE KNEE.
YOU STUDIED IN ENGLAND?
AT CAMBRIDGE.
DO YOU KNOW, "HINC LUCEM ET POCULA SACRA?"
"FROM THIS PLACE, WE GAIN ENLIGHTENMENT AND PRECIOUS KNOWLEDGE."
AMEN!

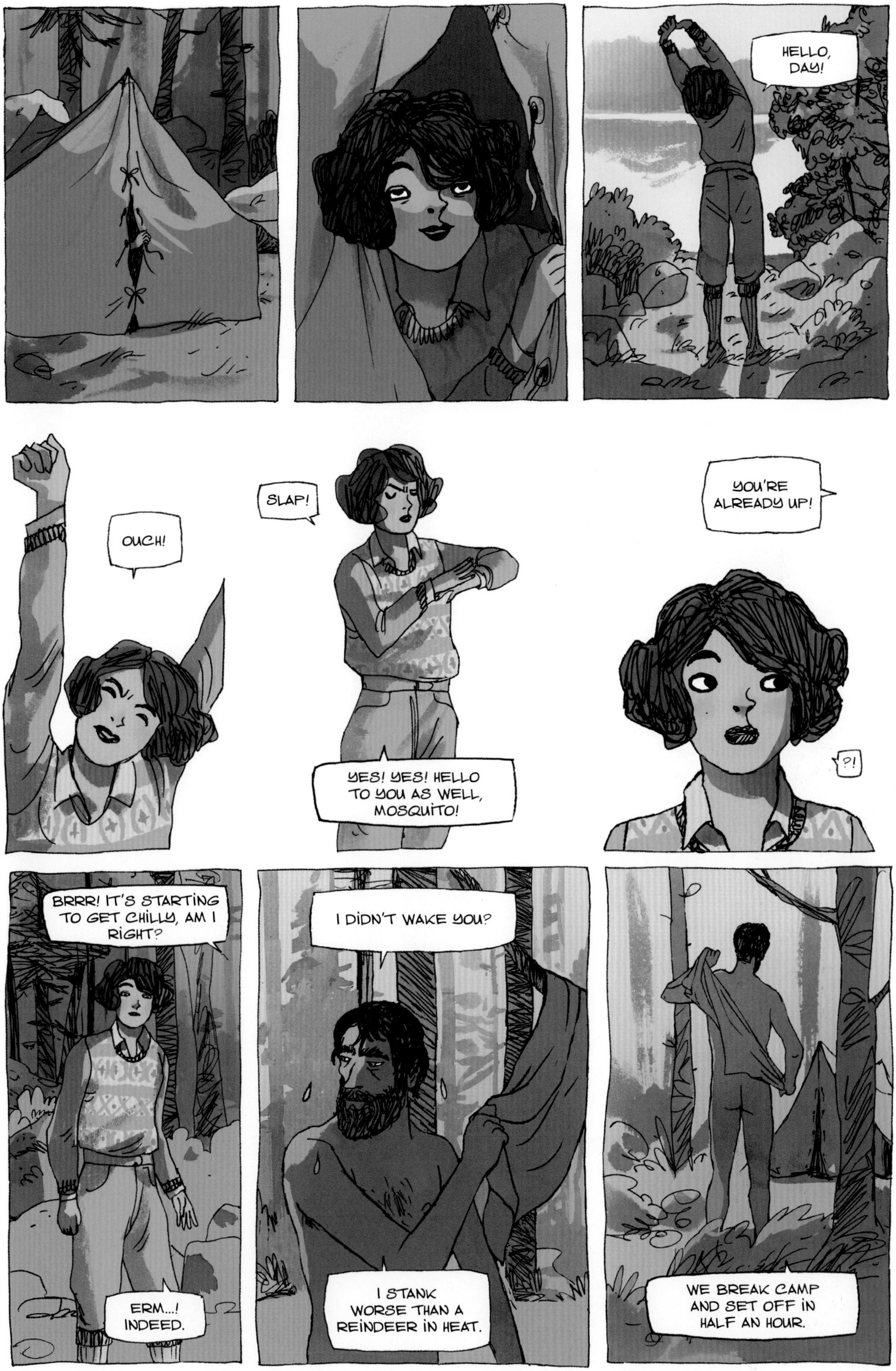
HELLO, DAY!
OUCH!
SLAP!
YES! YES! HELLO TO YOU AS WELL, MOSQUITO!
YOU'RE ALREADY UP!
?!
BRRR! IT'S STARTING TO GET CHILLY, AM I RIGHT?
ERM...! INDEED.
I DIDN'T WAKE YOU?
I STANK WORSE THAN A REINDEER IN HEAT.
WE BREAK CAMP AND SET OFF IN HALF AN HOUR.

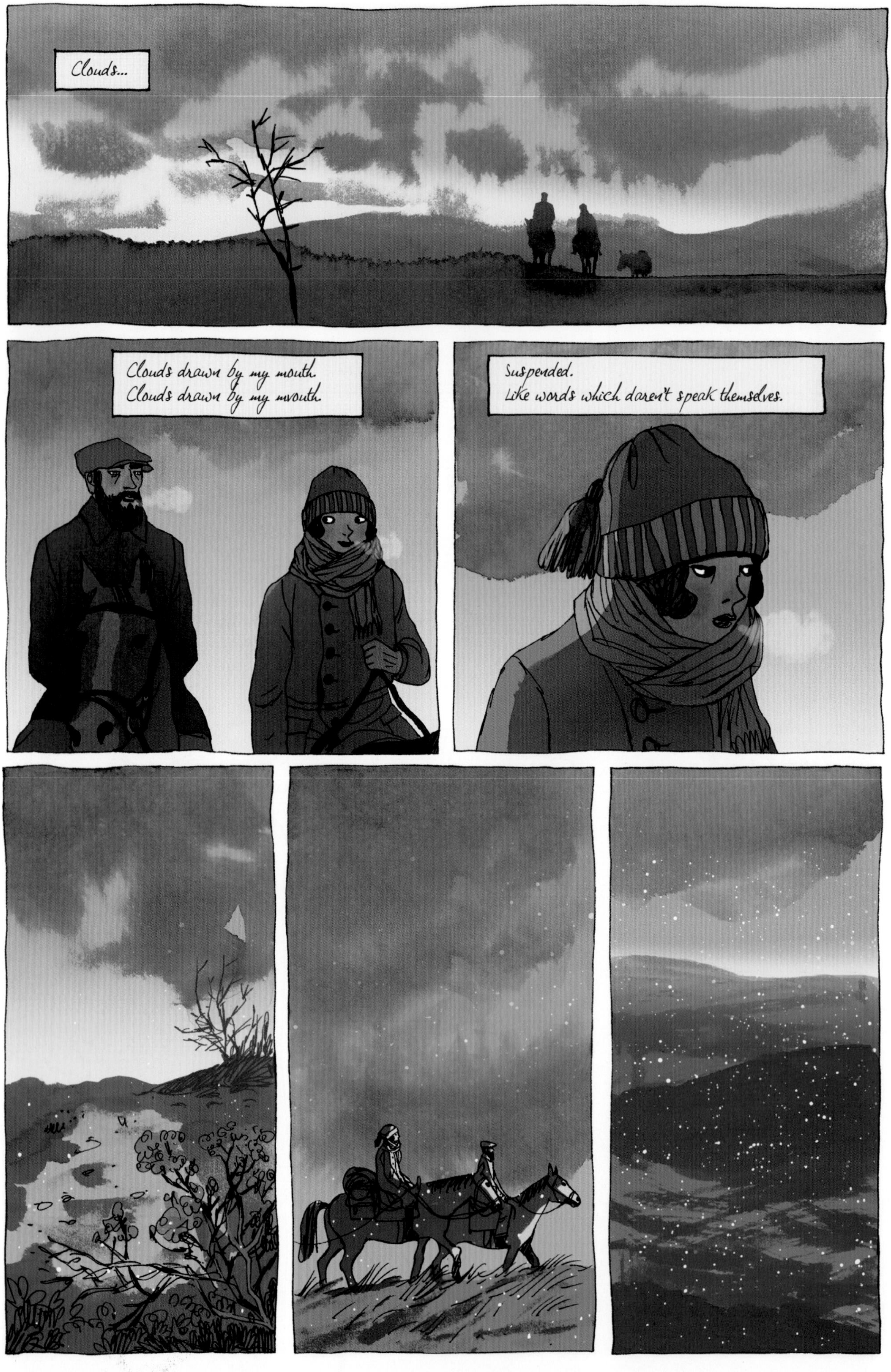
Clouds...
Clouds drawn by my mouth
Clouds drawn by my mouth
Suspended.
Like words which daren't speak themselves.

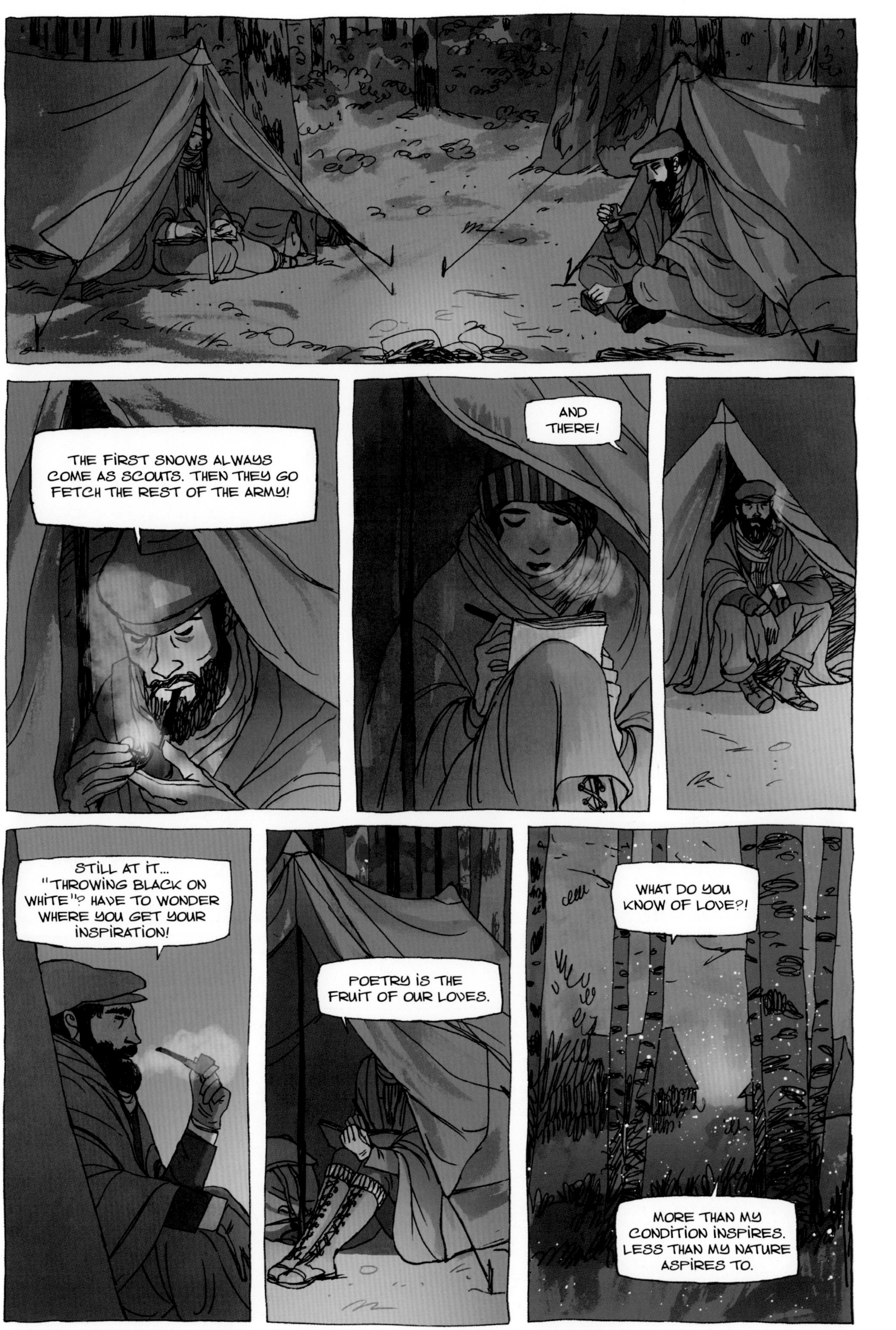
THE FIRST SNOWS ALWAYS COME AS SCOUTS. THEN THEY GO FETCH THE REST OF THE ARMY!
AND THERE!
STILL AT IT... "THROWING BLACK ON WHITE"? HAVE TO WONDER WHERE YOU GET YOUR INSPIRATION!
POETRY IS THE FRUIT OF OUR LOVES.
WHAT DO YOU KNOW OF LOVE?!
MORE THAN MY CONDITION INSPIRES. LESS THAN MY NATURE ASPIRES TO.

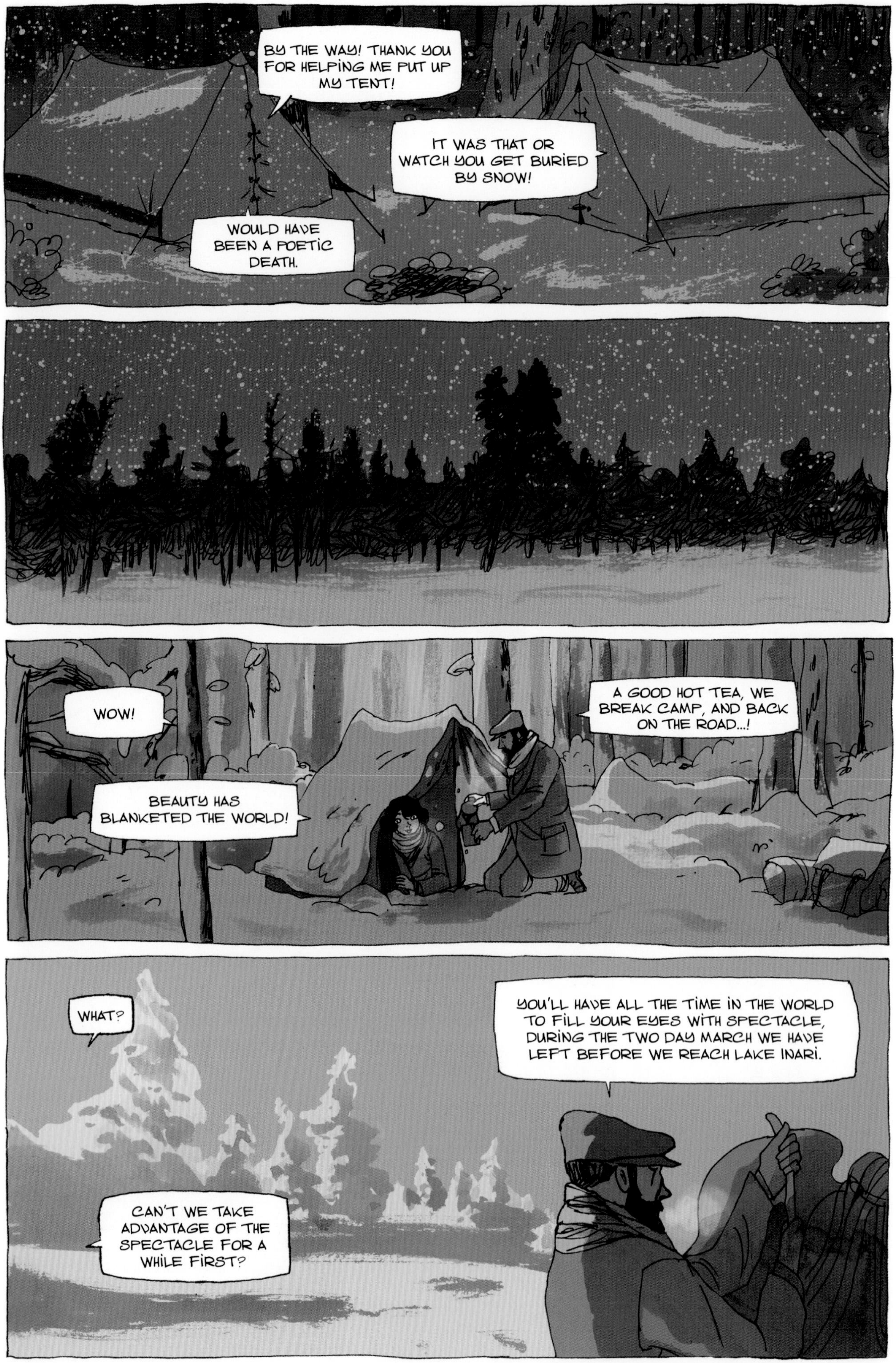
BY THE WAY! THANK YOU FOR HELPING ME PUT UP MY TENT!
IT WAS THAT OR WATCH YOU GET BURIED BY SNOW!
WOULD HAVE BEEN A POETIC DEATH.
WOW!
BEAUTY HAS BLANKETED THE WORLD!
A GOOD HOT TEA, WE BREAK CAMP, AND BACK ON THE ROAD...!
WHAT?
YOU'LL HAVE ALL THE TIME IN THE WORLD TO FILL YOUR EYES WITH SPECTACLE, DURING THE TWO DAY MARCH WE HAVE LEFT BEFORE WE REACH LAKE INARI.
CAN'T WE TAKE ADVANTAGE OF THE SPECTACLE FOR A WHILE FIRST?

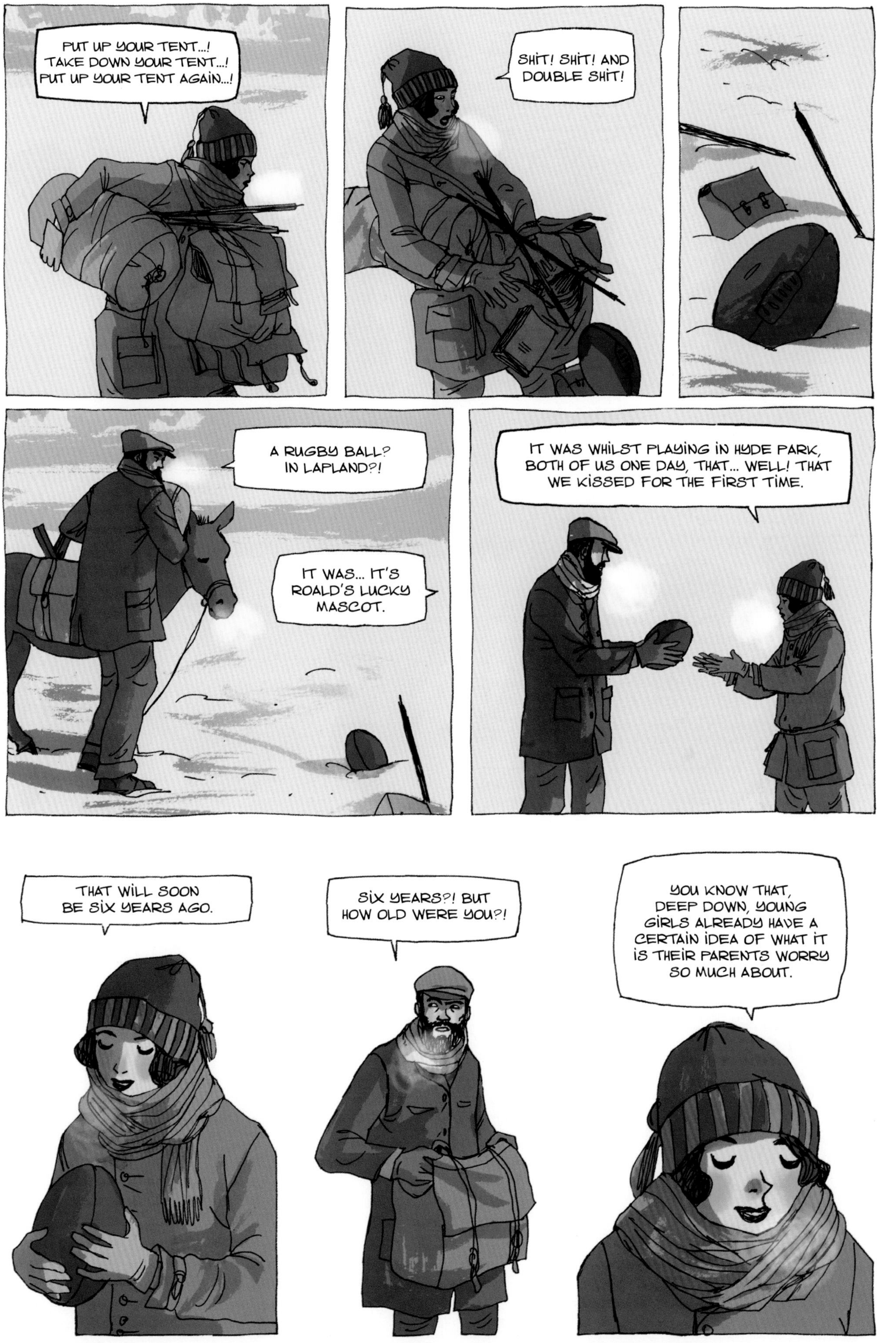
PUT UP YOUR TENT...! TAKE DOWN YOUR TENT...! PUT UP YOUR TENT AGAIN...!
SHIT! SHIT! AND DOUBLE SHIT!
A RUGBY BALL? IN LAPLAND?!
IT WAS... IT'S ROALD'S LUCKY MASCOT.
IT WAS WHILST PLAYING IN HYDE PARK, BOTH OF US ONE DAY, THAT... WELL! THAT WE KISSED FOR THE FIRST TIME.
THAT WILL SOON BE SIX YEARS AGO.
SIX YEARS?! BUT HOW OLD WERE YOU?!
YOU KNOW THAT, DEEP DOWN, YOUNG GIRLS ALREADY HAVE A CERTAIN IDEA OF WHAT IT IS THEIR PARENTS WORRY SO MUCH ABOUT.

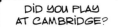
DID YOU PLAY AT CAMBRIDGE?

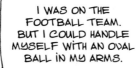
I WAS ON THE FOOTBALL TEAM. BUT I COULD HANDLE MYSELF WITH AN OVAL BALL IN MY ARMS.

WE'LL SOON SEE!

?!

NICE THROW!

...AT TACKLING!!!

I WAS EVEN BETTER...

"BEWILDERING HER VIKING OPPONENT, THE YOUNG BRITISH PRODIGY RUSHES TOWARD A VICTORIOUS TRY!"

"BUT, WITH THE RECKLESSNESS OF YOUTH, SHE FORGETS ONE DETAIL...

"...IN THE SNOW, VIKINGS RUN CONSIDERABLY FASTER THAN THE SUBJECTS OF HIS GLORIOUS MAJESTY, GEORGE THE 5TH!"

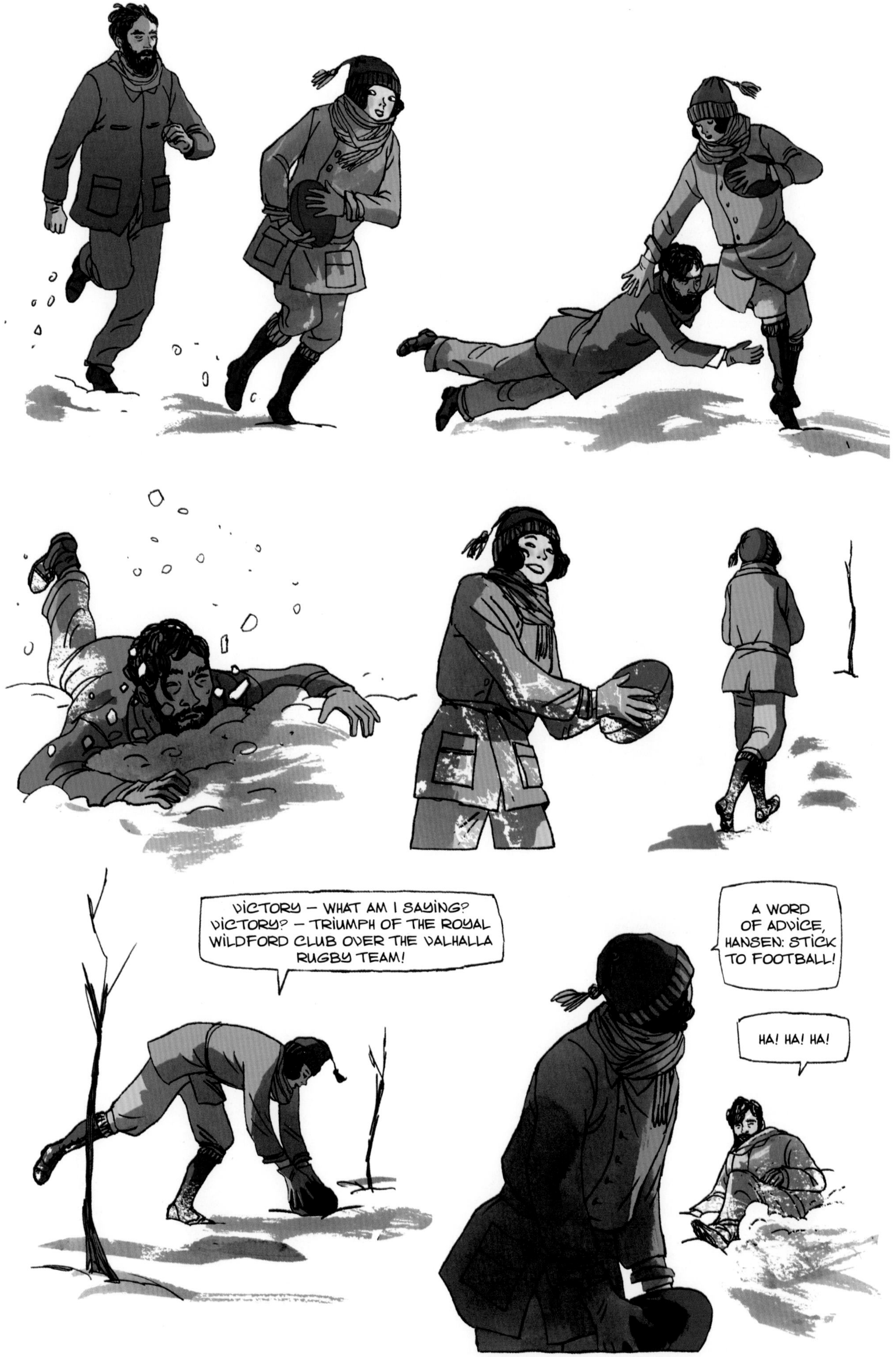
VICTORY – WHAT AM I SAYING? VICTORY? – TRIUMPH OF THE ROYAL WILDFORD CLUB OVER THE VALHALLA RUGBY TEAM!
A WORD OF ADVICE, HANSEN: STICK TO FOOTBALL!
HA! HA! HA!

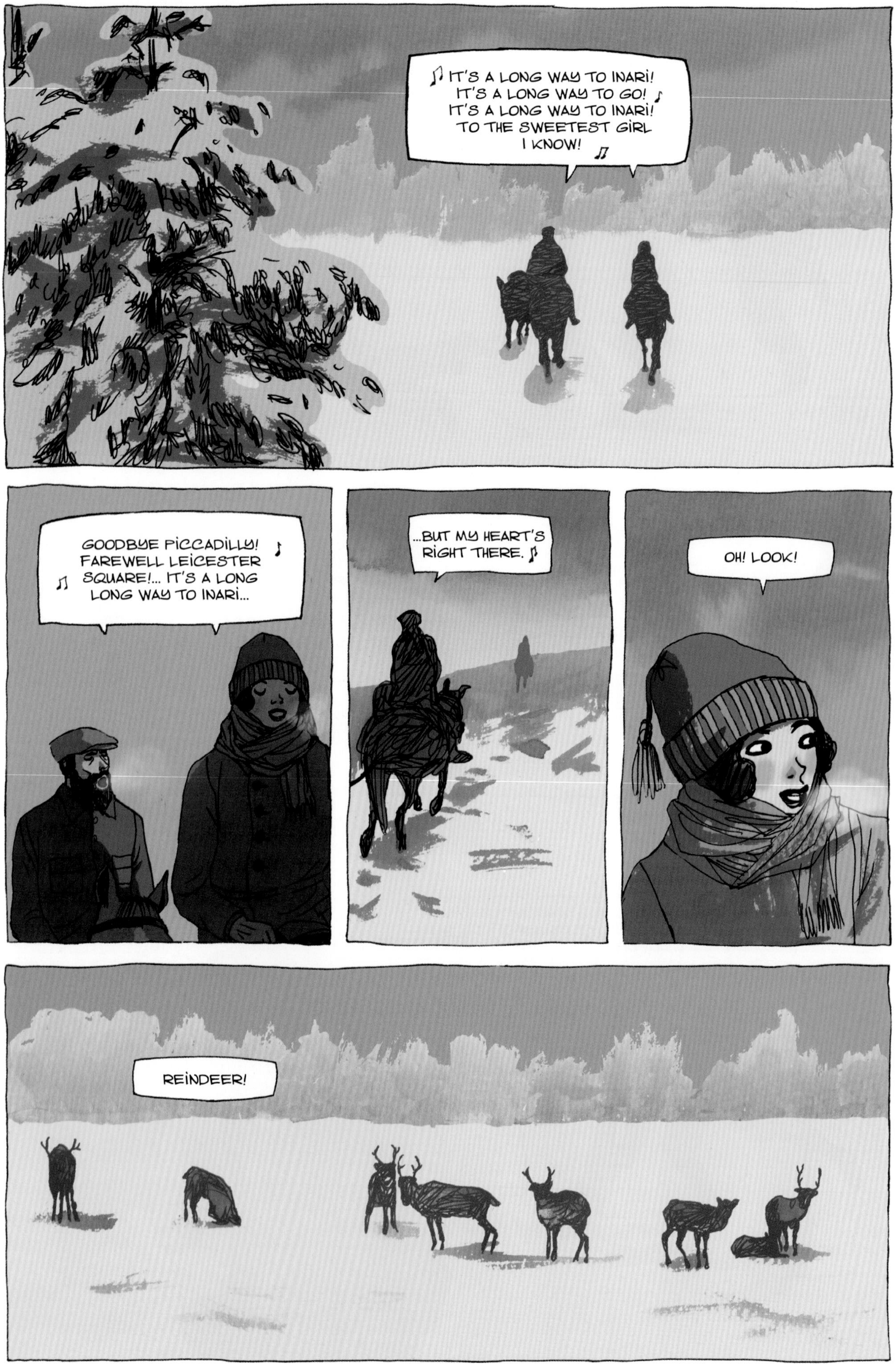
♫ IT'S A LONG WAY TO INARI! IT'S A LONG WAY TO GO! ♪ IT'S A LONG WAY TO INARI! TO THE SWEETEST GIRL I KNOW! ♫
GOODBYE PICCADILLY! ♪ FAREWELL LEICESTER SQUARE!... IT'S A LONG ♫ LONG WAY TO INARI...
...BUT MY HEART'S RIGHT THERE. ♪
OH! LOOK!
REINDEER!

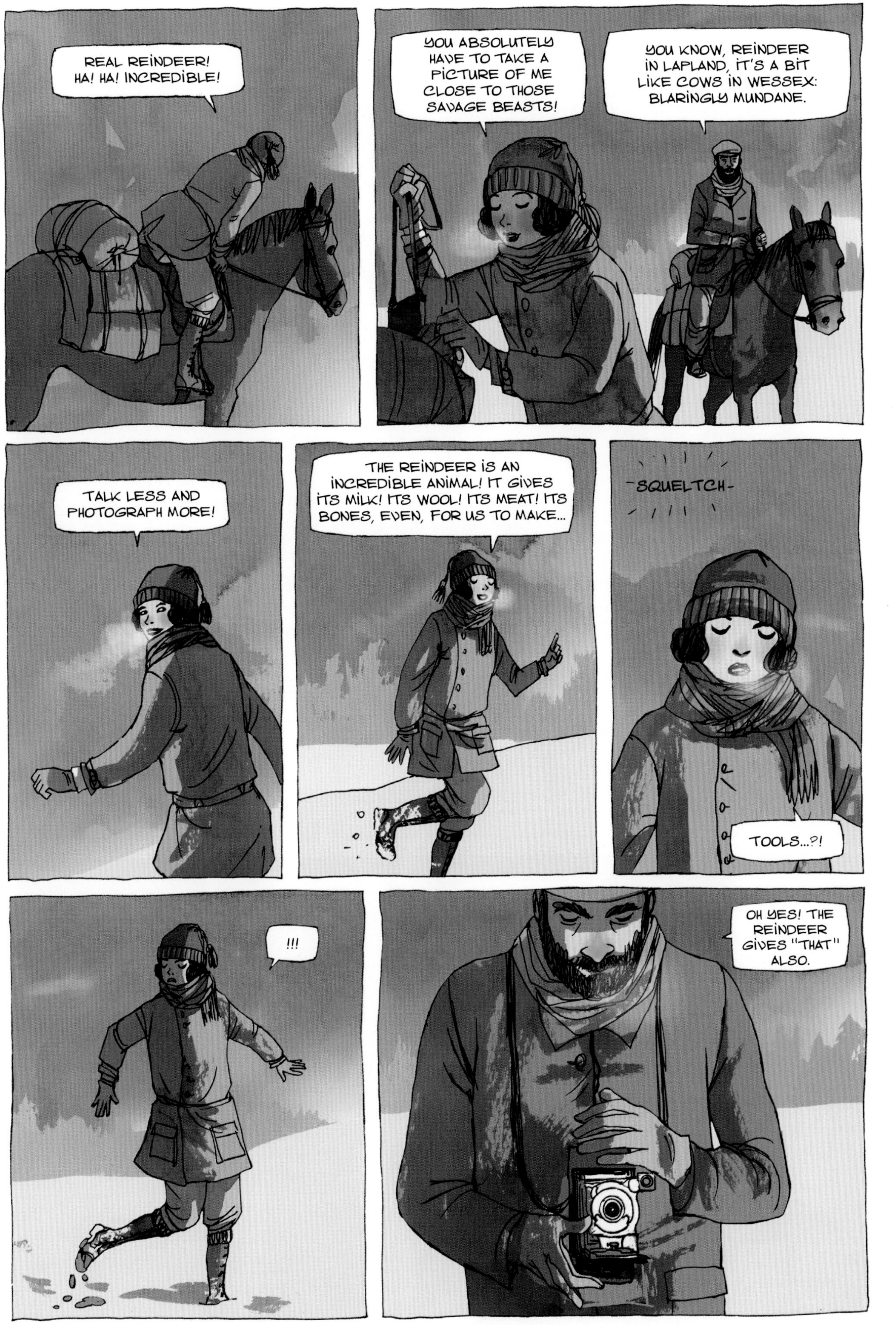
REAL REINDEER! HA! HA! INCREDIBLE!
YOU ABSOLUTELY HAVE TO TAKE A PICTURE OF ME CLOSE TO THOSE SAVAGE BEASTS!
YOU KNOW, REINDEER IN LAPLAND, IT'S A BIT LIKE COWS IN WESSEX: BLARINGLY MUNDANE.
TALK LESS AND PHOTOGRAPH MORE!
THE REINDEER IS AN INCREDIBLE ANIMAL! IT GIVES ITS MILK! ITS WOOL! ITS MEAT! ITS BONES, EVEN, FOR US TO MAKE...
-SQUELTCH-
TOOLS...?!
!!!
OH YES! THE REINDEER GIVES "THAT" ALSO.

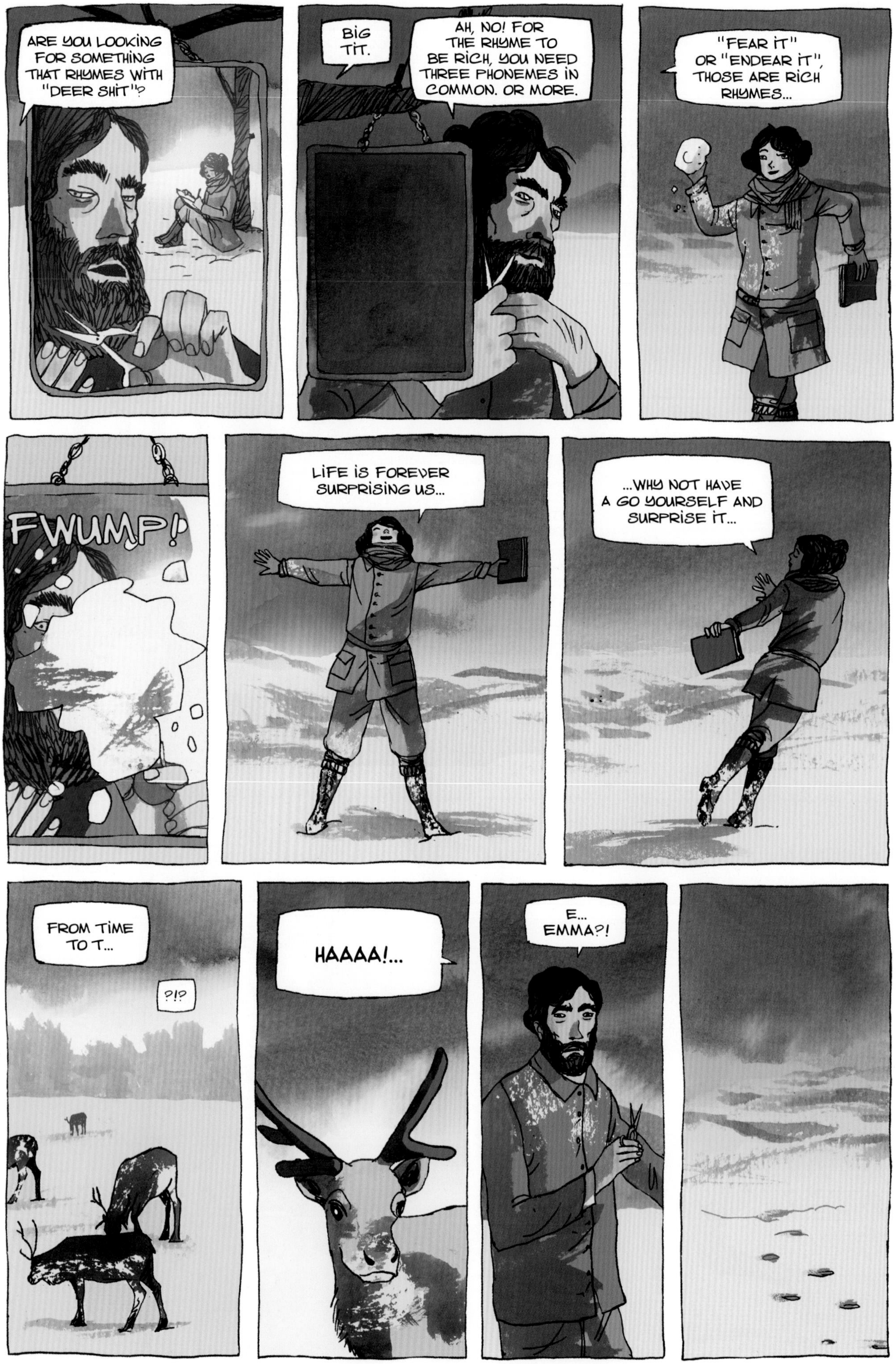
ARE YOU LOOKING FOR SOMETHING THAT RHYMES WITH "DEER SHIT"?
BIG TIT.
AH, NO! FOR THE RHYME TO BE RICH, YOU NEED THREE PHONEMES IN COMMON. OR MORE.
"FEAR IT" OR "ENDEAR IT", THOSE ARE RICH RHYMES...
FWUMP!
LIFE IS FOREVER SURPRISING US...
...WHY NOT HAVE A GO YOURSELF AND SURPRISE IT...
FROM TIME TO T...
?!?
HAAAA!...
E... EMMA?!

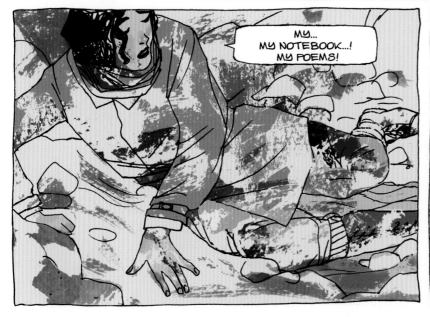

MY...
MY NOTEBOOK...!
MY POEMS!

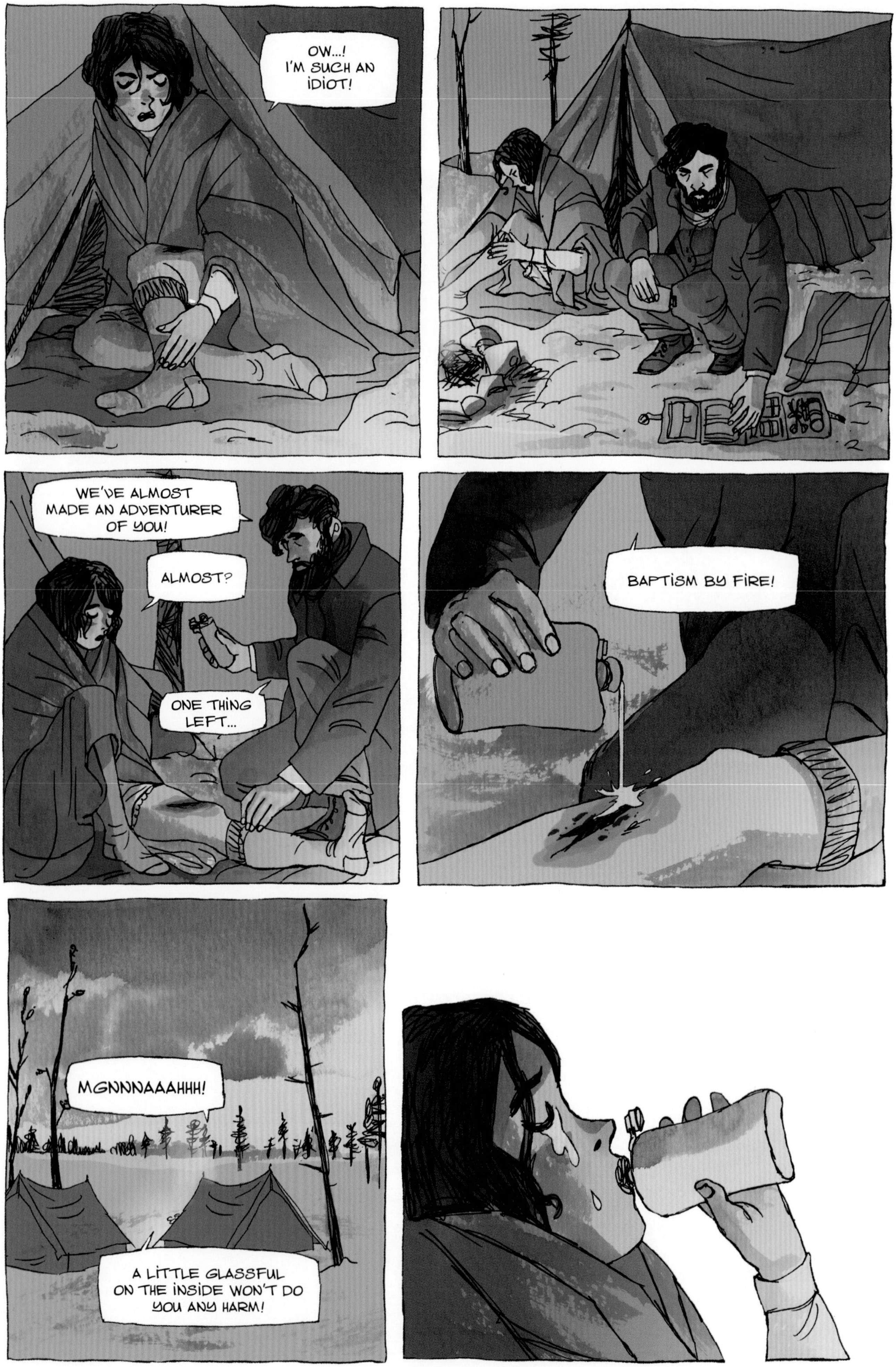
OW...! I'M SUCH AN IDIOT!
WE'VE ALMOST MADE AN ADVENTURER OF YOU!
ALMOST?
ONE THING LEFT...
BAPTISM BY FIRE!
MGNNNAAAHHH!
A LITTLE GLASSFUL ON THE INSIDE WON'T DO YOU ANY HARM!

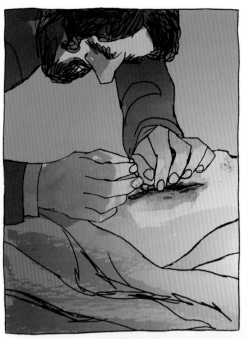

WE'LL STAY HERE A DAY OR TWO UNTIL YOU'VE RECOVERED YOUR STRENGTH.

BUT... WHAT IF THE HEAVY SNOWS COME?

IN THAT CASE...

...YOU'LL HAVE THE POETIC DEATH THAT YOU WERE DREAMING OF!

KNOCK KNOCK!

IF YOU'D BE SO KIND AND LEAVE THE TRAY AND NEWSPAPER BY THE DOOR, THANK YOU!

HOW ARE YOU? WERE YOU ABLE TO SLEEP, DESPITE THE PAIN?

THE STITCHES PULLED A BIT, BUT NOTHING MORE. IT'S THE BUMP ON MY HEAD WHICH HURTS.

OH!

I DID WHAT I COULD TO DRY YOUR NOTEBOOK, BUT...

LET ME HAVE A LOOK AT YOUR LEG.

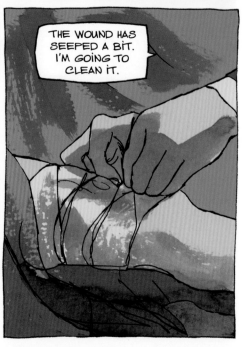

THE WOUND HAS SEEPED A BIT. I'M GOING TO CLEAN IT.

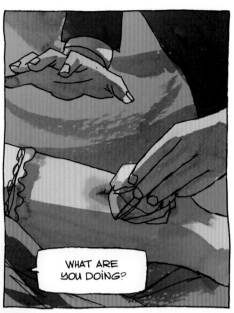

WHAT ARE YOU DOING?

EXCUSE ME, EMMA...

WHY DID YOU...

...REMOVE YOUR HAND?

GO HIGHER UP!

HIGHER UP!

HIGHER...

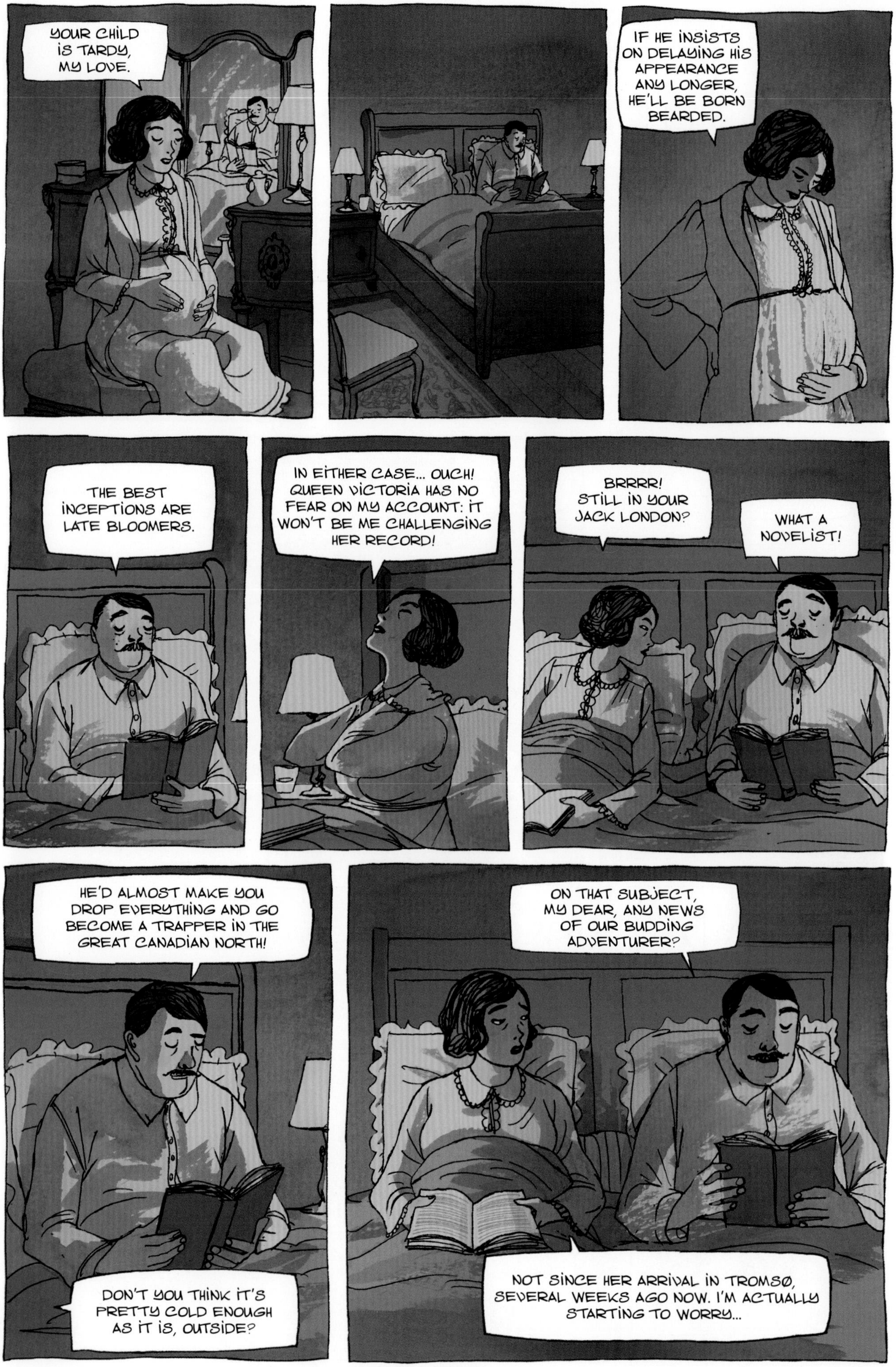
YOUR CHILD IS TARDY, MY LOVE.
IF HE INSISTS ON DELAYING HIS APPEARANCE ANY LONGER, HE'LL BE BORN BEARDED.
THE BEST INCEPTIONS ARE LATE BLOOMERS.
IN EITHER CASE... OUCH! QUEEN VICTORIA HAS NO FEAR ON MY ACCOUNT: IT WON'T BE ME CHALLENGING HER RECORD!
BRRRR! STILL IN YOUR JACK LONDON?
WHAT A NOVELIST!
HE'D ALMOST MAKE YOU DROP EVERYTHING AND GO BECOME A TRAPPER IN THE GREAT CANADIAN NORTH!
DON'T YOU THINK IT'S PRETTY COLD ENOUGH AS IT IS, OUTSIDE?
ON THAT SUBJECT, MY DEAR, ANY NEWS OF OUR BUDDING ADVENTURER?
NOT SINCE HER ARRIVAL IN TROMSØ, SEVERAL WEEKS AGO NOW. I'M ACTUALLY STARTING TO WORRY...

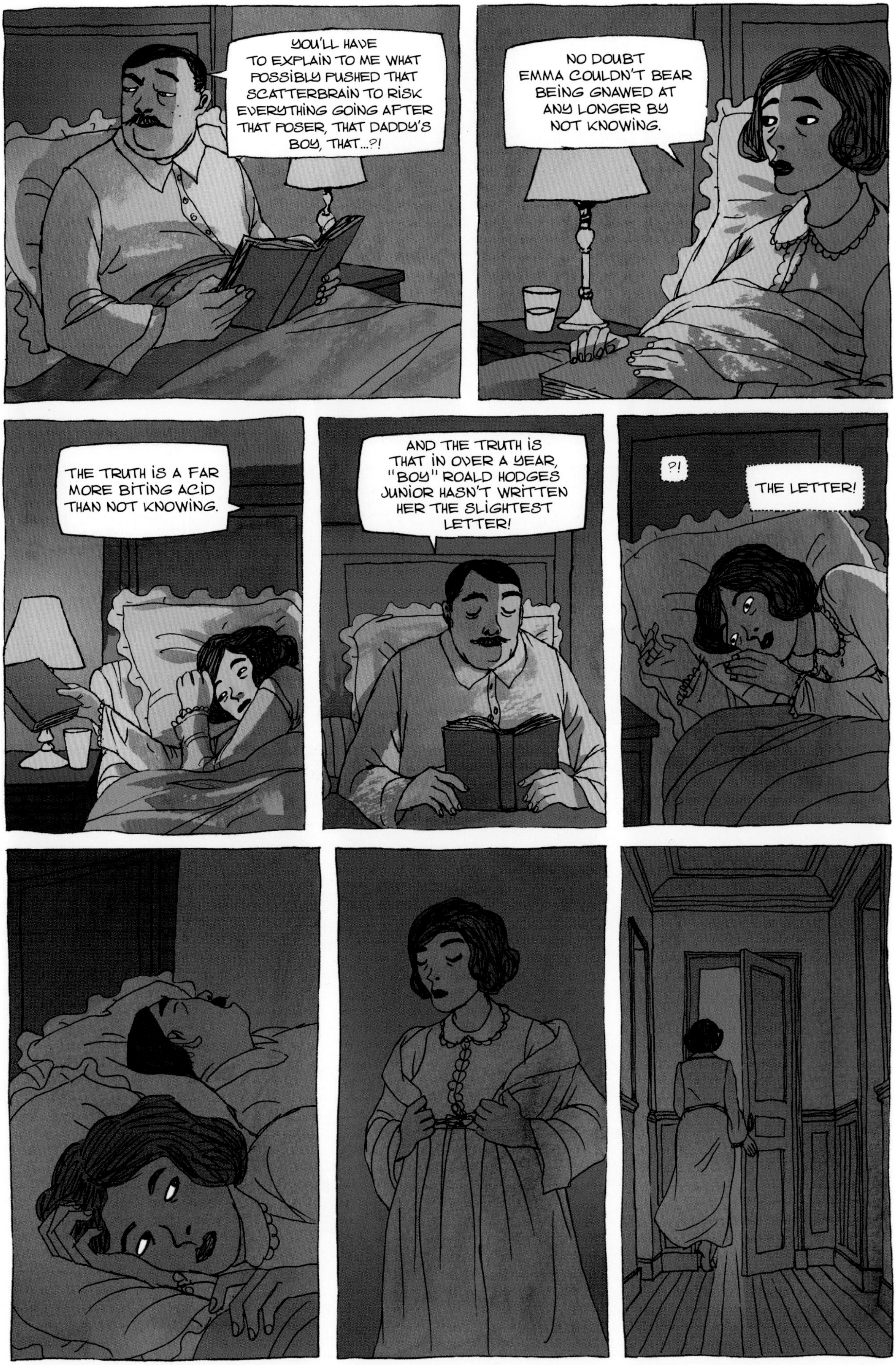
YOU'LL HAVE TO EXPLAIN TO ME WHAT POSSIBLY PUSHED THAT SCATTERBRAIN TO RISK EVERYTHING GOING AFTER THAT POSER, THAT DADDY'S BOY, THAT...?!
NO DOUBT EMMA COULDN'T BEAR BEING GNAWED AT ANY LONGER BY NOT KNOWING.
THE TRUTH IS A FAR MORE BITING ACID THAN NOT KNOWING.
AND THE TRUTH IS THAT IN OVER A YEAR, "BOY" ROALD HODGES JUNIOR HASN'T WRITTEN HER THE SLIGHTEST LETTER!
?!
THE LETTER!

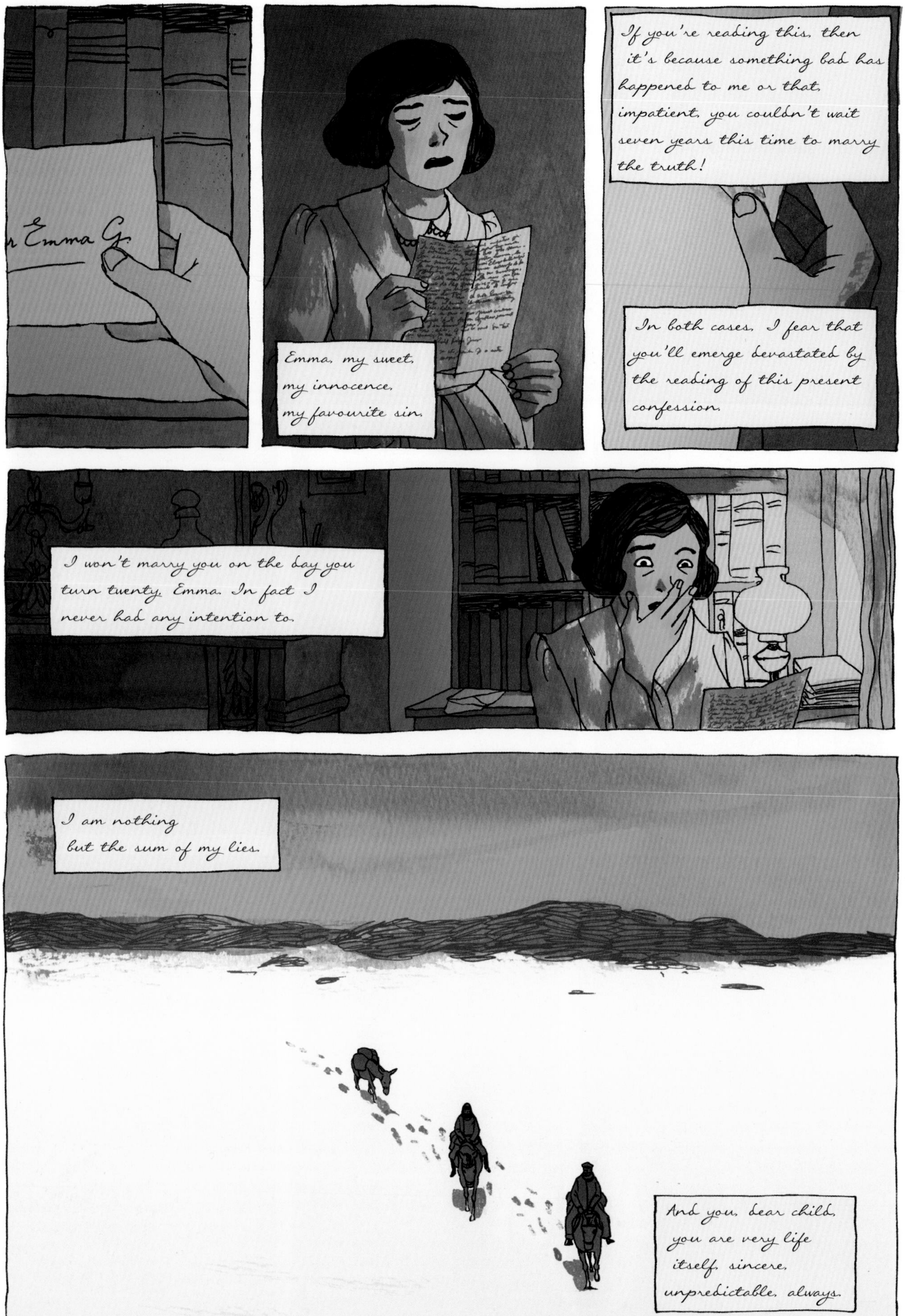

...r Emma G.
Emma, my sweet, my innocence, my favourite sin.
If you're reading this, then it's because something bad has happened to me or that, impatient, you couldn't wait seven years this time to marry the truth!
In both cases, I fear that you'll emerge devastated by the reading of this present confession.
I won't marry you on the day you turn twenty, Emma. In fact I never had any intention to.
I am nothing but the sum of my lies.
And you, dear child, you are very life itself, sincere, unpredictable, always.

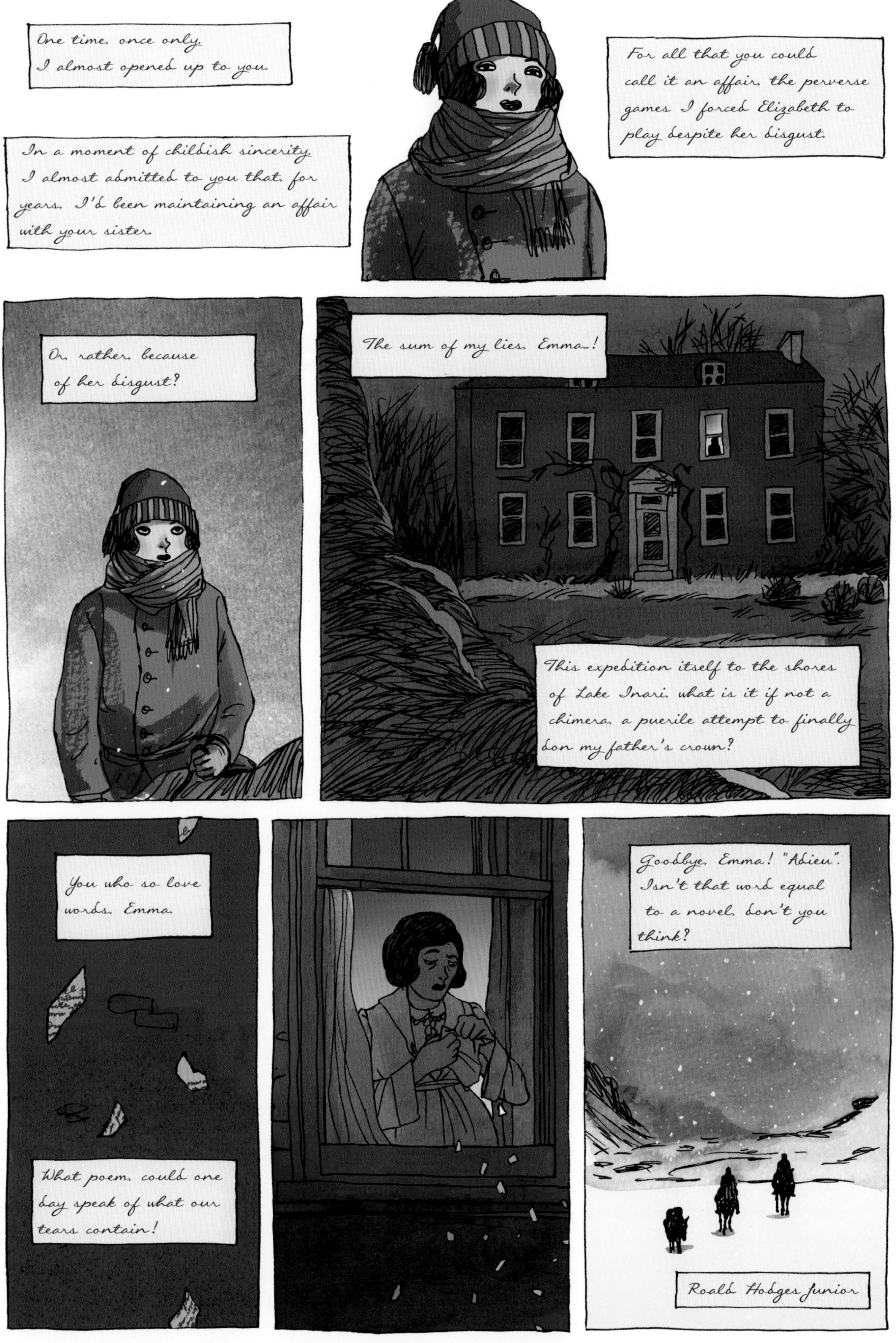
One time, once only.
I almost opened up to you.
In a moment of childish sincerity, I almost admitted to you that, for years, I'd been maintaining an affair with your sister.
For all that you could call it an affair, the perverse games I forced Elizabeth to play despite her disgust.
Or, rather, because of her disgust?
The sum of my lies, Emma...!
This expedition itself to the shores of Lake Inari, what is it if not a chimera, a puerile attempt to finally don my father's crown?
You who so love words, Emma.
What poem, could one day speak of what our tears contain!
Goodbye, Emma! "Adieu". Isn't that word equal to a novel, don't you think?
Roald Hodges Junior

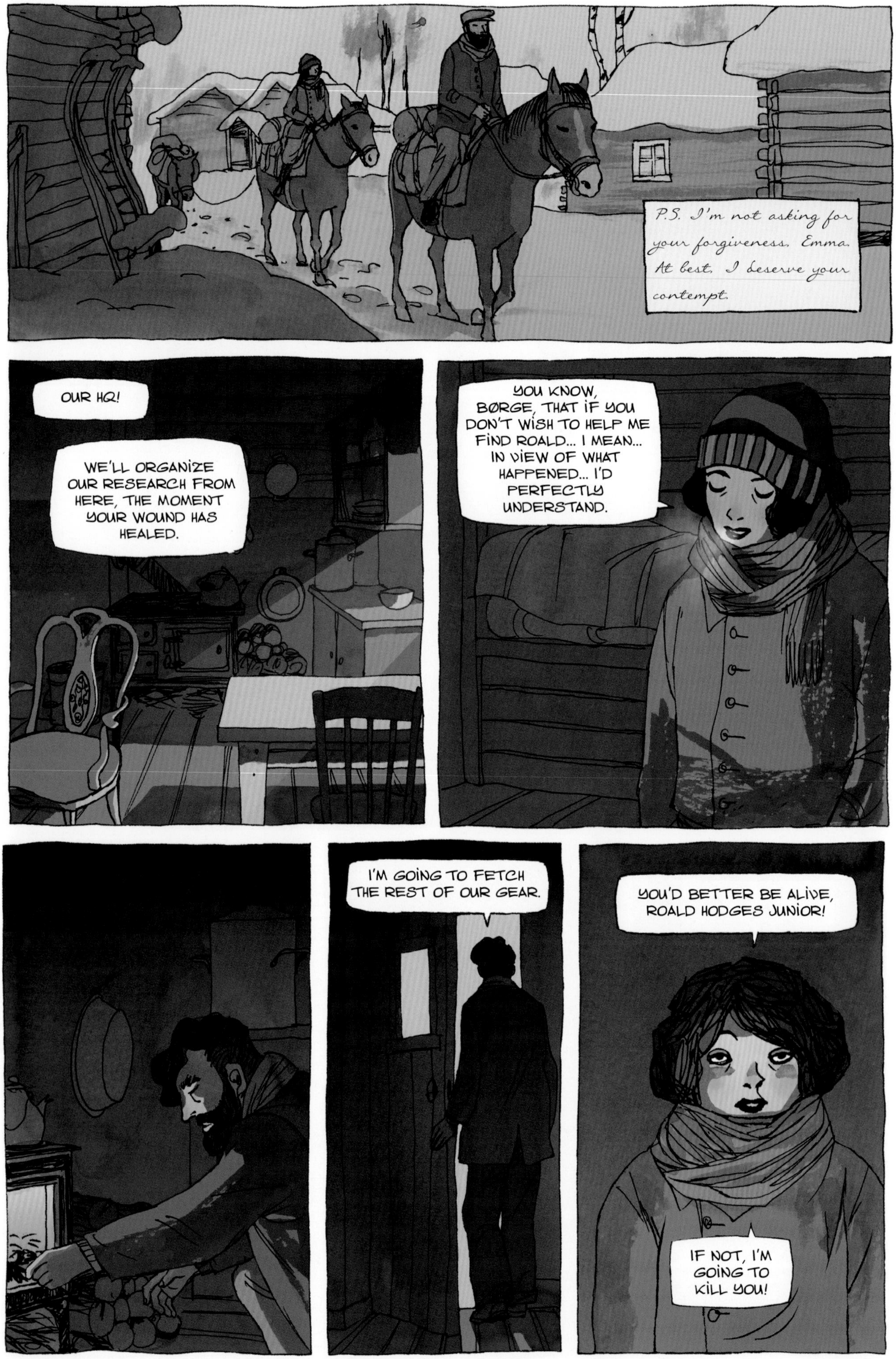
P.S. I'm not asking for your forgiveness, Emma. At best, I deserve your contempt.
OUR HQ!
WE'LL ORGANIZE OUR RESEARCH FROM HERE, THE MOMENT YOUR WOUND HAS HEALED.
YOU KNOW, BØRGE, THAT IF YOU DON'T WISH TO HELP ME FIND ROALD... I MEAN... IN VIEW OF WHAT HAPPENED... I'D PERFECTLY UNDERSTAND.
I'M GOING TO FETCH THE REST OF OUR GEAR.
YOU'D BETTER BE ALIVE, ROALD HODGES JUNIOR!
IF NOT, I'M GOING TO KILL YOU!

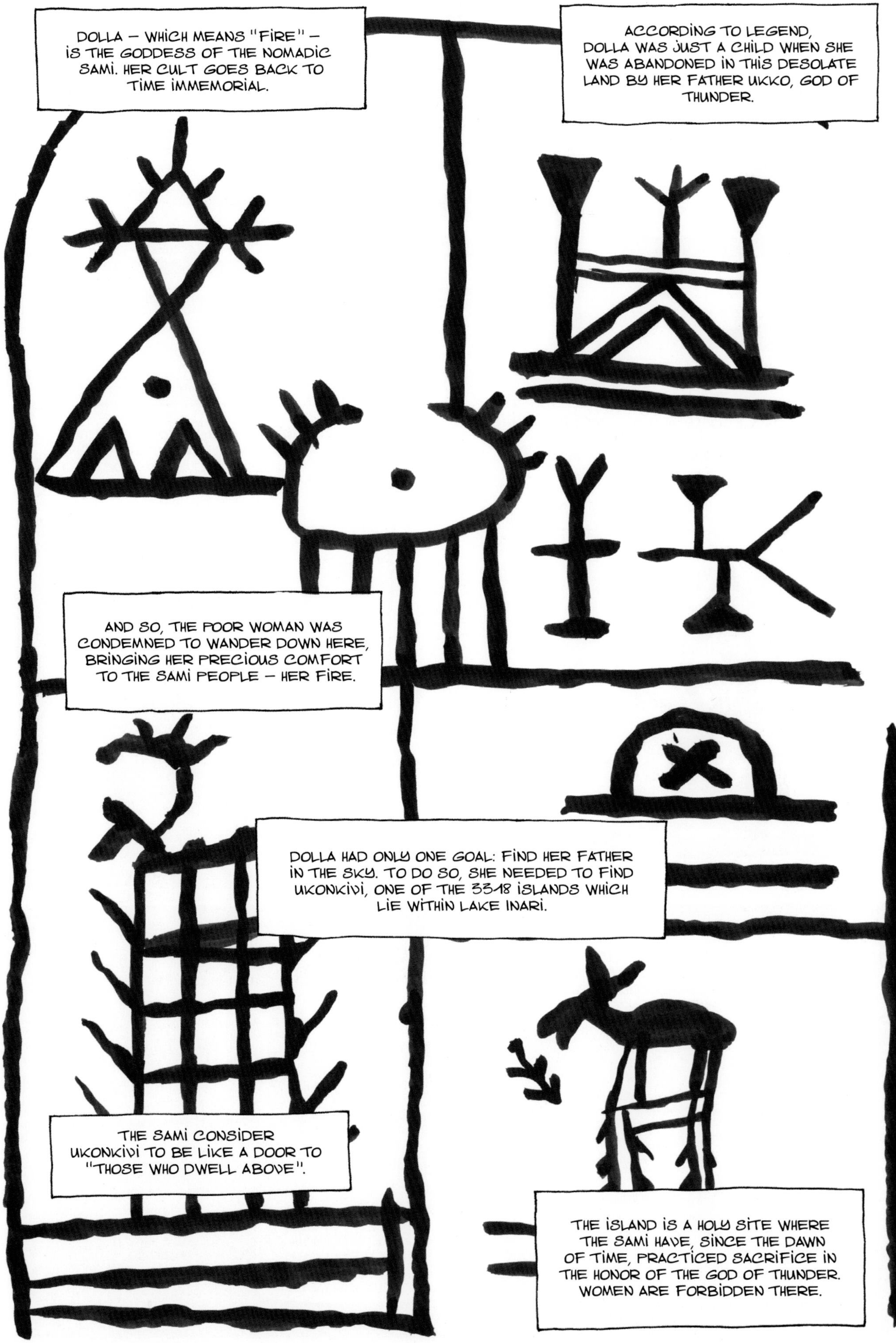
DOLLA – WHICH MEANS "FIRE" – IS THE GODDESS OF THE NOMADIC SAMI. HER CULT GOES BACK TO TIME IMMEMORIAL.
ACCORDING TO LEGEND, DOLLA WAS JUST A CHILD WHEN SHE WAS ABANDONED IN THIS DESOLATE LAND BY HER FATHER UKKO, GOD OF THUNDER.
AND SO, THE POOR WOMAN WAS CONDEMNED TO WANDER DOWN HERE, BRINGING HER PRECIOUS COMFORT TO THE SAMI PEOPLE – HER FIRE.
DOLLA HAD ONLY ONE GOAL: FIND HER FATHER IN THE SKY. TO DO SO, SHE NEEDED TO FIND UKONKIVI, ONE OF THE 3318 ISLANDS WHICH LIE WITHIN LAKE INARI.
THE SAMI CONSIDER UKONKIVI TO BE LIKE A DOOR TO "THOSE WHO DWELL ABOVE".
THE ISLAND IS A HOLY SITE WHERE THE SAMI HAVE, SINCE THE DAWN OF TIME, PRACTICED SACRIFICE IN THE HONOR OF THE GOD OF THUNDER. WOMEN ARE FORBIDDEN THERE.

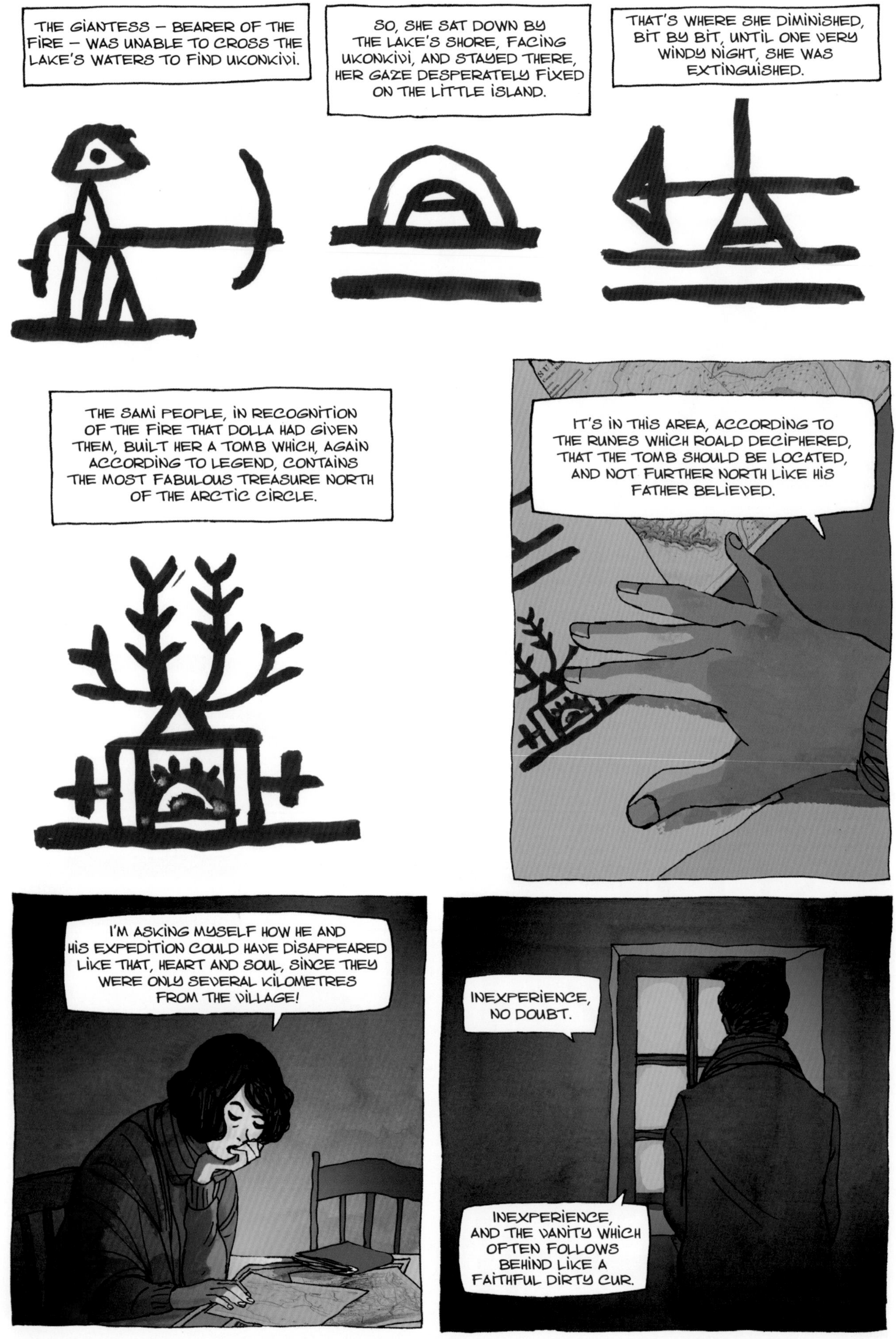
THE GIANTESS – BEARER OF THE FIRE – WAS UNABLE TO CROSS THE LAKE'S WATERS TO FIND UKONKIVI.
SO, SHE SAT DOWN BY THE LAKE'S SHORE, FACING UKONKIVI, AND STAYED THERE, HER GAZE DESPERATELY FIXED ON THE LITTLE ISLAND.
THAT'S WHERE SHE DIMINISHED, BIT BY BIT, UNTIL ONE VERY WINDY NIGHT, SHE WAS EXTINGUISHED.
THE SAMI PEOPLE, IN RECOGNITION OF THE FIRE THAT DOLLA HAD GIVEN THEM, BUILT HER A TOMB WHICH, AGAIN ACCORDING TO LEGEND, CONTAINS THE MOST FABULOUS TREASURE NORTH OF THE ARCTIC CIRCLE.
IT'S IN THIS AREA, ACCORDING TO THE RUNES WHICH ROALD DECIPHERED, THAT THE TOMB SHOULD BE LOCATED, AND NOT FURTHER NORTH LIKE HIS FATHER BELIEVED.
I'M ASKING MYSELF HOW HE AND HIS EXPEDITION COULD HAVE DISAPPEARED LIKE THAT, HEART AND SOUL, SINCE THEY WERE ONLY SEVERAL KILOMETRES FROM THE VILLAGE!
INEXPERIENCE, NO DOUBT.
INEXPERIENCE, AND THE VANITY WHICH OFTEN FOLLOWS BEHIND LIKE A FAITHFUL DIRTY CUR.

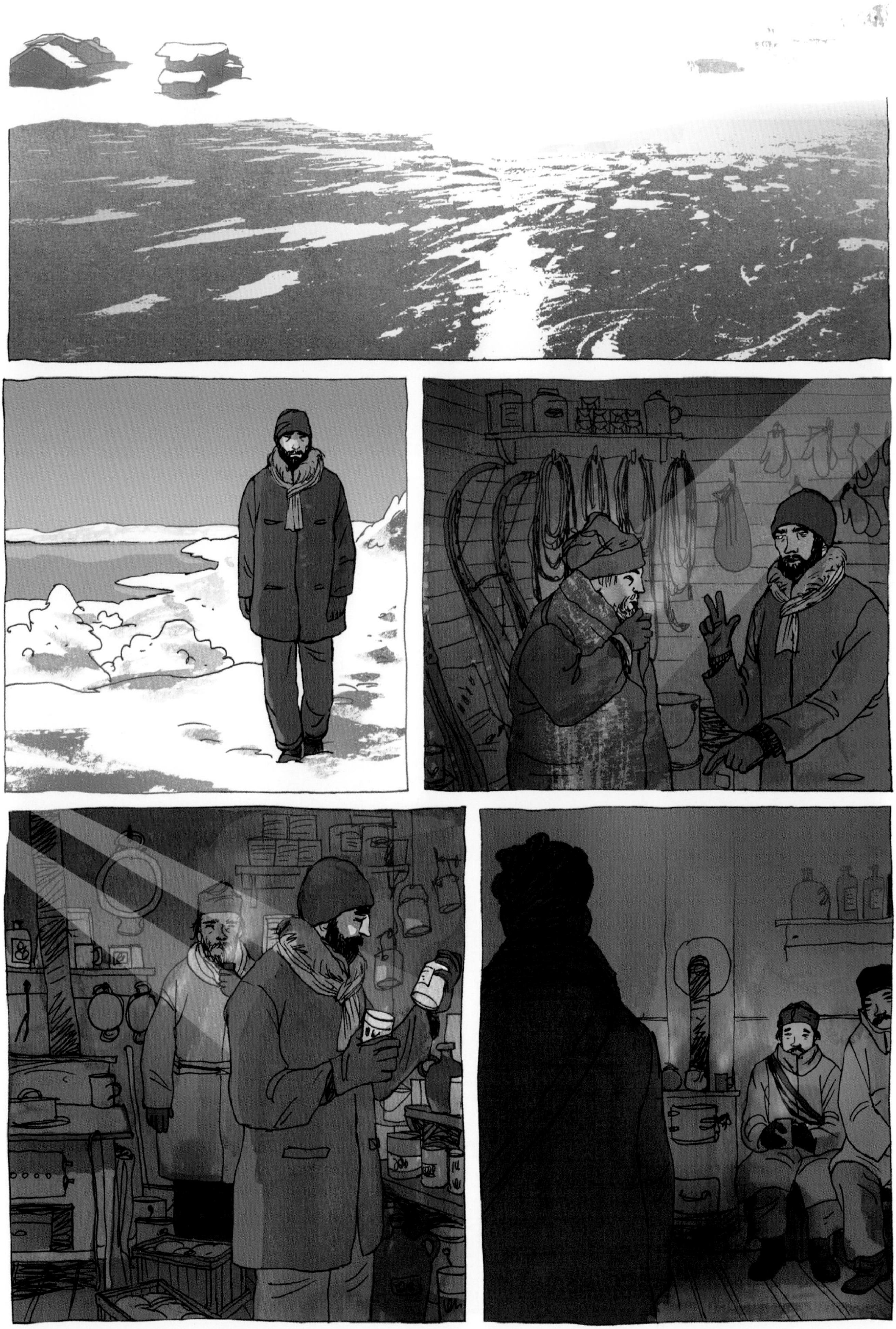

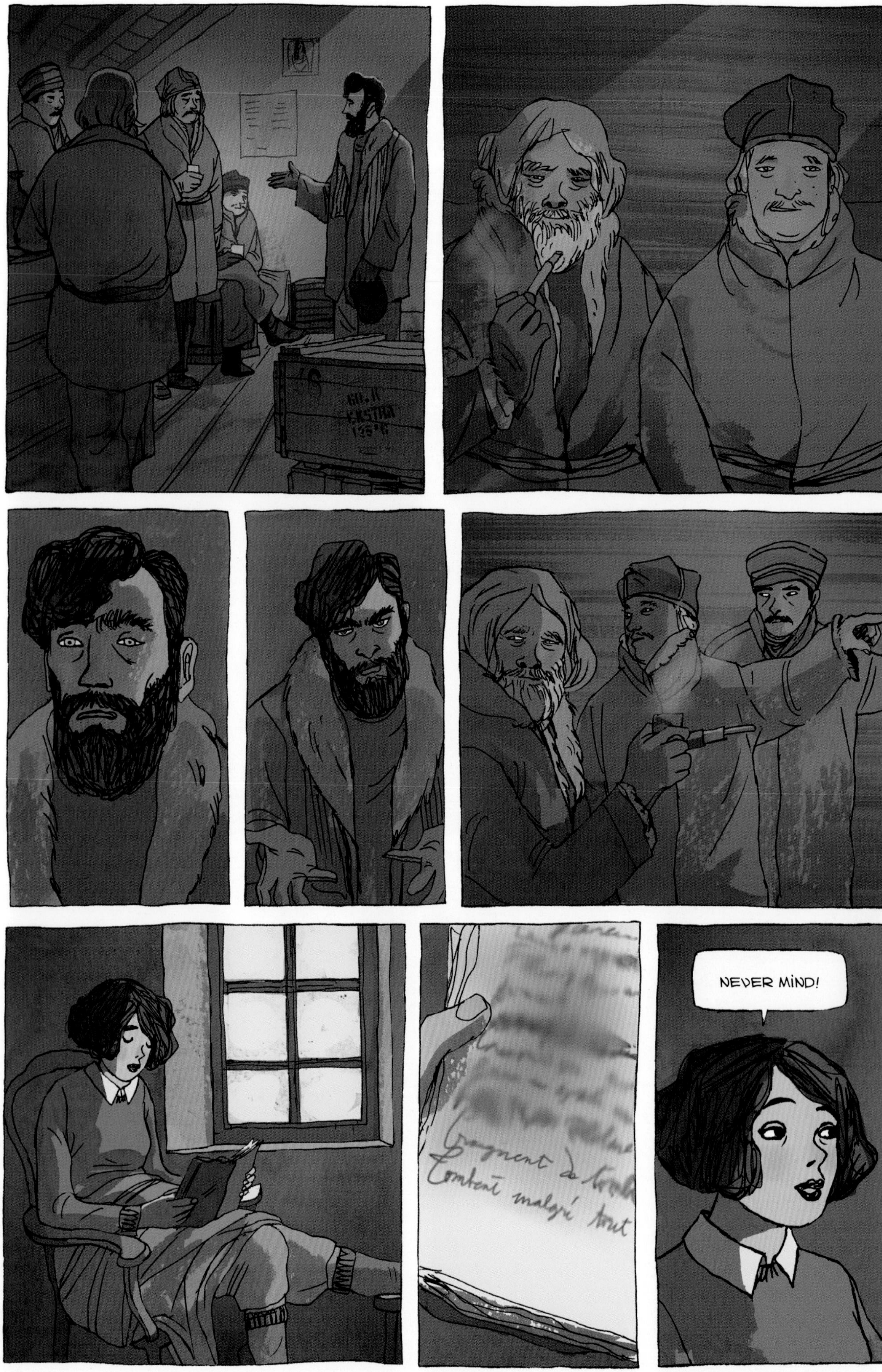
NEVER MIND!

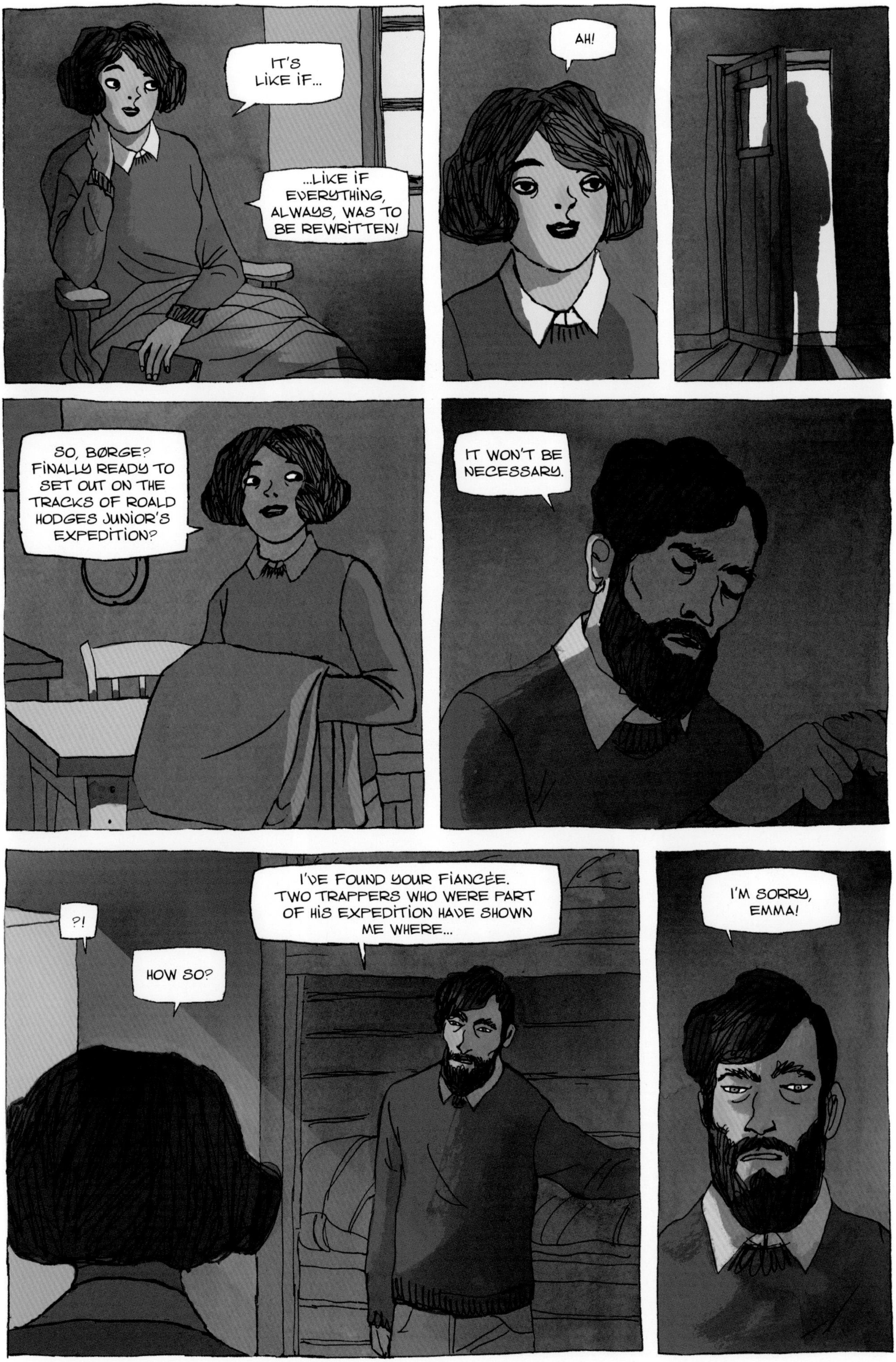
IT'S LIKE IF...
...LIKE IF EVERYTHING, ALWAYS, WAS TO BE REWRITTEN!
AH!
SO, BØRGE? FINALLY READY TO SET OUT ON THE TRACKS OF ROALD HODGES JUNIOR'S EXPEDITION?
IT WON'T BE NECESSARY.
I'VE FOUND YOUR FIANCÉE. TWO TRAPPERS WHO WERE PART OF HIS EXPEDITION HAVE SHOWN ME WHERE...
?!
HOW SO?
I'M SORRY, EMMA!

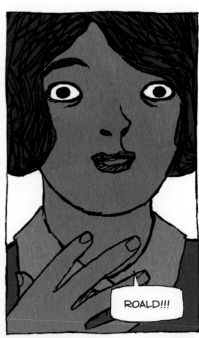

ROALD!!!

EMMA?

... DARLING?

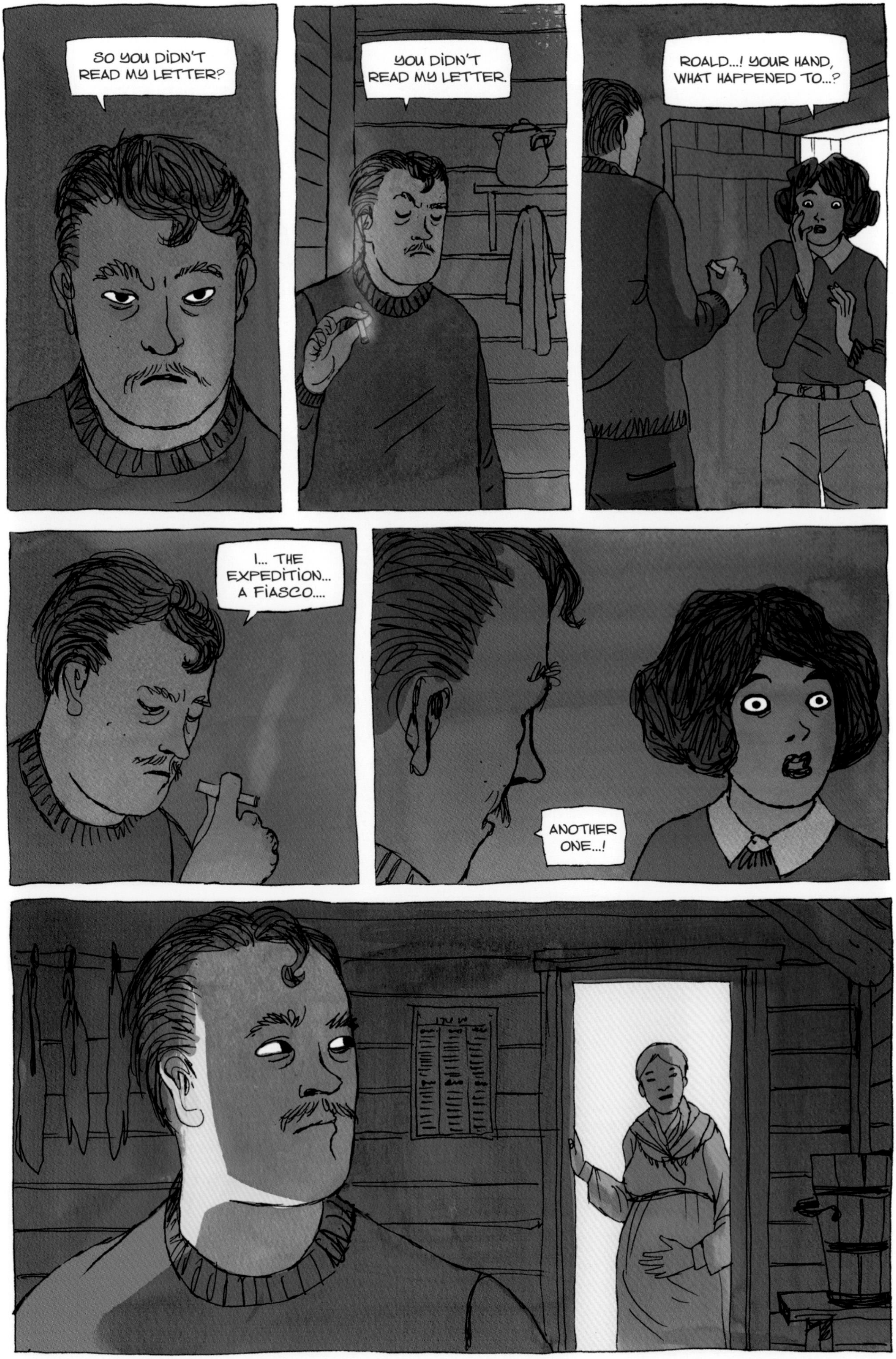
SO YOU DIDN'T READ MY LETTER?
YOU DIDN'T READ MY LETTER.
ROALD...! YOUR HAND, WHAT HAPPENED TO...?
I... THE EXPEDITION... A FIASCO....
ANOTHER ONE...!

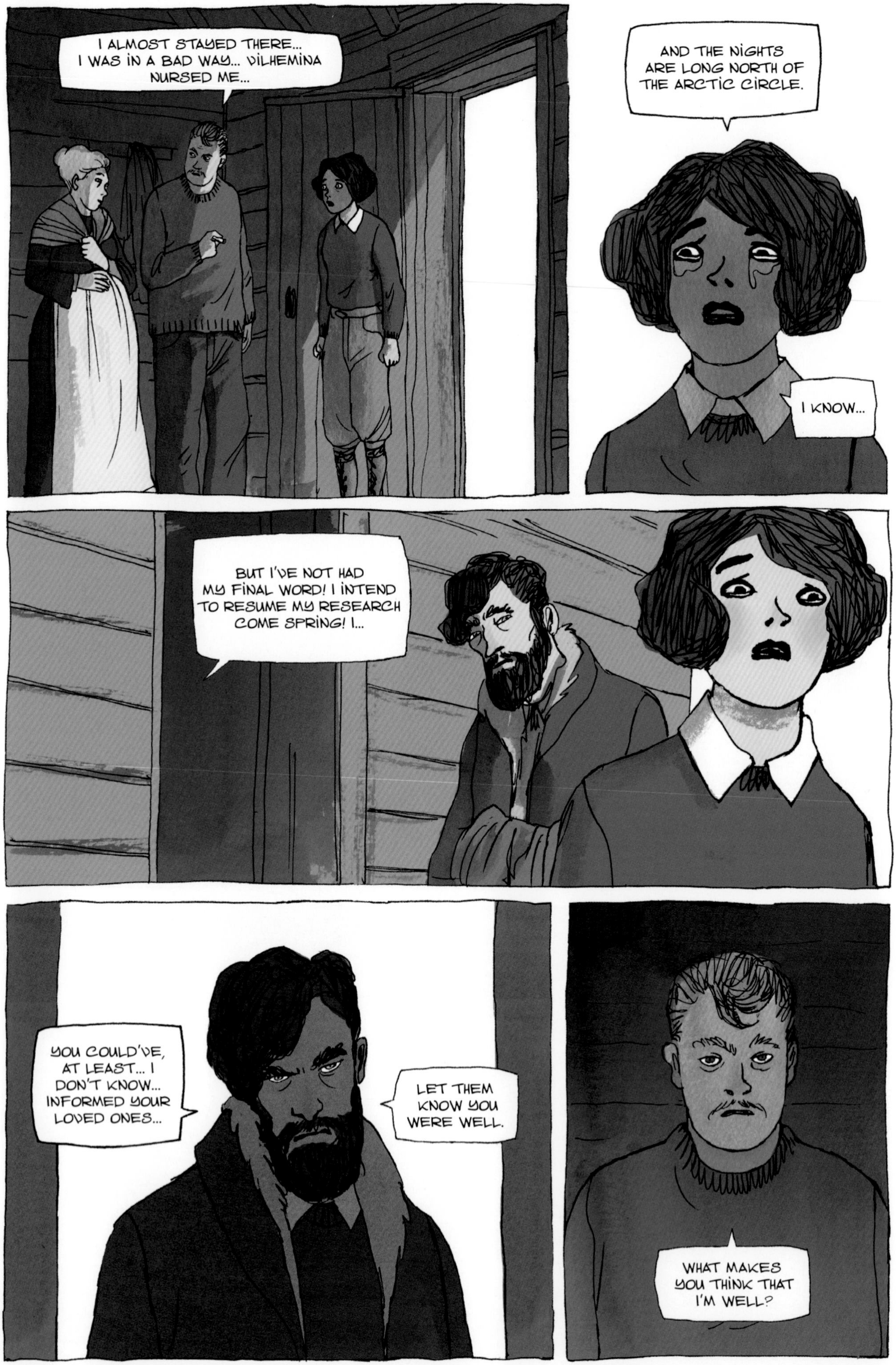
I ALMOST STAYED THERE... I WAS IN A BAD WAY... VILHEMINA NURSED ME...
AND THE NIGHTS ARE LONG NORTH OF THE ARCTIC CIRCLE.
I KNOW...
BUT I'VE NOT HAD MY FINAL WORD! I INTEND TO RESUME MY RESEARCH COME SPRING! I...
YOU COULD'VE, AT LEAST... I DON'T KNOW... INFORMED YOUR LOVED ONES...
LET THEM KNOW YOU WERE WELL.
WHAT MAKES YOU THINK THAT I'M WELL?

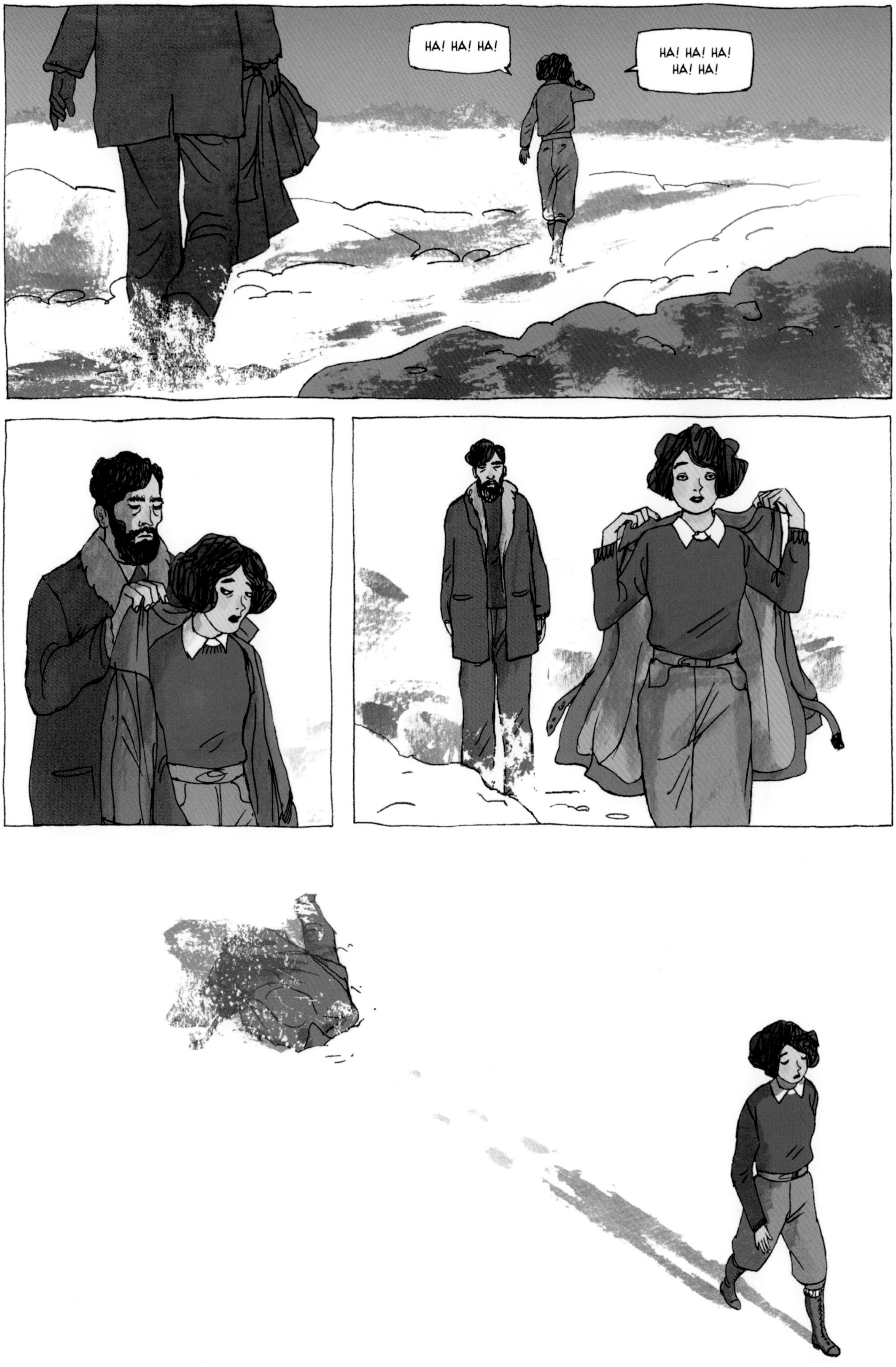
HA! HA! HA!
HA! HA! HA!
HA! HA!

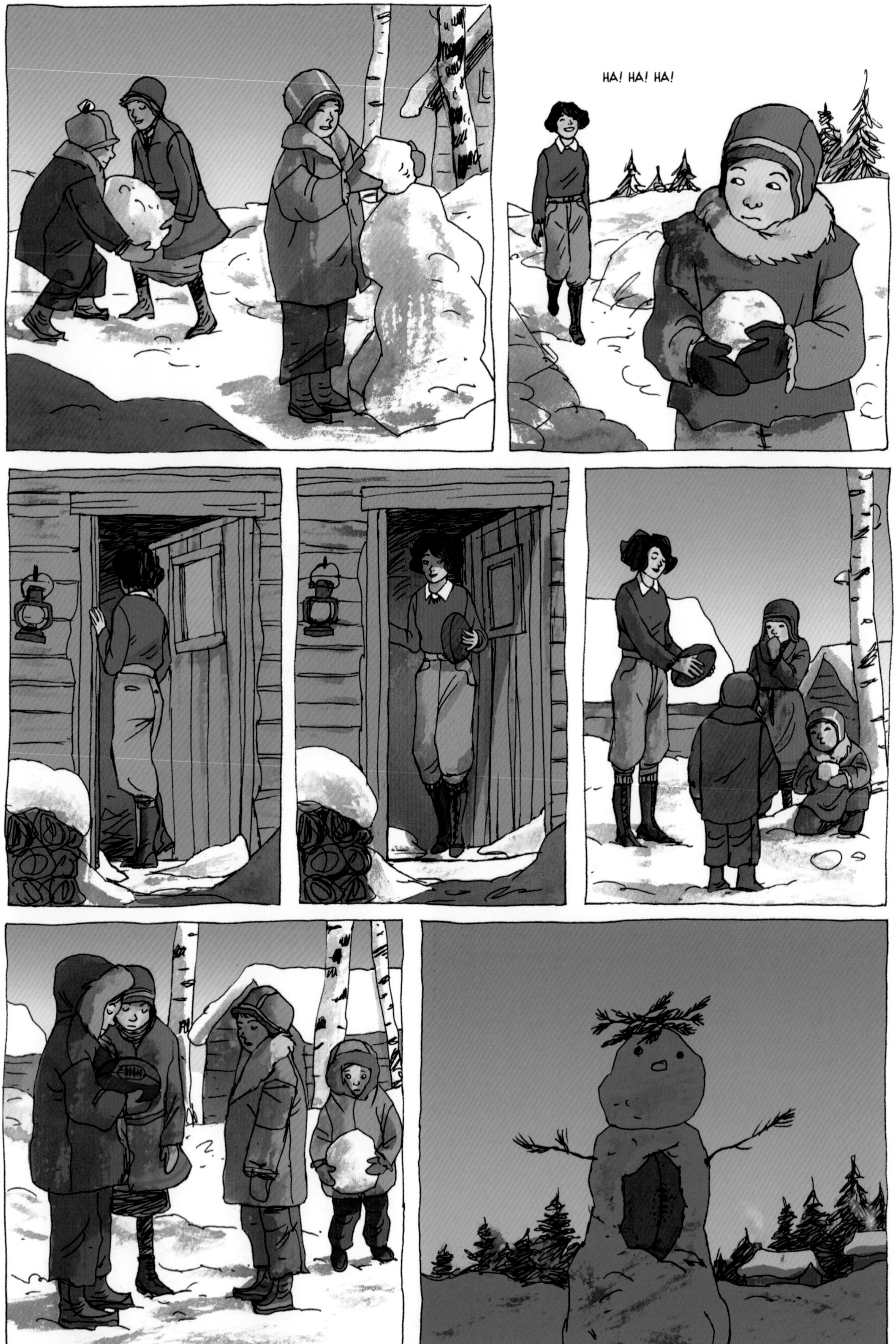
HA! HA! HA!

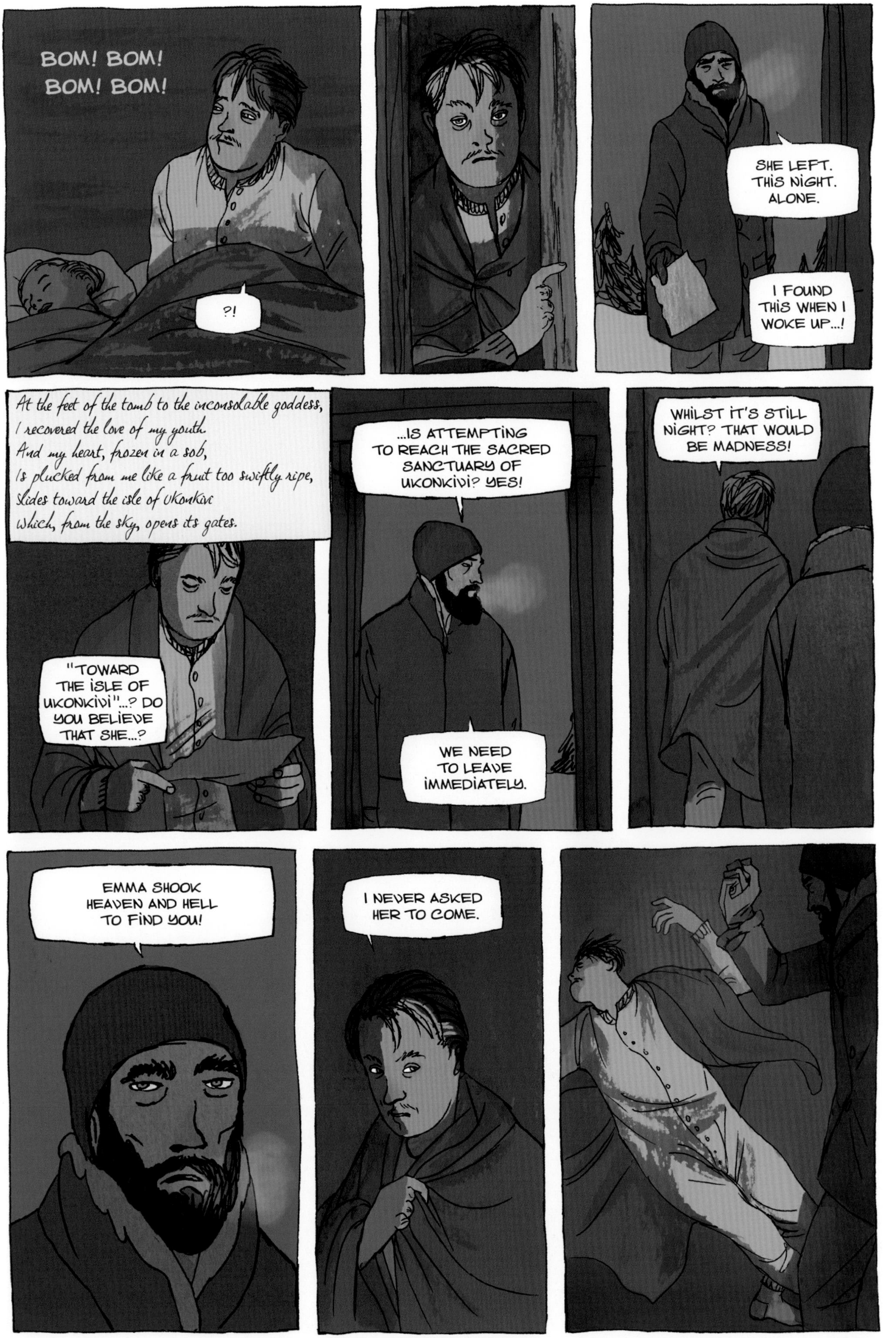
BOM! BOM! BOM! BOM!
?!
SHE LEFT. THIS NIGHT. ALONE.
I FOUND THIS WHEN I WOKE UP...!
At the feet of the tomb to the inconsolable goddess,
I recovered the love of my youth
And my heart, frozen in a sob,
Is plucked from me like a fruit too swiftly ripe,
Slides toward the isle of Ukonkivi
Which, from the sky, opens its gates.
"TOWARD THE ISLE OF UKONKIVI"...? DO YOU BELIEVE THAT SHE...?
...IS ATTEMPTING TO REACH THE SACRED SANCTUARY OF UKONKIVI? YES!
WE NEED TO LEAVE IMMEDIATELY.
WHILST IT'S STILL NIGHT? THAT WOULD BE MADNESS!
EMMA SHOOK HEAVEN AND HELL TO FIND YOU!
I NEVER ASKED HER TO COME.

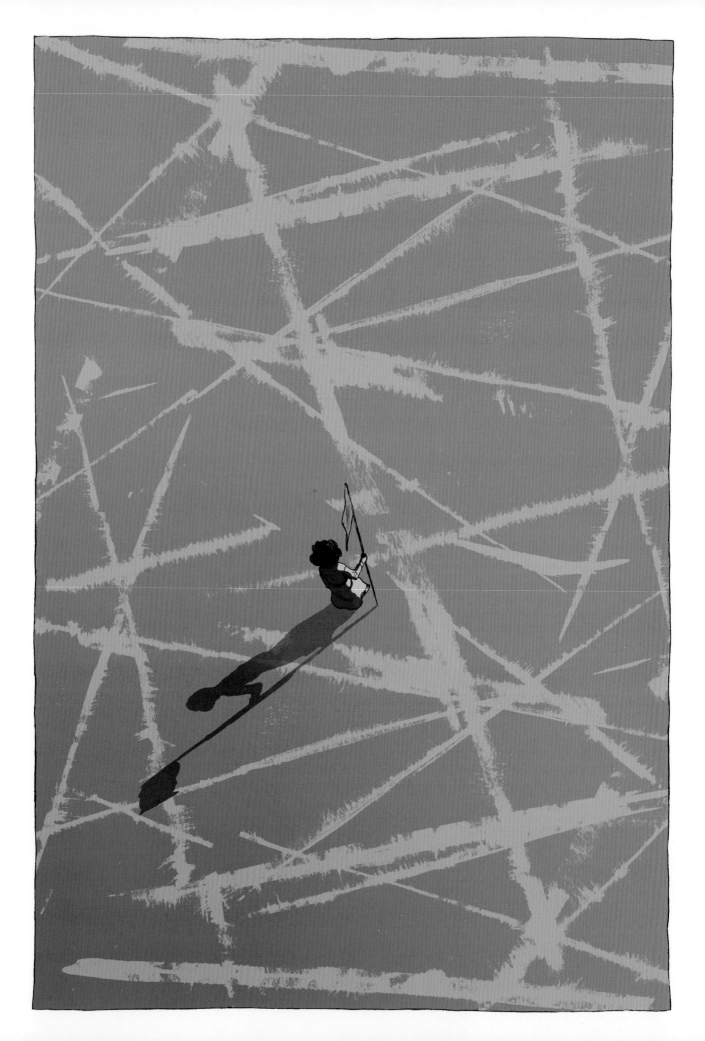

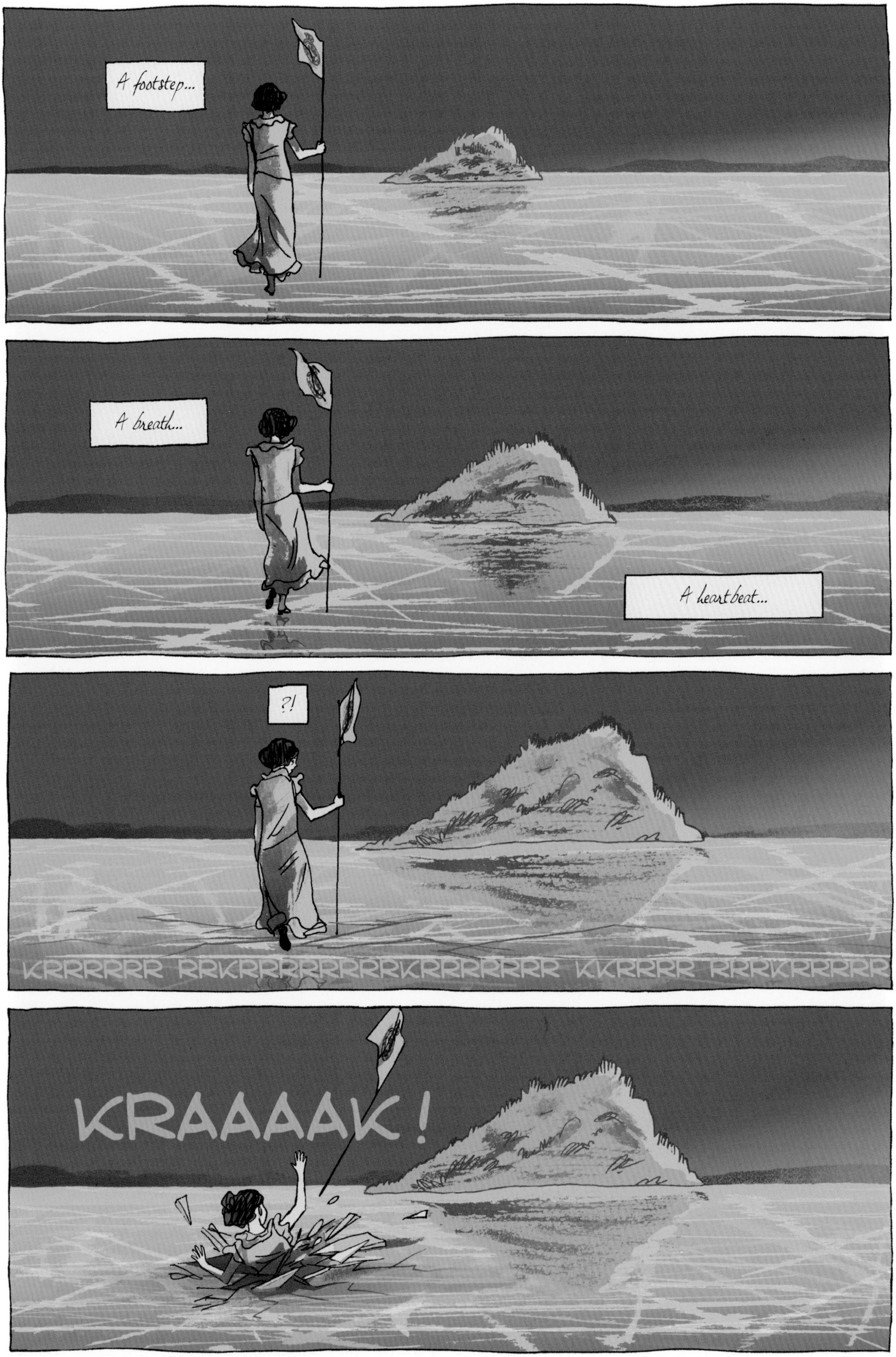
A footstep...
A breath...
A heartbeat...
?!
KRRRRRR RRKRRRRRRRRRKRRRRRRRR KKRRRR RRRKRRRRRR
KRAAAAK!

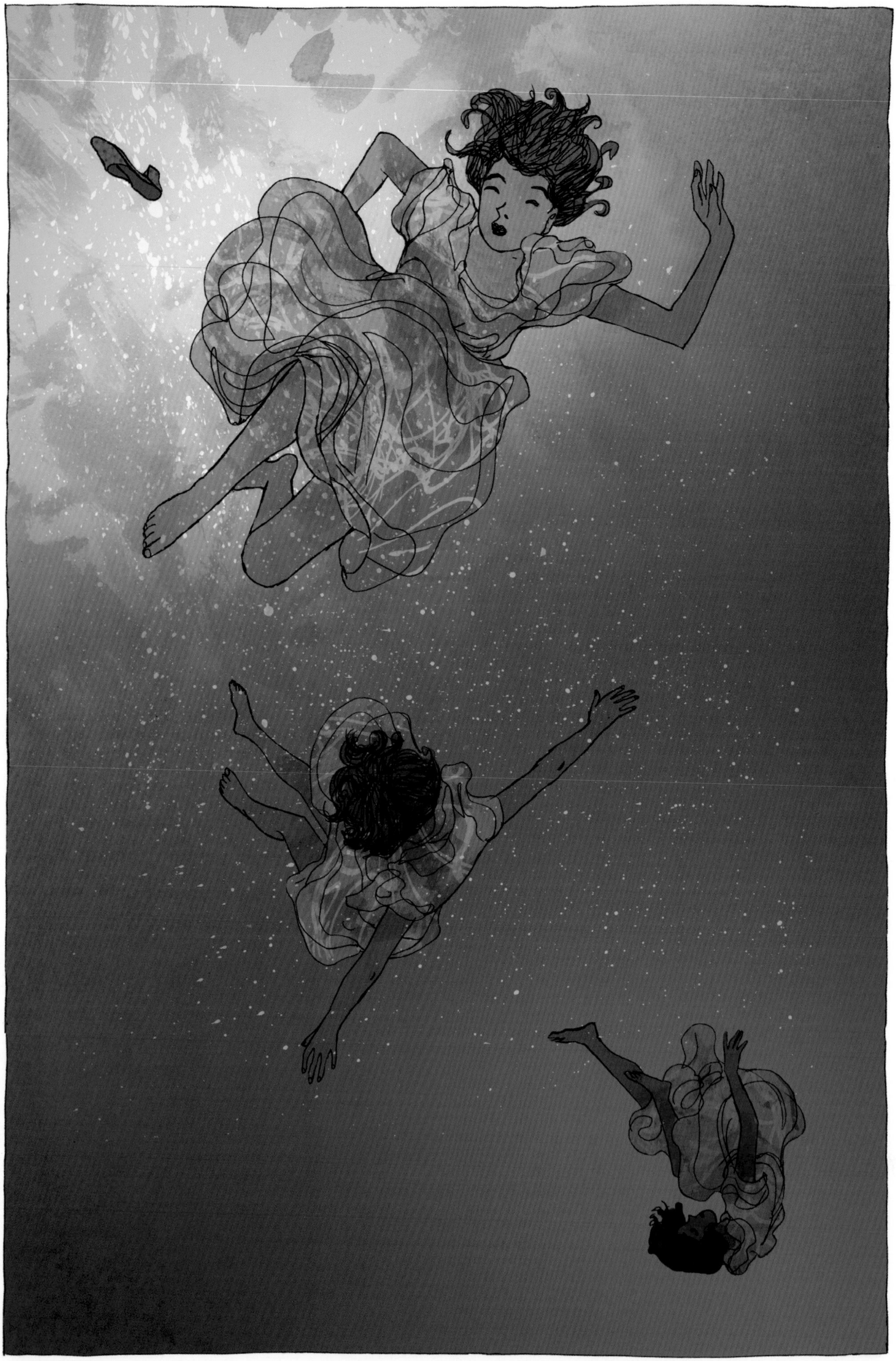

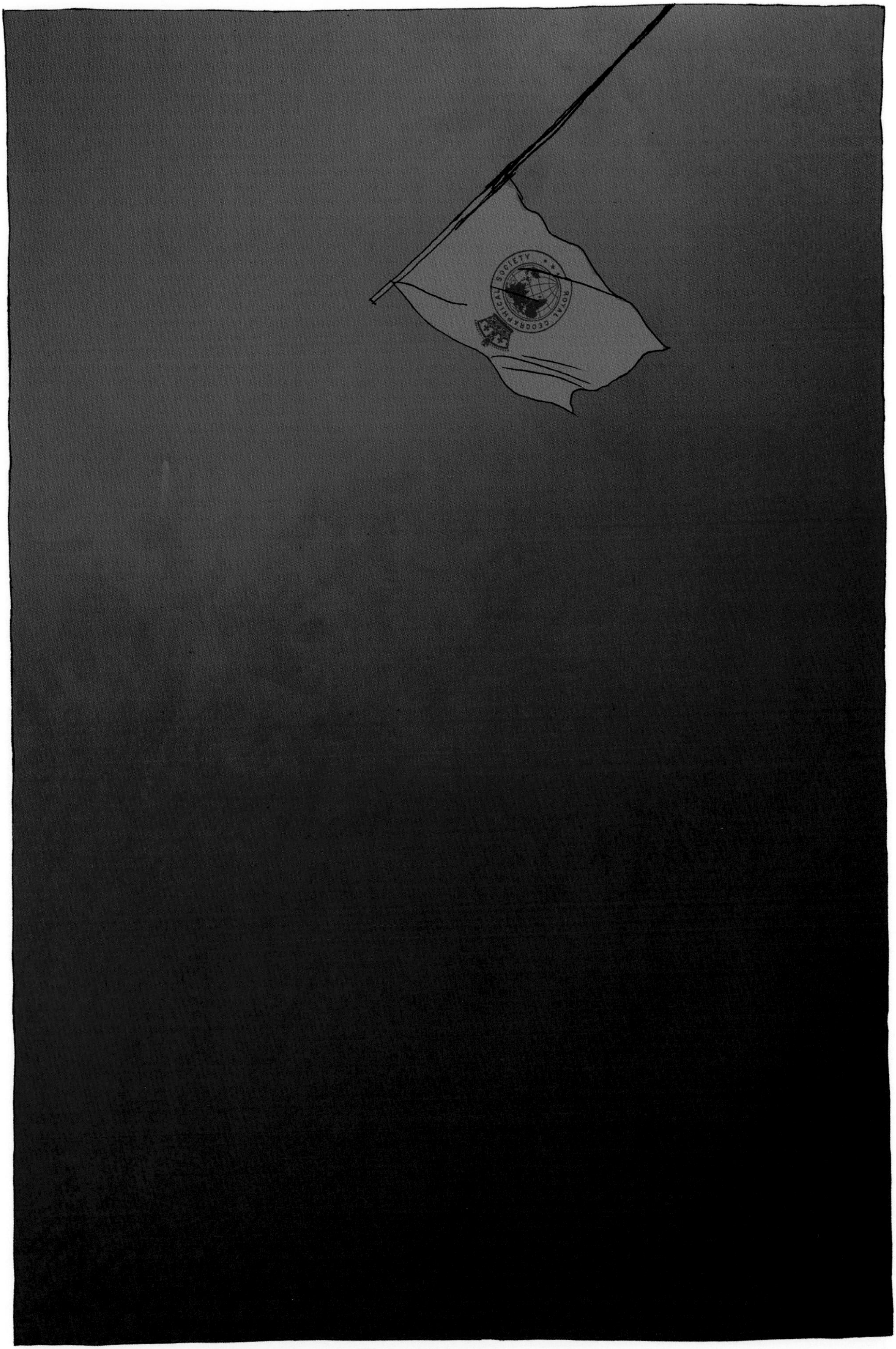
ROYAL GEOGRAPHICAL SOCIETY

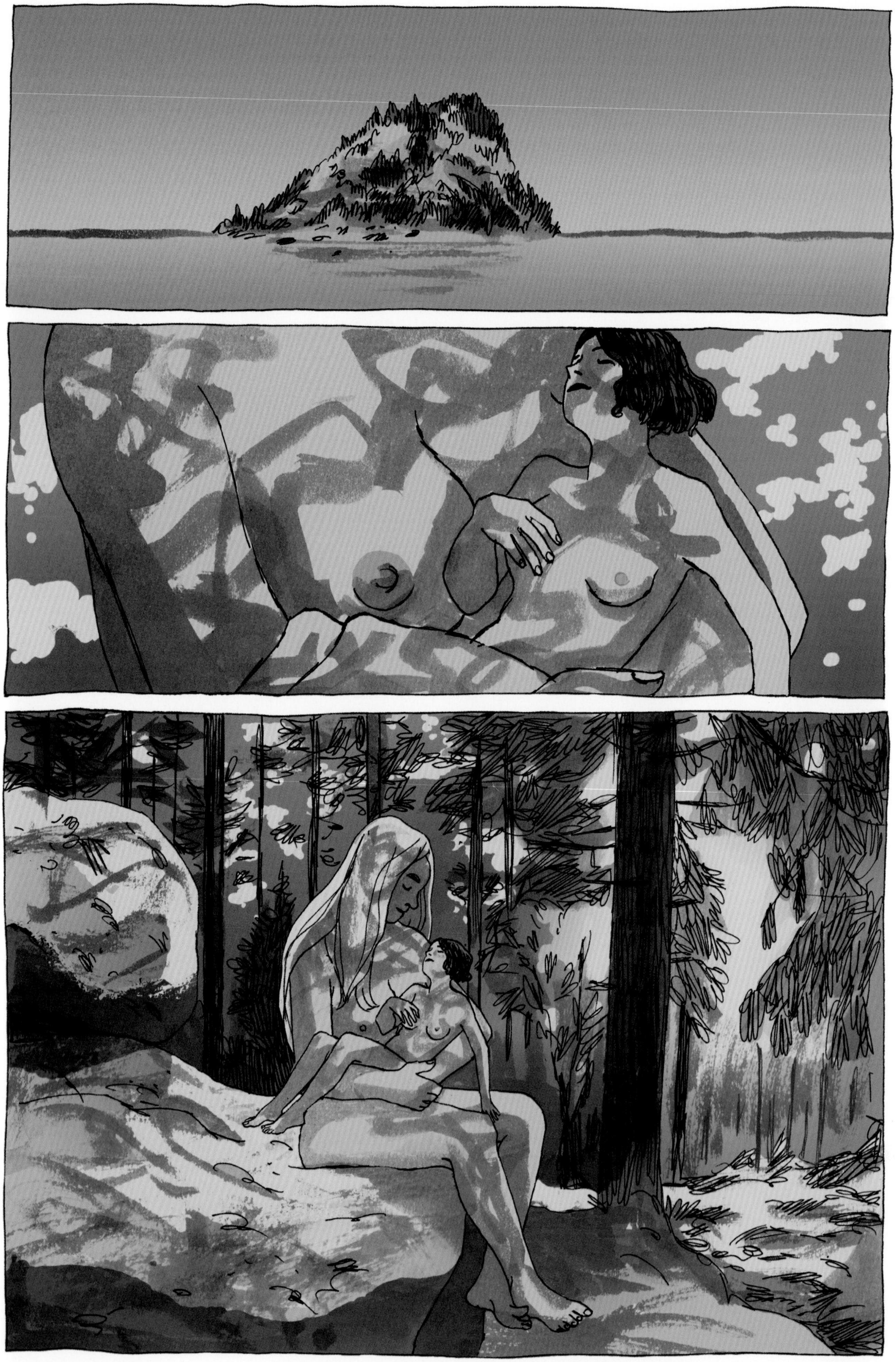

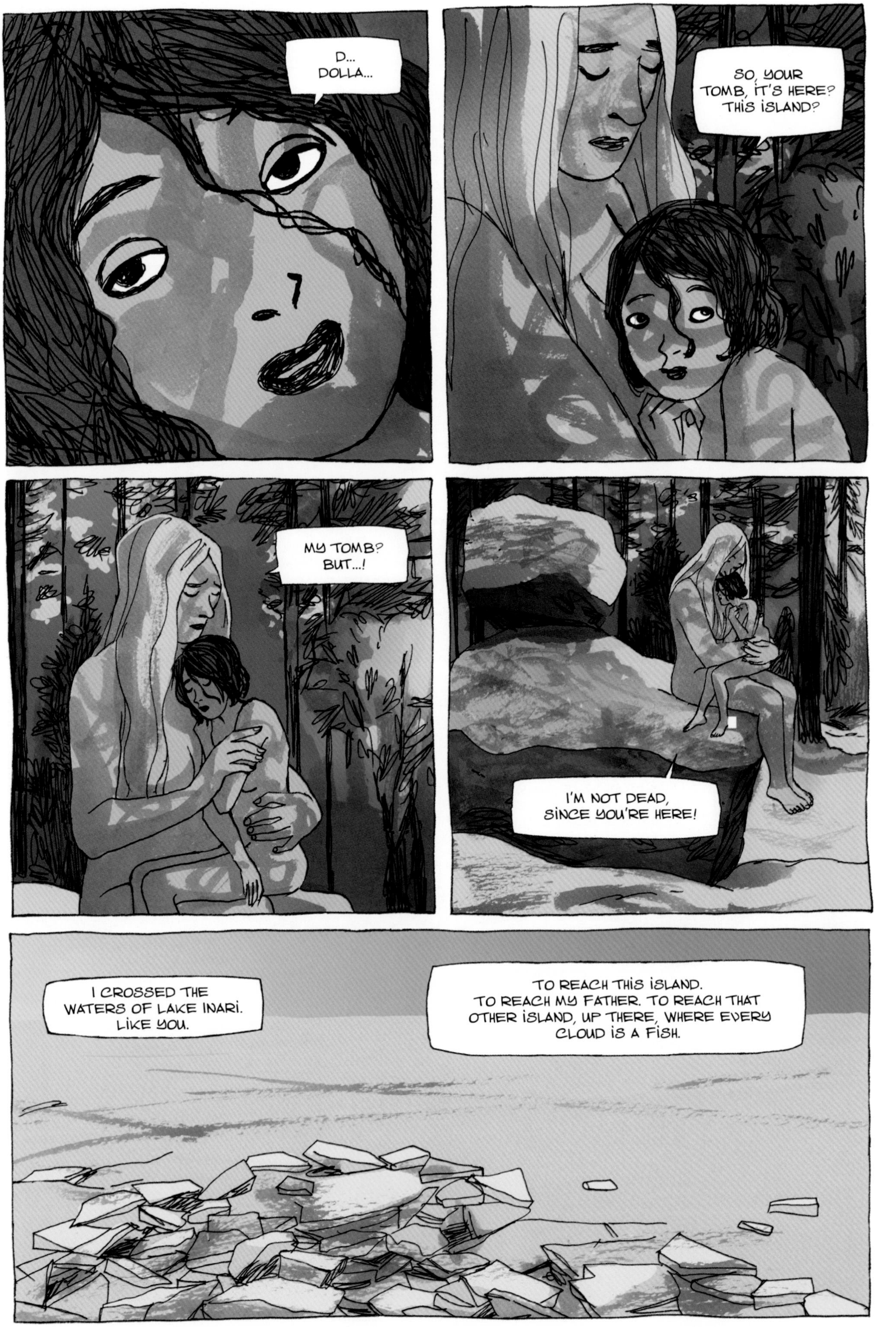
D... DOLLA...
SO, YOUR TOMB, IT'S HERE? THIS ISLAND?
MY TOMB? BUT...!
I'M NOT DEAD, SINCE YOU'RE HERE!
I CROSSED THE WATERS OF LAKE INARI. LIKE YOU.
TO REACH THIS ISLAND. TO REACH MY FATHER. TO REACH THAT OTHER ISLAND, UP THERE, WHERE EVERY CLOUD IS A FISH.

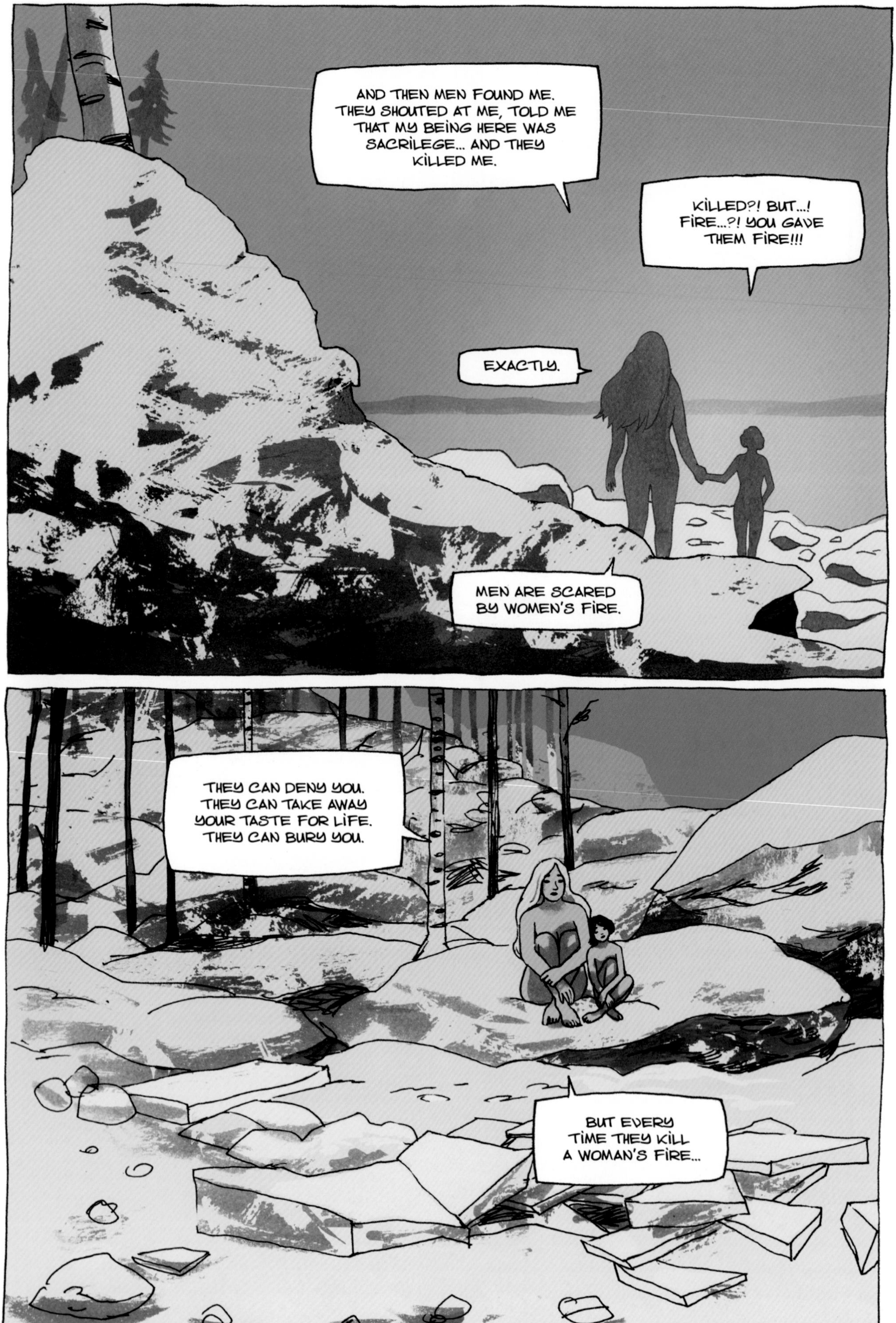
AND THEN MEN FOUND ME. THEY SHOUTED AT ME, TOLD ME THAT MY BEING HERE WAS SACRILEGE... AND THEY KILLED ME.
KILLED?! BUT...! FIRE...?! YOU GAVE THEM FIRE!!!
EXACTLY.
MEN ARE SCARED BY WOMEN'S FIRE.
THEY CAN DENY YOU. THEY CAN TAKE AWAY YOUR TASTE FOR LIFE. THEY CAN BURY YOU.
BUT EVERY TIME THEY KILL A WOMAN'S FIRE...

...THE FIRE IN ANOTHER WOMAN, ELSEWHERE, IS LIT.

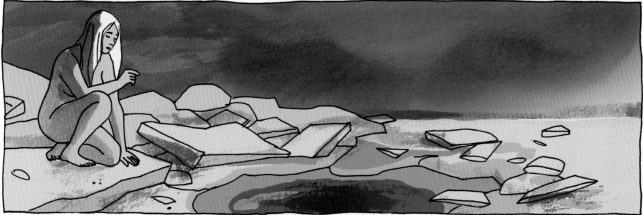

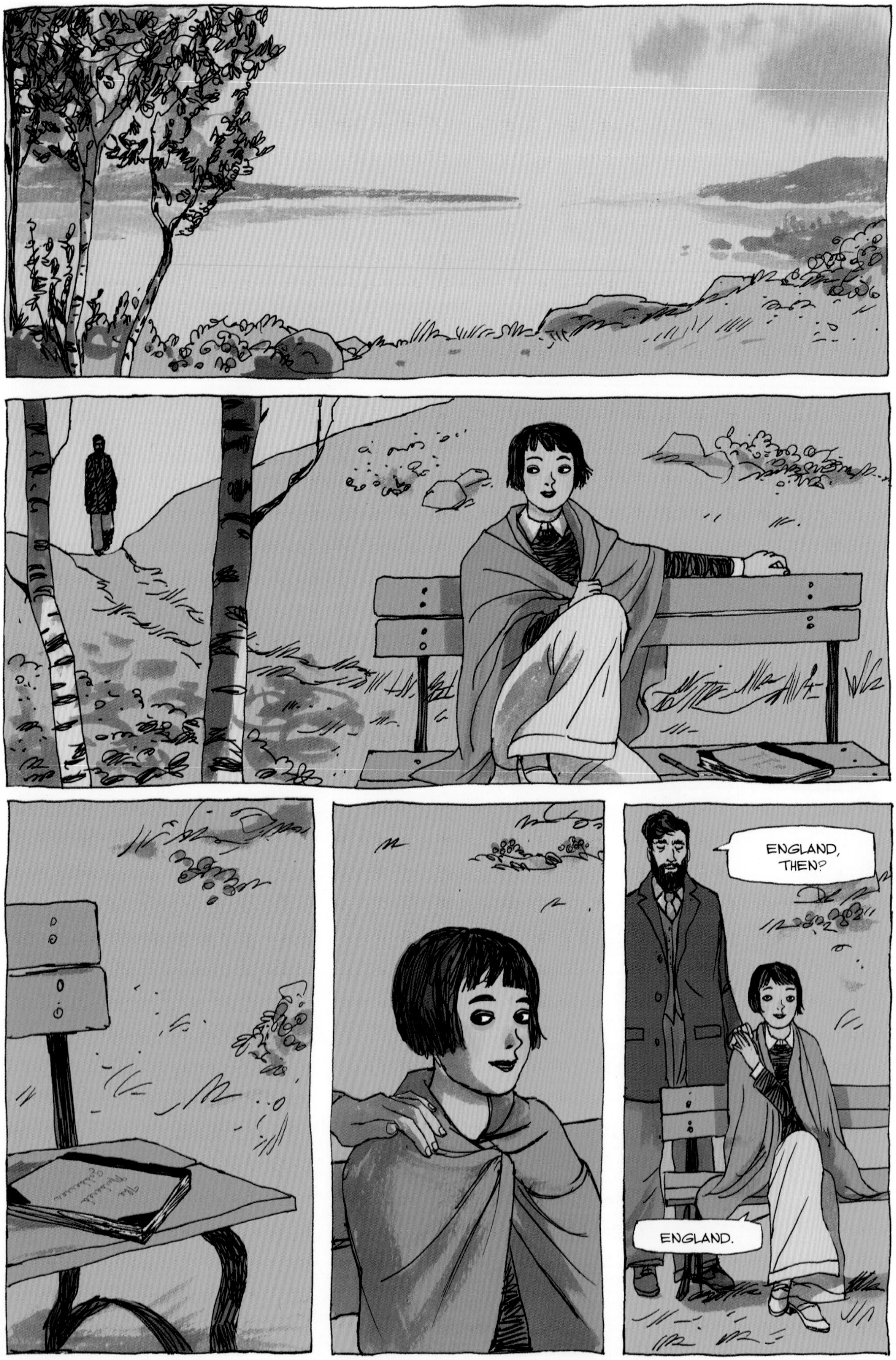
ENGLAND, THEN?
ENGLAND.

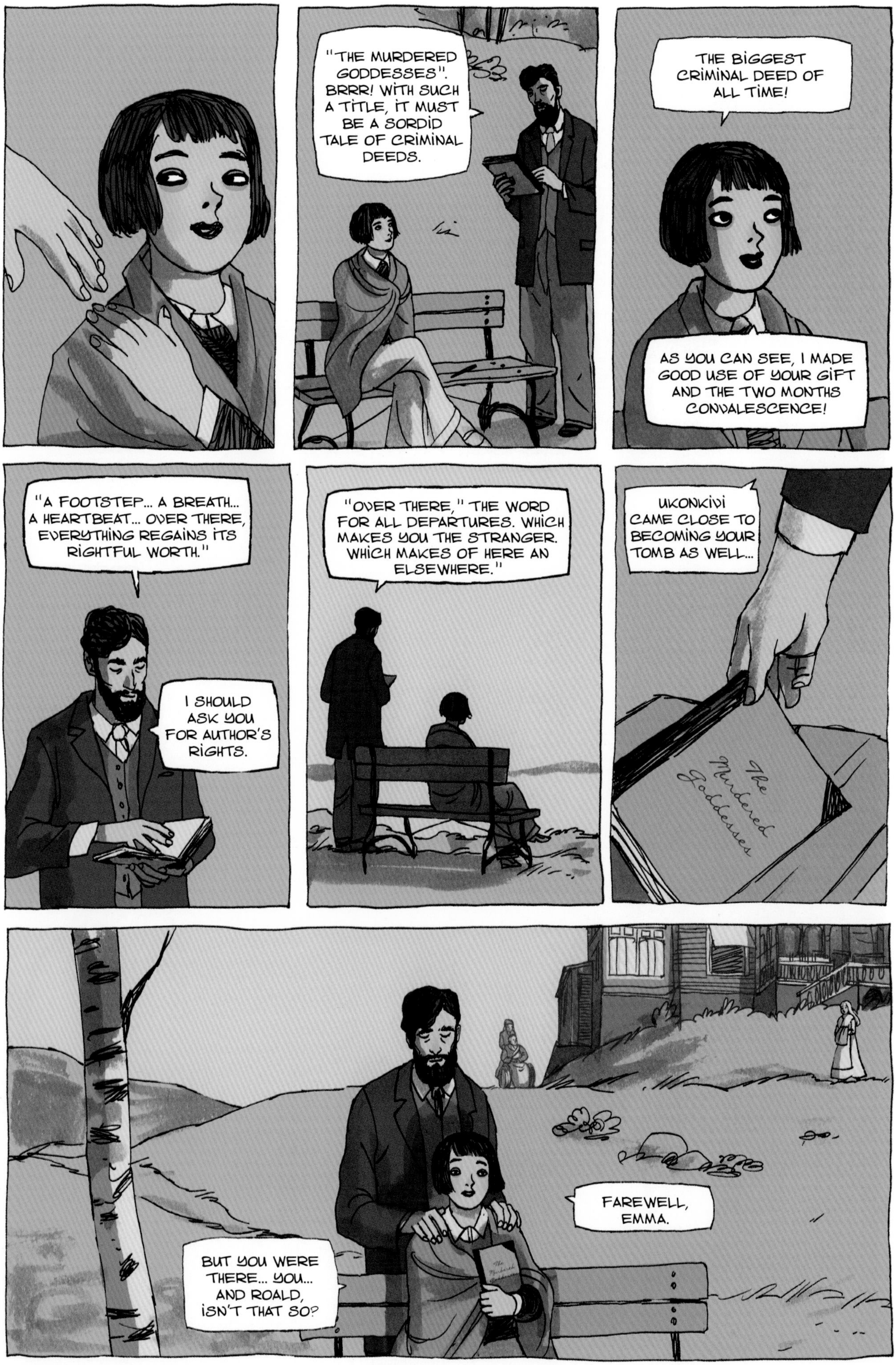
"THE MURDERED GODDESSES". BRRR! WITH SUCH A TITLE, IT MUST BE A SORDID TALE OF CRIMINAL DEEDS.
THE BIGGEST CRIMINAL DEED OF ALL TIME!
AS YOU CAN SEE, I MADE GOOD USE OF YOUR GIFT AND THE TWO MONTHS CONVALESCENCE!
"A FOOTSTEP... A BREATH... A HEARTBEAT... OVER THERE, EVERYTHING REGAINS ITS RIGHTFUL WORTH."
I SHOULD ASK YOU FOR AUTHOR'S RIGHTS.
"OVER THERE," THE WORD FOR ALL DEPARTURES. WHICH MAKES YOU THE STRANGER. WHICH MAKES OF HERE AN ELSEWHERE."
UKONKIVI CAME CLOSE TO BECOMING YOUR TOMB AS WELL...
The Murdered Goddesses
FAREWELL, EMMA.
BUT YOU WERE THERE... YOU... AND ROALD, ISN'T THAT SO?

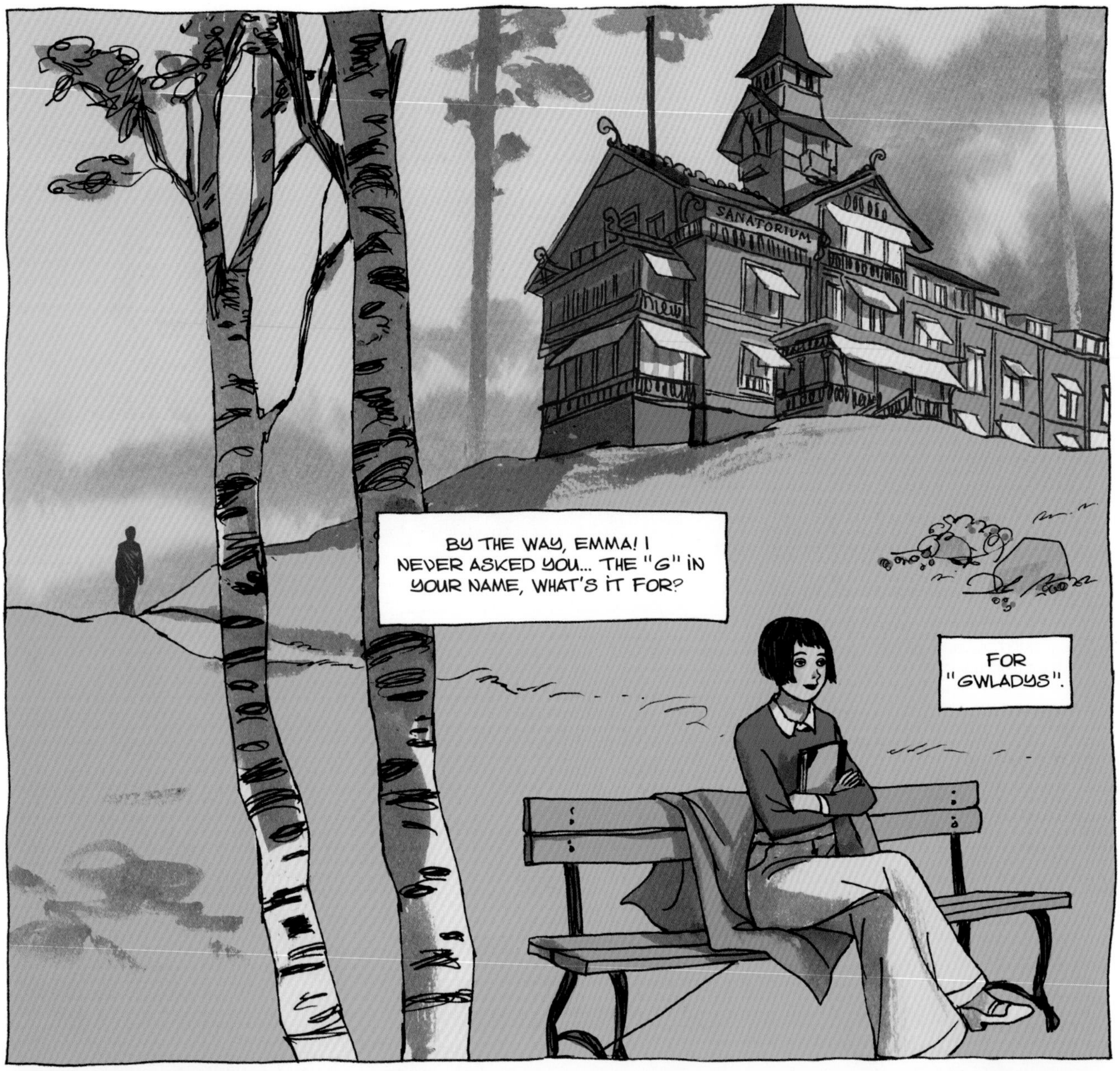
SANATORIUM
BY THE WAY, EMMA! I NEVER ASKED YOU... THE "G" IN YOUR NAME, WHAT'S IT FOR?
FOR "GWLADYS".

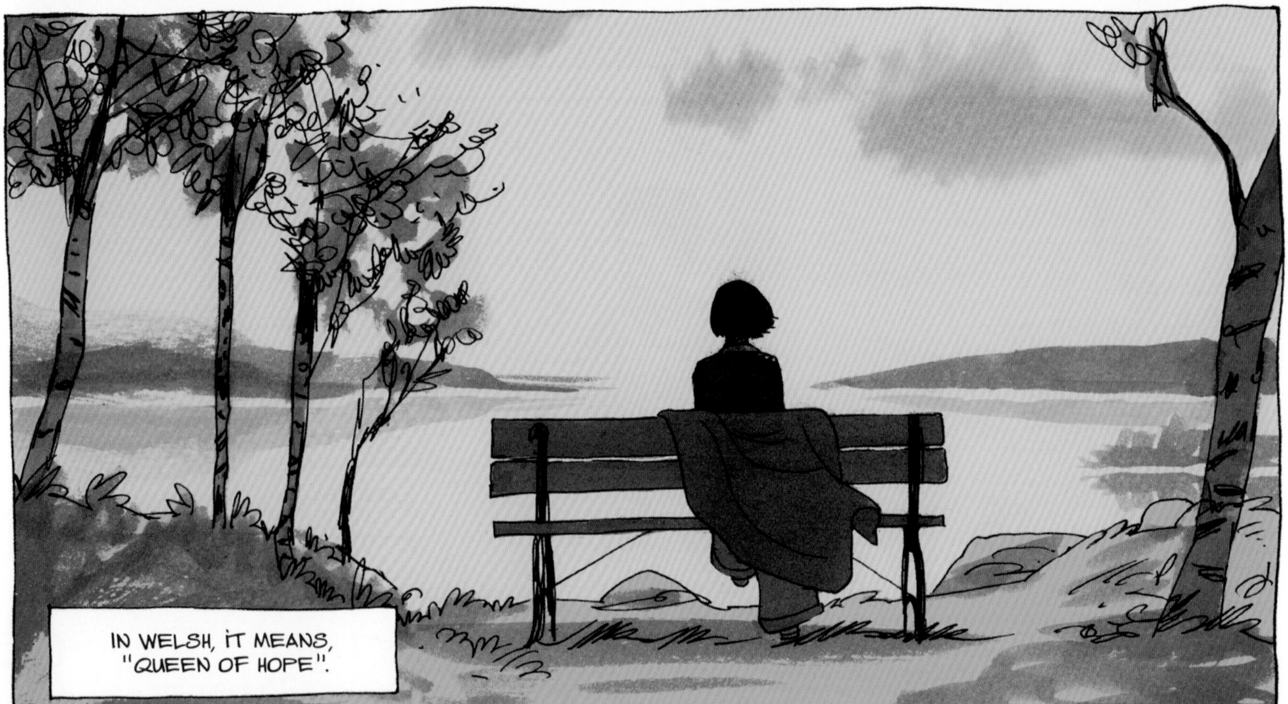
IN WELSH, IT MEANS, "QUEEN OF HOPE".

BONUS
FEATURES

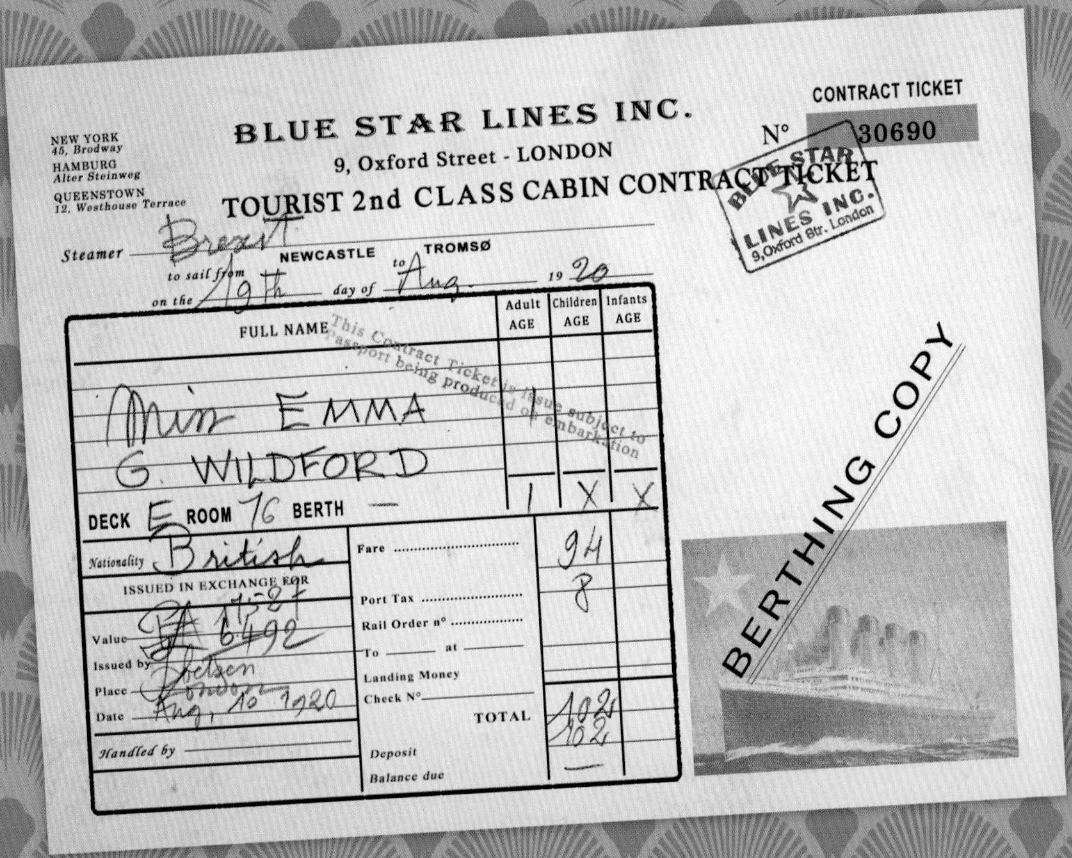
CONTRACT TICKET

N° 30690

BLUE STAR LINES INC.

NEW YORK
45, Brodway
HAMBURG
Alter Steinweg
QUEENSTOWN
12, Westhouse Terrace

9, Oxford Street - LONDON

TOURIST 2nd CLASS CABIN CONTRACT TICKET

BLUE STAR LINES INC. 9, Oxford Str. London

Steamer Brexit
to sail from NEWCASTLE to TROMSØ
on the 19th day of Aug. 1920

FULL NAME	Adult AGE	Children AGE	Infants AGE
Miss EMMA G. WILDFORD	1	X	X

This Contract Ticket is issue subject to Passport being produced at embarkation

DECK E ROOM 76 BERTH —

Nationality British

ISSUED IN EXCHANGE FOR	Fare	94
Value PA 15-27 6492	Port Tax	8
Issued by Joetsen	Rail Order n°	
Place London	To at	
Date Aug. 10 1920	Landing Money	
	Check N°	
	TOTAL	102
Handled by	Deposit	102
	Balance due	—

BERTHING COPY

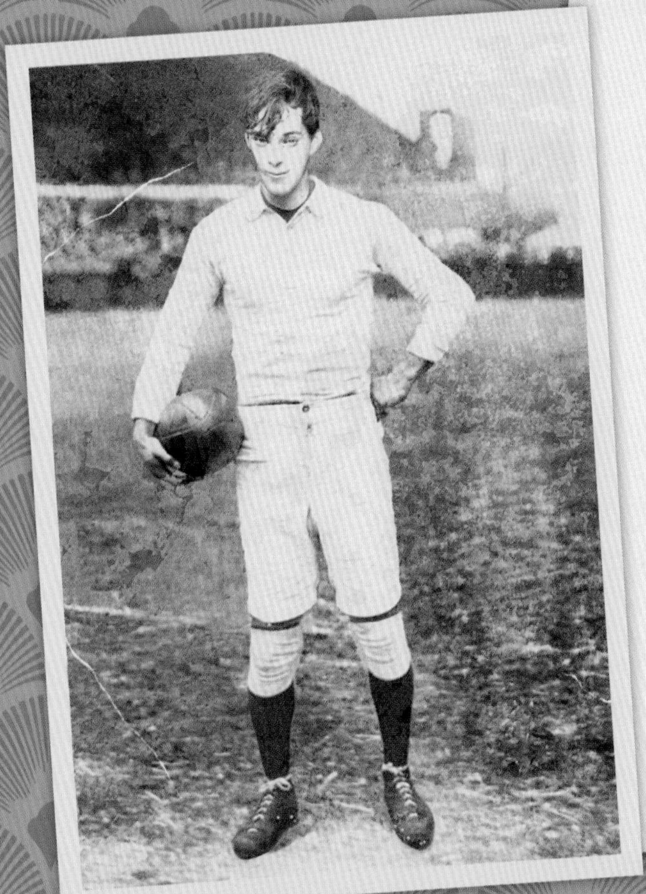

Roald proud with his first love
1912.

Wentworth Photography - 21, Needle Street - LONDON

Emma,

My sweet, my innocence, my favourite sin.
If you're reading this, then it's because something
bad has happened to me or that, impatient, you
couldn't wait seven years this time to marry the
truth!

    In both cases, I fear that you'll emerge devastated
by the reading of this present confession.

I won't marry you on the day you turn twenty,
    Emma. In fact I never had any intention to.
The cat doesn't bite the mouse it likes to play with.

You gave me everything. Whereas I, I took it all.
Including your delusions, once this letter has
buried itself to the hilt in your heart.

    I am nothing but the sum of my lies. And you,
    dear child, you are very life itself, sincere, unpre-
dictable, always.

    One time, once only, I almost opened up to you.

    That day, drunk with rage, you told me how that
banker of a brother-in-law tried to violate you.

In a moment of childish sincerity, I almost admitted to you that, for years, I'd been maintaining an affair with your sister.

For all that you could call it an affair, the perverse games I forced Elizabeth to play despite her disgust. Or, rather, because of her disgust?

The sum of my lies, Emma...!

This expedition itself to the shores of Lake Inari, what is it if not a chimera, a puerile attempt to finally don my father's crown?

You who so love words, Emma. Emma, you who makes lovers of them, strokes them, lays them on the paper, tell me.

What poem, could one day speak of what our tears contain!

What song could ever capture the hurt of a love deceived?

Goodbye, Emma! "Adieu". Isn't that word equal to a novel, dont you think?

Roald Hodges Junior

P.S. I'm not asking for your forgiveness, Emma. At best, I deserve your contempt.

TRANSLATED BY
MARC BOURBON-CROOK

EDITOR
JONATHAN STEVENSON

DESIGNER
DONNA ASKEM

ASSISTANT EDITOR
DAN BOULTWOOD

MANAGING & LAUNCH EDITOR
ANDREW JAMES

ART DIRECTOR
OZ BROWNE

SENIOR PRODUCTION CONTROLLER
JACKIE FLOOK

PRODUCTION SUPERVISOR
MARIA PEARSON

PRODUCTION CONTROLLER
PETER JAMES

PRODUCTION ASSISTANT
RHIANNON ROY

SENIOR SALES MANAGER
STEVE TOTHILL

CIRCULATION EXECUTIVE
FRANCES HALLAM

PRESS OFFICER
WILL O'MULLANE

COMICS BRAND MANAGER
CHRIS THOMPSON

ADS & MARKETING ASSISTANT
BELLA HOY

DIRECT SALES & MARKETING MANAGER
RICKY CLAYDON

COMMERCIAL MANAGER
MICHELLE FAIRLAMB

PUBLISHING MANAGER
DARRYL TOTHILL

PUBLISHING DIRECTOR
CHRIS TEATHER

OPERATIONS DIRECTOR
LEIGH BAULCH

EXECUTIVE DIRECTOR
VIVIAN CHEUNG

PUBLISHER
NICK LANDAU

EMMA G. WILDFORD
9781785869280
PUBLISHED BY TITAN COMICS
A DIVISION OF TITAN PUBLISHING GROUP LTD.
144 SOUTHWARK ST., LONDON, SE1 0UP.
TITAN COMICS IS A REGISTERED TRADEMARK OF TITAN PUBLISHING GROUP, LTD.
ALL RIGHTS RESERVED.

ORIGINALLY PUBLISHED IN FRENCH © 2017 ÉDITIONS SOLEIL / ZIDROU / EDITH.

A CIP CATALOGUE RECORD FOR THIS TITLE IS AVAILABLE FROM THE
BRITISH LIBRARY

10 9 8 7 6 5 4 3 2 1
FIRST PUBLISHED NOVEMBER 2018
PRINTED IN CHINA.
TITAN COMICS.

ALSO FROM TITAN COMICS AND STATIX PRESS

2021: LOST CHILDREN

ALISIK: FALL

ATLAS & AXIS

THE BEAUTIFUL DEATH

CENTURY'S END

THE CHIMERA BRIGADE - BOOK 1

THE CHIMERA BRIGADE - BOOK 2

THE CHIMERA BRIGADE - BOOK 3

THE CHRONICLES OF LEGION - BOOK 1: RISE OF THE VAMPIRES

THE CHRONICLES OF LEGION - BOOK 2: THE THREE LIVES OF DRACULA

THE CHRONICLES OF LEGION - BOOK 3: THE BLOOD BROTHERS

THE CHRONICLES OF LEGION - BOOK 4: THE THREE FACES OF EVIL

DEAD LIFE

THE DEATH OF STALIN

DEATH TO THE TSAR

DOCTOR RADAR

EMMA G. WILDFORD

EXTERMINATOR 17

FACTORY

HERCULES: WRATH OF THE HEAVENS

KHAAL

KONUNGAR: WAR OF CROWNS

THE 6 VOYAGES OF LONE SLOANE

LONE SLOANE: DELIRIUS

LONE SLOANE: GAIL

MANCHETTE'S FATALE

MASKED: RISE OF THE ROCKET

MCCAY

MONIKA - BOOK 1: MASKED BALL

MONIKA - BOOK 2: VANILLA DOLLS

THE NIKOPOL TRILOGY

NORMAN - VOLUME 1

NORMAN - VOLUME 2: TEACHER'S PET

NORMAN - VOLUME 3: THE VENGEANCE OF GRACE

NORMAN: THE FIRST SLASH

OSCAR MARTIN'S SOLO: THE SURVIVORS OF CHAOS

PACIFIC

THE QUEST FOR THE TIME BIRD

THE RAGE - BOOK 1: ZOMBIE GENERATION

THE RAGE - BOOK 2: KILL OR CURE

RAVINA THE WITCH?

RE-MIND

ROYAL BLOOD

SALAMMBÔ

SAMURAI: THE ISLE WITH NO NAME

SAMURAI: BROTHERS IN ARMS

THE SEASON OF THE SNAKE

SHERLOCK FOX

SHOWMAN KILLER - BOOK 1: HEARTLESS HERO

SHOWMAN KILLER - BOOK 2: THE GOLDEN CHILD

SHOWMAN KILLER - BOOK 3: THE INVISIBLE WOMAN

SKY DOLL: SPACESHIP

SKY DOLL: DECADE

SKY DOLL: SUDRA

SNOWPIERCER: THE ESCAPE

SNOWPIERCER: THE EXPLORERS

SNOWPIERCER: TERMINUS

THE THIRD TESTAMENT - BOOK 1: THE LION AWAKES

THE THIRD TESTAMENT - BOOK 2: THE ANGEL'S FACE

THE THIRD TESTAMENT - BOOK 3: THE MIGHT OF THE OX

THE THIRD TESTAMENT - BOOK 4: THE DAY OF THE RAVEN

UNDER: SCOURGE OF THE SEWER

UNIVERSAL WAR ONE

VOID

WORLD WAR X

YRAGAËL / URM THE MAD